The Citizen and the Alien

The Citizen and the Alien

DILEMMAS OF CONTEMPORARY MEMBERSHIP

Linda Bosniak

PRINCETON UNIVERSITY PRESS

PRINCETON AND OXFORD

Copyright ©2006 by Princeton University Press
Published by Princeton University Press, 41 William Street, Princeton, New Jersey 08540
In the United Kingdom: Princeton University Press, 6 Oxford Street,
Woodstock, Oxfordshire OX20 1TW

Second printing, and first paperback printing, 2008
Paperback ISBN: 978-0-691-13828-2

The Library of Congress has cataloged the cloth edition of this book as follows

Bosniak, Linda
The citizen and the alien : dilemmas of contemporary membership / Linda Bosniak.
p.   cm.
Includes bibliographical references and index.
ISBN-13: 978-0-691-11622-8 (hardcover : alk. paper)
ISBN-10: 0-691-11622-9 (hardcover : alk. paper)
1. Citizenship. 2. Aliens. I. Title.
K3224.B67 2006
323.6—dc22   2005034124

British Library Cataloging-in-Publication Data is available

This book has been composed in Sabon

Printed on acid-free paper. ∞

press.princeton.edu

Printed in the United States of America

10   9   8   7   6   5   4   3   2

For Andrew, for Tanya, and for Jessica

Sometimes noisily and sometimes sneakily, borders have *changed place*. Whereas traditionally, and in conformity with both their juridical definition and 'cartographical' representation as incorporated in national memory, they should be *at the edge of the territory*, marking the point where it ends, it seems that borders and the institutional practices corresponding to them have been transported *into the middle of political space*.
　　　　　—Etienne Balibar, *We the People of Europe*

To claim that the universal has not yet been articulated is to insist that the "not yet" is proper to an understanding of the universal itself: that which remains unrealized by the universal constitutes it essentially.
　　　　　—Judith Butler, *Sovereign Performatives in the Contemporary Scene of Utterance*

Contents

Acknowledgments

THIS IS A BOOK about membership. Its writing has been shaped by my own membership in several exceptional institutional communities. Rutgers Law School has provided a supportive and stimulating environment in which to work over the past several years. I appreciate the support of Dean Ray Solomon, former Dean Roger Dennis, and my colleagues, past and present, especially David Frankford, Sheila Foster, Ann Freedman, Sally Goldfarb, Phil Harvey, Beth Hillman, Earl Maltz, Rand Rosenblatt, Allan Stein, Beth Stephens, and Alice Dueker. My students at Rutgers have helped me immeasurably to deepen my thinking about citizenship and noncitizenship in its various forms. I have also had the assistance of several outstanding research assistants at Rutgers who contributed in important ways to this book. These include Sue Raufer, Josh Byrne, Cullen Grace, Kate McDonnell, Kelly Breslin, Carolyn Buccerone, Amy Cores Sailer, and Georgette Fries.

The Rutgers University Center for the Critical Analysis of Contemporary Culture (CCACC) served as an intellectual home twice during this book's gestation. Bruce Robbins and Pedro Caban directed the stimulating 1998–1999 CCACC seminar, "The American Century in the Americas." More recently, the Center's seminar on citizenship in 2003–2004 provided an extraordinary site of intellectual fellowship. I am grateful to Yoav Peled, Peggy Somers, David Abraham, Ethel Brooks, Phil Harvey, Dorothy Hodgson, Ana Yolanda Ramos-Zayas, Leslie McCall, Dorothy Hodgson, Mara Sidney, Jimmy Swenson, Edward Ramsamy, Denniston Bonadie, Joe Bonica, Eric Boehme, Brian Norman, and Sandrine Sanos for a year of rich exchange on the subject of citizenship, as well as to Carolyn Williams, George Levine, Link Larsen, and Wendy Creevy for gracious institutional support.

I spent an exceptionally fruitful year as a Faculty Fellow at Princeton University's Program in Law and Public Affairs (LAPA) in 2001–2002. Chris Eisgruber, Christina Burnett, Fionuala Ni'Aolain, Oren Gross, Phil Weiser, Gil Seinfeld, Wilf Prest, Alan Patten, Dirk Hartog, and Carol Greenhouse were astute and generous colleagues. Kathy Applegate and Cindy Schoeneck made everything run seamlessly.

I have delivered parts of this book as talks in workshops or at conferences at several institutions, including the University of Chicago, Brooklyn Law School, Hofstra Law School, the University of Minnesota Law School, the University of Colorado Law School, Georgetown Law School,

Cardozo Law School, Fordham School of Law, Princeton University, Yale University, New York University Law School, the Radcliffe Institute, the University of Toronto Law School, and the American Bar Foundation. I am grateful for the invitations and for the comments and questions of participants. The biennial Immigration Law Teachers workshops have provided lively and collegial settings for the development of some of these ideas as well.

I have been fortunate to have many colleagues and friends who have generously read and insightfully commented on parts or all of this book in its earlier incarnations. These readers include David Abraham, Alex Aleinikoff, Amy Bartholomew, Jackie Bhabba, Christina Burnett, Andrew Bush, Joe Carens, Richard Delgado, Chris Eisgruber, Karen Engle, David Frankford, Abner Greene, Susan Gzesh, Joel Handler, Phil Harvey, Bonnie Honig, Vicki Jackson, David Jacobson, Ken Karst, Karl Klare, Audrey Macklin, Earl Maltz, David Martin, Leslie McCall, Linda McClain, Gerry Neuman, Mae Ngai, Alan Patten, Kunal Parker, Yoav Peled, Noah Pickus, Jamie Raskin, Bruce Robbins, Jeffrey Rubin, Saskia Sassen, Peter Schuck, Rogers Smith, Peggy Somers, Allan Stein, Dan Tichenor, Mark Tushnet, and Ari Zolberg. Special thanks to Fionuala Ni'Aolain for encouraging me at a critical moment to bring the strands of this project together, to Peter Spiro, Hiroshi Motomura, and Leti Volpp for ever-perceptive commentary over the years, and to Chuck Myers for his sensible editorial guidance.

This is a book about belonging. I am grateful to the many family members and friends who have provided a foundation of belonging from which I have been able to explore the ambiguities of marginality and membership. I want especially to acknowledge the support of Mort Bosniak, Tommie Hager Bosniak, David Christie, Michael Christie, Ellie Clark, Donna Lehman Geller, Wally Bush, Leonore Shohan, and the late Minnie Singer. I also appreciate the wise friendship and steadfast support I have received from Sheldon Weiss and Anne Finkelstein over the years.

My greatest debt is to my immediate family. Andrew Bush has contributed to this book's conception and its writing in countless ways. My daughters, Jessica Bush and Tanya Bush, inspire, encourage, and challenge me in all endeavors, including this one. I am exceptionally fortunate to belong with all three.

Earlier versions of some chapters were previously published as follows:

Chapter 3: Linda S. Bosniak, *Membership, Equality and the Difference That Alienage Makes*, 69 New York University Law Review 1047 (1994).

Chapter 4: Linda Bosniak, *Constitutional Citizenship Through the Prism of Alienage*, 63 Ohio State Law Journal 1286 (2002).

Chapter 2 contains excerpts from Linda Bosniak, *Citizenship*, in Oxford Handbook of Legal Studies (Peter Cane and Mark Tushnet, eds., Oxford University Press, 2003), by permission of Oxford University Press.

The Citizen and the Alien

CHAPTER 1

Divided Citizenships

POLITICAL AND LEGAL thought today are suffused with talk of citizenship. Whether the focus is equal citizenship or democratic citizenship or social citizenship or multicultural citizenship, whether the preoccupation is with civil society citizenship or workplace citizenship or corporate citizenship or postnational citizenship, some version of *citizenship* is now vital to the intellectual projects of scholars across the disciplines. Citizenship talk pervades our popular political discourse as well.

Citizenship, however, is a more confounding concept than most who employ the word usually recognize. Citizenship is commonly portrayed as the most desired of conditions, as the highest fulfillment of democratic and egalitarian aspiration. But this, I believe, reflects a habit of citizenship romanticism that tends to obscure the deeper challenges that the concept poses. These challenges derive from citizenship's basic ethical ambiguity. The idea of citizenship is commonly invoked to convey a state of democratic belonging or inclusion, yet this inclusion is usually premised on a conception of a community that is bounded and exclusive. Citizenship as an ideal is understood to embody a commitment against subordination, but citizenship can also represent an axis of subordination itself.

The fact that citizenship leads us in these contrasting directions is, in one respect, an idiosyncrasy of rhetoric. Certainly, citizenship is an overworked term, and its ubiquity inevitably leads to confusion. But the trouble goes deeper: the divided nature of citizenship as an idea also implicates core issues of political and social theory. It leads us especially to focus on questions about *who it is* that rightfully constitutes the subjects of the citizenship that we champion. To the extent that we express our ideals of justice and democratic belonging by way of the concept of citizenship, we need to be particularly sensitive to the questions of exclusion implicated in the discussion. Citizenship of, and for, exactly whom?

CITIZENSHIP'S "WHO" QUESTION

We tend to answer citizenship's "who" question differently depending on our analytical starting point. Sometimes we view citizenship from an internal or endogenous perspective. From this vantage, citizenship is understood to designate the nature and quality of relations among presumed members of an already established society. As a normative matter, citizenship in this internal sense is understood to stand for a universalist ethic—for the inclusion and incorporation of "everyone."[1] Most of the citizenship revival that has occurred in the academy has taken place within this inward-looking framework.

At other times we approach citizenship by attending to the community's boundaries. Here the concern is not the internal life of the political community but its edges; our focus is the ways in which that community—usually a nation-state—is constituted and maintained *as* a community in the first instance. In normative terms, boundary-focused citizenship is understood to denote not only community belonging but also community exclusivity and closure. The status of citizenship in any given state is rationed, and the limitations on its availability mark the limitations on belonging.

As a matter of intellectual sociology, there has been a surprisingly limited degree of interchange between these inward-looking and boundary-conscious worlds of citizenship discourse. What has happened is that citizenship's boundary questions are usually taken up by a specialized group of scholars across the disciplines in the field of immigration studies. Just about everyone else tends to *presume* the boundaries, or, more often, they presume away any world outside the nation altogether. The national society is treated as the total universe of analytical focus and normative concern, and citizenship then has to do with the nature of the relationships prevailing among already assumed members. Certainly, there have been some encounters and mutual incursions across this intellectual divide, but there has not been as much sustained dialogue as is necessary. I believe we need to deepen the conversation between inward-looking and boundary-conscious approaches to citizenship, in the interest of illuminating the dilemmas of inclusion and exclusion that are implicated by the concept. This book's purpose is to advance that conversation.

The Citizenship of Aliens

My own initial interest in citizenship developed from my work as an immigration scholar—as someone who was thinking about citizenship's boundaries. I was preoccupied with questions of exclusion from formal citizenship status and what that means for people residing in liberal democratic states like the United States. It was within that context that I began to read other bodies of citizenship-related literature. These were the aspirational, inward-looking strands in constitutional and political and social theory, which treat citizenship as the fulfillment of all that is socially good and valuable. In some respects, I found this literature inspiring; I identified with the progressive message expressed through ideas like "democratic citizenship" and "equal citizenship," and I wanted to embrace it.

But I was also nervous about it. It seemed clear to me that these citizenships referenced nationally circumscribed conceptions of justice and well-being, though they were usually not acknowledged as such. And I wondered whether it was a good idea to use the language of citizenship in this aspirational way, given the potentially exclusionary implications of doing so, at least rhetorically. There was, first of all, the question of citizenship's applicability to people beyond the boundaries of the national society. Could citizenship-linked conceptions of justice extend to such people?

But even leaving aside the difficult questions of transnational justice, and given my interests in issues of immigration, I wondered, in particular, about the meaning of this discourse for those people living within liberal democratic societies who lack citizenship by legal definition. If citizenship is treated as the highest measure of social and political inclusion, can people designated as *noncitizens* as a matter of status be among the universe of the included?

On first reflection, the answer is obviously no: common sense tells us that citizenship is—of course—only *for citizens*. Further reflection, though, greatly complicates the answer. In the United States, as in other liberal democratic societies, status noncitizens are, in fact, not always and entirely outside the scope of those institutions and practices and experiences we call citizenship. Indeed, many of citizenship's core attributes do not depend on formal citizenship status at all but are extended to individuals based on the facts of their personhood and national territorial presence. The experiences of being a citizen and enjoying citizenship, it turns out, are not always aligned as a practical matter; status noncitizens are the subjects of what many call citizenship in a variety of contexts.

Recognizing that it is not necessarily incoherent to speak of the "citizenship of noncitizens"—or the citizenship of aliens, in legal terminology—is analytically important in a discursive context in which *citizenship* has become so central.[2] It makes clear that citizenship is not a unitary or monolithic whole: the concept is comprised of distinct discourses designating a range of institutions and experiences and social practices that are overlapping but not always coextensive. Citizenship is a divided concept.

The fact that citizenship is divided in this way might suggest that my initial apprehension about the increasing salience of citizenship talk among progressives is misplaced. Strictly speaking, to embrace citizenship as our normative benchmark is not necessarily to exclude status noncitizens. The trouble, however, is that we tend not to speak or to hear strictly. In conventional usage, citizenship's meanings are conflated. It is easy and no doubt common to hear a reference to citizenship and to think simultaneously of universal citizenship and of the citizenship of borders, or to be uncertain which meaning is intended. It is hardly surprising that, when the term is used aspirationally, we tend to suppose that what is at stake is universal citizenship for formal holders of citizenship status.

In one respect, what we have here is a semantic problem: the term citizenship has multiple meanings, and this creates confusion. But the trouble runs deeper than sloppiness of rhetoric. In fact, I have come to believe that the confusions of citizenship rhetoric are themselves a symptom of a more profound condition, one of substantive political theory. Citizenship is not just divided conceptually, it is divided normatively, and the ambiguities that plague our citizenship-talk often reflect this ethical divide.

CITIZENSHIP'S JURISDICTIONS

Citizenship in liberal democratic states stands, as I have said, for both universalist and exclusionary commitments. Usually, however, these contrasting normative orientations are not understood as conflicting but rather as complementary, with each one relevant to, and operative in, a different jurisdictional domain. Universalism, in this understanding, is applicable within the national political community, while exclusion applies at its edges. This division of normative labor is functional for many purposes, and indeed, it has come to represent our commonsense understanding of the way citizenship works. Citizenship, we tend to think, is *hard on the outside and soft on the inside*, with hard edges and soft interior together constituting a complete citizenship package.

Yet the complementarity aspired to in this construct of citizenship can stand only so long as the hard outer edge actually separates inside from outside. And in a world of porous borders, real separation is often elusive. This is nowhere clearer than in the context of transnational migration, where foreigners enter the bounded national territory from the outside and, once present, are assigned the status of alienage. These noncitizen immigrants have entered the spatial domain of universal citizenship, but they remain outsiders in a significant sense: the border effectively follows them inside. The question then becomes, which citizenship norms apply? In theory, both sets are relevant and applicable. The fact that they are— the fact that "hard" threshold norms have now come to occupy the same (internal) terrain as the "soft" interior ones—leads to uncertainty and conflict. Determining which set of norms should prevail when they conflict, and under what circumstances, is always difficult, in practice and in theory.

Recognizing that alienage lies at the interface of these normatively contrasting citizenship regimes, and that this liminality inevitably produces normative and policy conflict, is clearly important as a matter of immigration theory. Doing so enables us to understand why it is that noncitizens, although marginalized and subordinated in significant ways, are also in some respects treated as citizenship's subjects. It makes clear, in other words, why the apparently paradoxical idea of "noncitizen citizenship" can make a certain kind of sense, while remaining a source of contestation as well.

But addressing the hybrid condition of alienage is equally important, I believe, for the development of citizenship theory beyond the immigration field. Exponents of citizenship in its inward-looking mode have been able, by virtue of the prevailing conception of spatially divided citizenship regimes, to avoid contending with citizenship's bounded dimension. Citizenship's exclusionary commitments (to the extent they are acknowledged at all) are viewed as relevant and operative not within the national territory but rather "out there," at the community's edges. Yet it is in the very nature of alienage to bring those boundaries to bear in the territorial inside: alienage entails the introjection of borders. Bringing alienage into view, therefore, requires inward-looking citizenship theory to attend to the national border, and in the process, to reflect on the scope and nature of the universality which it professes to champion. Citizenship, once again, of, and for, precisely whom?

The Nationalism of Citizenship Theory

Several of this book's chapters begin with an observation (at times, a complaint) about the analytical and normative nationalism that characterizes discussions of citizenship in mainstream constitutional and political theory. Most such discussions presume that citizenship is enacted within bounded national societies. Ordinarily, these presumptions are unspoken and unacknowledged: theorists tend to treat both a national setting and a state of boundedness as already satisfied conditions for the practices and institutions and experiences of citizenship. Making these assumptions permits them to focus their attention on what citizenship requires and entails in substantive terms within these pre-given boundaries.

More often than not, in fact, this literature appears to presume not merely that citizenship is national as a matter of current fact, but also that it is national as a matter of necessity or nature. One of the arguments I make in chapter 2 is that the automatic correspondence commonly presumed between citizenship and nation-state is unfounded. Citizenship's intimate relationship to the nation-state is not intrinsic but contingent and historical, and the forms and locations of citizenship, as we conventionally understand the term, are more varied than ordinarily acknowledged. Citizenship has been, can be, and arguably should sometimes be enacted not merely within national borders but beyond and across them, as well.

There is, however, no denying that many of the institutions and practices and experiences that we call citizenship today take a prevailingly national form. "Postnational" or "transnational" forms of citizenship remain a real but limited part of the citizenship landscape. For this reason, it is essential that scholars attend to the complex practices and institutions and experiences that we call citizenship within the national society. Doing so is a central aim of this book.

But to say that nationally situated citizenship requires scholarly focus is not to endorse the kind of insular framework that so many scholars of citizenship employ in their studies. To state the problem briefly, inward-looking citizenship scholars often treat the national society as the total universe of analytical and moral concern. They rely on the kind of analytical premise made explicit by Rawls, whose theory of justice presupposed a conception of a "democratic society [that is] a complete and closed social system."[3] In his most influential work, Rawls aimed to develop principles "for the basic structure of society conceived for the time being as a closed system isolated from other societies."[4]

Yet to the extent that a society's completion and closure are the analytical starting points, these premises obviously escape critical examination themselves, and simultaneously serve to preordain an insularity of focus. As some of Rawls's critics have pointed out, moreover, community closure and autonomy are empirically untenable and normatively unsatisfying premises on which to ground any political theory of justice and governance.[5] These presumptions, it seems to me, are equally (if not more) untenable as a backdrop for any convincing account of citizenship.

They are lacking, to begin with, because they are implausible. Few if any political societies are hermetically sealed, and certainly those that are the subject of most citizenship theorists' interest—liberal democratic societies—are deeply imbricated, economically and socially and politically, with other societies in a larger world landscape. Cross-border relationships have always existed, but their intensity has accelerated to the point that most of us are embedded, irremediably, in various fields of interaction that traverse national borders. Transborder movements of consumer goods, production processes, money, crime, information, music, disease, religion (the list is long), as well as people, are less tightly constrained today by the territorial and institutional parameters of individual nation-states than they have ever been.

THE THEORETICAL COSTS OF NATIONAL INSULARITY

This growing (though uneven) permeability of national borders, often described under the rubric of "globalization," has become axiomatic in much social and economic scholarship. Yet these trends have registered surprisingly little in inward-looking theoretical work on citizenship, particularly among those scholars concerned with "equal" or "democratic" or "social" citizenship. The problem is not that these citizenship theorists fail to make globalization the direct object of their study, for as I have said, the nature of citizenship within national societies is itself a necessary object of analysis. The problem is that their disregard of the larger world frame and of the permeability of national borders serves to distort and limit any account these scholars may offer of the practices and institutions and experiences of citizenship as it is practiced *within* the nation-state.

There are several reasons for this. First, reliance on the premises of completion and closure permit scholars to avoid a host of crucial normative questions intimately linked to the debates over citizenship: those regarding the rightful scope of solidarity and the proper reach of justice claims. Questions, in particular, about the scope of our moral identifications—about the defensibility of national solidarities and the possibilities for, and desirability of, responsibilities and identifications extending beyond the class of one's compatriots—are simply bracketed out of discussion[6] or are consigned, if acknowledged at all, to the seemingly utopian preserve of moral cosmopolitan theory. Analysts maintain a presumption of national priority without the need for either its acknowledgment or its defense. Their moral nationalism appears not to be a normative choice but a metaphysical given.

In addition, and of particular concern to me here, the presumptions of completion and closure inevitably thwart the development of a full descriptive accounting of the nature of citizenship as it is enacted within the national society. The inward-looking citizenship literature presumes or posits a firm separation between national inside and outside, yet in fact, the line between inside and outside—both social and territorial—is often very difficult to draw. Politically, borders are neither fixed nor static; what counts as part of the inside or outside is subject to ongoing negotiation and contestation. And whatever the prevailing understanding of their character and location, as a practical matter national borders are very often tested, stretched, permeated, or breached. Any vision of the world that presumes a stark dichotomy between a political society's inside and out, in other words, is unequipped to contend with the complex interpenetration of institutions and practices and persons across borders that characterizes the contemporary landscape. A habit of dichotomous inside/outside thinking disables theorists from seeing, among other things, that the global is not merely situated "out there" but is also located, increasingly, within national borders.[7]

The internalization of the global is nowhere more vividly instantiated than in the case of cross-national migration. Cross-border movements of people are hardly new; they are a longstanding feature of the modern international system (and, of course, they precede it as well). Yet the rate of cross-national migration for labor and family reunification and humanitarian purposes has accelerated in recent years: large numbers of migrants from abroad have traveled to live and work in many liberal national societies each year. According to recent estimates, nearly 180 million people—more than three percent of the world's population today—have migrated across national borders during their lifetimes.[8] Many former countries of emigration, particularly in Europe, have become net importers of people, thereby joining the ranks of the traditional countries of immigration. In the United States, the numbers of foreign-born persons in residence is estimated to have reached 28 million—higher than it has ever been, even at the turn of the twentieth century.[9]

Although the United States and other liberal democratic immigrant-receiving states are precisely the kinds of societies that are of principal concern to most citizenship theorists, the subject of immigration, as I have said, has been neglected in much of their work.[10] The presumptions of completion and closure that so often frame this work tend to keep immigration policy questions off the agenda. Questions concerning the substantive standards and decisional processes for admission and exclusion of foreigners and questions having to do with the status and treatment of foreigners who reside within the national state without citizenship are almost invariably treated as the grist of the immigration specialists, who have lately produced a large and diverse body of scholarship on these issues.

The fact that there is such a division of labor among scholars of citizenship is not entirely surprising. No one can address every issue in a wide and complex field; specialization is inevitable, and lines have to be drawn somewhere. In the end, though, the occupational and conceptual divide between the inward-focused and border-conscious citizenship literatures is misleading and unproductive.

To begin with, the divide is nonsensical in purely formal terms. Two decades ago, Michael Walzer pointed out that the study of distributive relationships within a political community (or within political communities in general) always begs the prior question of how that community was constituted and is maintained in the first instance. At stake is what Walzer called the distribution of membership: "The primary good that we distribute to one another is membership in some human community," he wrote. Political communities' membership decisions are those that concern "their present and future populations."[11] These are threshold citizenship matters, matters pertaining to the formation and maintenance of the community *within which* matters of substantive citizenship are enacted.[12]

There is no way to coherently address the substantive citizenship dynamics within a community until we contend with the citizenship questions of who belongs and how decisions about who belongs are to be reached.

In descriptive terms, furthermore, a thoroughgoing separation of threshold and internal citizenship concerns is impossible in any event.[13] The regulation of national boundaries is not confined to the specific domain of the nation-state's physical or territorial border[14] but extends into the territorial interior as well, and shapes the pursuit of democratic/equal citizenship within the national society.[15] This introgression of the border is precisely what occurs in the case of immigrants who reside within a liberal democratic society as status noncitizens, who live within the national territory and enjoy important rights and recognition by virtue of their presence but who remain outsiders under the community's threshold-regulating citizenship rules. That outsider status, which the law calls alienage, shapes their experience and identity within the community in profound ways. Among other disabilities, aliens are denied the vote and most significant welfare benefits, and, notwithstanding the ties they may have developed in and with the community, they are always potentially subject to deportation by the state.

The point is, there is no firm separation possible between the domains of citizenship at the border and citizenship within. Instead, the two domains are overlapping and interpenetrated in various respects. Citizenship theory needs to be able to address the ways in which the institutions and norms of citizenship at the threshold and in the interior meet and shape and constrain one another. This book seeks to map this interplay in legal thought and practice; its focus is how these twin citizenship regimes—one committed to inclusion of persons, the other to the exclusion of strangers—converge to produce the ambiguities of alien status in liberal democratic societies.[16]

ALIENAGE AND SUBORDINATION

A book about the condition of noncitizens in liberal democratic societies necessarily implicates important questions about the nature of status inequality and social subordination more generally, and I address these questions in various ways throughout this book. The category of alienage puts pressure on our conceptualizations of inequality and subordination in challenging ways. To begin with, my discussion often treats aliens in the aggregate, as a social group; but it is not always clear to what extent, and in what respects, status noncitizens can be said to represent a social group in the conventional sense. At one level, they plainly do: they are categorized as such by the state, and in objective terms, their condition is "linked to their being so categorized . . . with respect to the relevant interactions or allocations of benefits and burdens."[17] On the other hand, it is less than clear that noncitizens specifically identify themselves *as* noncitizens or aliens, beyond what Iris Young calls the simple "passbook" meaning of identity, as in "an acknowledgement of the power of the rules over my life because of my lineage or bureacratic status."[18] Deeper forms of identification and solidarity based specifically on this status have not been the rule in the case of noncitizens.[19] Still, this may be changing, as evidenced by the Immigrant Freedom Rides in the United States in 2003 and by recent campaigns to obtain local voting rights for some noncitizen immigrants.[20]

The category "alienage," futhermore, can be misleading unifying. In objective terms, the people who comprise the group of aliens are socially divided in many significant ways. Some of these differences are a matter of legal status. There are crucial distinctions between lawful and unlawfully present aliens and between those in the United States temporarily and those here permanently, and each of these distinctions is itself divided by legal category in ways that matter for the experience of the people involved. There are also social differences, including gender differences and ethnic, national, racial, and class distinctions, that affect noncitizens' experiences in ways that frequently compound, and frequently ameliorate, the disadvantage associated with alienage status.[21] For these reasons it is often not very meaningful to talk about aliens as a unitary class.

Nevertheless, it seems clear that there are certain characteristics of alienage that structurally shape the lives of most noncitizens, usually in disadvantaging forms. Aliens' lack of formal citizenship status has rendered them politically disenfranchised; they are formally ineligible for many aspects of "social citizenship," or the public provision of basic needs; and they are always subject to the possibility of deportation from the territory.

Strikingly, these particular forms of disadvantage have often been overlooked by theorists who engage the subject of social subordination in general terms. In the critical literature across the disciplines, it is common to come upon laundry lists of the vectors of subordination—such as race, ethnicity, gender, class, sexual orientation, religion, disability, and appearance—that fail to include or even acknowledge the category of alienage. One reason for this disregard is the pervasiveness in legal, political, and social thought of the baseline premises of completion and closure, as described earlier. Within such a conceptual framework, "we are the world" entire, and the idea of citizenship is invoked to refer to the condition of full belonging and recognition among already presumed members of the nation. Ample attention is paid to "second-class citizenship" in various guises, but the issue of formal noncitizenship simply does not arise.

Still, I suspect that the reason for the traditional disregard of alienage goes deeper. Alienage presents real difficulties for antisubordination theorists. While it shares some characteristics with other forms of social subordination, it can also appear to be a different species of exclusion altogether: not social disadvantage but, instead, an instance of constitutive boundary maintenance, a necessary condition for preservation of the community *within which* the struggle against social subordination takes place. At different moments, aliens can appear as oppressed insiders and as relative strangers, with (at least temporarily) inadequate claims for full membership. Not infrequently they are viewed as embodying *both* identities—subordinated insiders and national strangers—at once. Given the confusions that these simultaneous perceptions can generate, and given the historically sensitive nature of immigration politics for the left more generally,[22] I suspect it has often been easier for progressive theorists to avoid these issues rather than to engage them head-on.

The widespread disregard of alienage in social theory may be changing. The category of "immigration status" has been appearing with greater frequency in various catalogues of subordination axes offered by commentators.[23] Any increasing attention paid to the condition of noncitizenship in status terms is a positive development, given the traditional disregard the subject has suffered in mainstream social and political theory. Yet it is not enough to add alienage to "the list," as if it were simply one more category of social exclusion. Instead, it is important to understand how, precisely, disadvantage based on alienage is both like and unlike other forms of disadvantage, and what these similarities and divergences reveal about our conventional understandings of subordination.

One way in which I approach this question throughout the book is to ask what it means for people to *lack* citizenship, not merely as a matter of formal status but in other respects as well. Like citizenship itself, noncitizenship is a complex and divided condition. I argue that, by recognizing the various forms of noncitizenship and by examining the relationships among them, we are able to think more productively about subordination and disadvantage in general. Taking account of the particular form of noncitizenship that alienage represents demonstrates the inadequacy of the national and territorial premises that characterize so much liberal and critical theory today.

CITIZENSHIP: THE CONCEPT

The term *citizenship* conventionally describes a certain set of institutions and practices and identities in the world, and this book is concerned with examining some of these. However, "citizenship" is also a contested political and constitutional concept whose scope of reference and application are subject to ongoing dispute. It is, therefore, not only citizenship's multiple referents but also the concept of citizenship itself that require scholarly attention. In substantial part, this book is concerned with examining the ways in which legal and political theorists employ the concept of citizenship in their arguments about the social and political world.[24]

Citizenship is one of those "keywords" in political language that are subject to much confusion and debate.[25] Misunderstandings and disagreements abound about what citizenship is, where it takes place, and who exactly can claim it. One of my principal aims is to sort out these various disagreements.

In one respect, however, the meaning of citizenship is not in contention at all. The term's normative valence—its appraisive meaning[26]—is almost unfailingly positive. To characterize practices or institutions or experiences in the language of citizenship is to afford them substantial political recognition and social value. It is for exactly this reason that political actors and scholars often vie to characterize practices and institutions and experiences *as* citizenship. Describing aspects of the world in the language of citizenship is a legitimizing political act.[27]

My approach rejects an essentialist notion of language, according to which words have intrinsic and unchanging meanings. Claims of this kind have frequently been made by participants in the debates over citizenship. Some commentators have maintained that citizenship has a fixed and true meaning that has been distorted in recent uses, sometimes beyond recognition.[28] Certainly, the notion of alien citizenship will be viewed by purists as linguistically nonsensical as well as provocative. I agree, however, with those analysts who view language as a field of political contest,[29] and who characterize efforts to recast key political terms as a kind of "political innovation."[30] In this view, there is no way to clarify the meaning of words once and for all, or to purify them of unconventional uses.[31] The task, instead, is to understand the source and nature and direction of these efforts and to recognize the debate's imbrication in the broader political landscape.

In the end, I argue, our understandings of citizenship will depend on the shape and the outcomes of the substantive debates in legal and political thought in which the conceptual debate is embedded. These debates center on two principal kinds of questions—questions of identity and questions of responsibility.[32] Uncertainties about who "we" are and to whom we maintain special commitments are perennial questions, of course, but they arise today in a particularly challenging environment, one in which the factual and normative presumptions of national closure that liberal democratic theory maintains are increasingly untenable. Our arguments about citizenship are, in large part, arguments about these questions.

The book is structured as follows. In chapter 2, I examine the idea of citizenship in largely conceptual terms. I first show how understandings and uses of citizenship are multiple and contested, but I also make clear that citizenship is by no means entirely indeterminate in scope and meaning. There are, in fact, common themes and common divides that have come to organize citizenship discourse both within and beyond legal studies. Broadly speaking, citizenship questions can be divided into three (inevitably overlapping) categories: those that concern the substance of citizenship (what citizenship is), those that concern its domain or location (where citizenship takes place), and those that concern citizenship's subjects (who is a citizen). Each of these questions in turn has elicited a range of conventionally acceptable answers that have served to structure the citizenship debates.

I also argue, however, that pressure has recently been brought to bear by scholars across the disciplines on the prevailing approaches to each of these questions in ways that seek to significantly redefine citizenship's scope and meaning. Briefly, scholars have sought to take the concept of citizenship beyond the strictly political, beyond the nation-state, beyond the individual, and beyond the ethical particularist and even humanist commitments usually associated with the concept. These efforts at redefinition are often supported by way of an appeal to citizenship's own expansive logic and ethics; the challengers purport to better capture the normative heart of the citizenship idea than prevailing approaches have thus far done.

I pay special attention in chapter 2 to the contested constitution of citizenship's subjects—to citizenship's "who" question. One of the persistent themes in the academic literature on citizenship concerns the question of how far citizenship extends in social terms: this is the question of who will constitute the class of citizenship's subjects. Because citizenship is conceived as representing political or social membership (almost always, as we have seen, in the context of the nation-state), the question of citizenship's subjects is consequently the question of who will be counted as (usually national) political or social members. But because membership is very differently conceived in different understandings of citizenship, the answers to citizenship's "who" question often vary as well. Some citizenship scholars treat citizenship principally as a universalist project, while others emphasize its exclusionary attributes. Much of the literature on citizenship's "who" question can be divided along this normative fault line.

The third and fourth chapters consider the legal structure of alienage and citizenship in American constitutional thought and practice. In chapter 3, I argue that alienage is an intrinsically hybrid legal category that is simultaneously the subject of two distinct domains of regulation and relationship. The first domain governs membership in the national community; it includes the government's immigration power, which the state regulates through the admission and exclusion of aliens and imposes conditions on their entry. In the landscape of current American public law, this power remains exceptionally unconstrained. The second domain governs the rights of persons within the national society. In this domain, government power to impose disabilities on people based on their status is far more limited: formal commitments to the elimination of caste-like status and to norms of equal treatment have significantly shaped our public law during the past several decades, and these developments have made aliens appear to be precisely the sort of social group that requires the law's protection.

Given the hybrid legal character of alienage, I contend, government discrimination against aliens is perenially burdened by the question of when and to what extent such discrimination is an expression, or a rightful extension, of the government's power to regulate the border—that is, to impose conditions on entry and to control the composition of the national community, and when it implicates a different sort of governmental authority, one shaped by interests not in sovereignty but in equality, and one subject to far greater constraints. When, in other words, is alienage a question of national borders, when is it a question of legal equality, and how are we to tell the difference? In chapter 3 I show how these questions both plague and structure U.S. law of alienage discrimination—constitutional, statutory, and common. I argue that the major strands of thought in legal and political theory on aliens' rights represent competing approaches to their resolution. In this chapter, I closely analyze the work of political theorist Michael Walzer, whose own approach to the status of alienage casts powerful light on the questions at stake.

Chapter 4 addresses what I take to be the ambiguous meaning of the category "citizenship" in the U.S. constitutional tradition. I contend that the Fourteenth Amendment can be read to approach citizenship at once as a kind of formal status and as the enjoyment of basic rights. My concern here is the relationship between these understandings. The pathway into this discussion is the question of how the increasing revival of interest in citizenship as a basis for rights in contemporary constitutional thought might affect aliens—people who lack citizenship by formal definition. More specifically, the chapter considers the question of whether aliens will necessarily suffer in the wake of the citizenship turn in constitutional law.

Although there is a good case to be made that aliens will be disadvantaged, some constitutional commentary from the 1970s provocatively suggests, though with little elaboration, that the position of aliens would not necessarily be undermined if we were to reorganize constitutional doctrine and house individual rights in the citizenship clause or the privileges or immunities clause of the Fourteenth Amendment. I argue in this chapter that the prospect of citizenship for aliens, however paradoxical, is not logically impossible. This is because in our law and conventional understandings, the status of citizenship and the rights we associate with citizenship are not always convergent. We typically talk about second-class citizens; these are people who enjoy status citizenship but who nevertheless are denied the enjoyment of citizenship rights, or "equal citizenship." Conversely, aliens could be said to enjoy certain incidents of "equal citizenship" in our society today by virtue of possessing an important range of fundamental rights despite their lack of status citizenship.

Although alien citizenship is not an incoherent construct per se, and although in some respects we could say that aliens do already enjoy certain incidents of equal citizenship, I argue that the equal citizenship that noncitizens can aspire to is limited in scope. This is because the constitutional ideal of equal citizenship is committed not only to universal rights (thereby including aliens) but also to an ethic of national solidarity and to practices of bounded national membership. It is by virtue of these nationalist commitments that aliens—so long as they remain aliens—can aspire to partial citizenship at best.

Chapter 5 examines the interplay of our competing conceptions of citizenship in a distinct intellectual and political context: that of the ongoing debates in feminist thought over the organization of domestic labor. Much of the discourse about women and work relies on the language of citizenship. Yet thinking clearly about work and gender requires thinking not just about equal citizenship or democratic citizenship or economic citizenship for women, conceived in universalist terms, but also about citizenship as an exclusive national status. And once we attend to status citizenship, we see that what many theorists describe as the achievement of "citizenship" for some women through participation in paid work depends increasingly on the labor of people from poorer countries who themselves lack status citizenship.

The question I ask in Chapter 5 is how to think about the configuration of citizenships embedded in this situation. It might initially appear that first-world women acquire their citizenship *at the expense of* the citizenship of their domestic workers. Rhetorically tempting as such an account might be, however, it fails to capture the nature of the relationship between equal citizenship and status citizenship as they are usually conceived. Citizenship is not a single quantity that can be transferred from some women to others in zero-sum fashion. Status citizenship and equal democratic citizenship are analytically distinct and nonfungible.

This is not to say that these citizenships are unrelated. But how should we understand their relationship? In the conventional account (to the extent the daulity even registers), they are viewed as complementary parts of a larger whole, with bounded citizenship providing the necessary bordered framework for the pursuit of equal/democratic citizenship within. This hard-on-the-outside, soft-on-the-inside conception of citizenship is broadly accepted, but it does not entirely capture important contemporary understandings and practices of citizenship. Most relevantly, bounded citizenship often operates inside the community's territorial perimeters, especially by way of exclusionary laws on immigration and alienage. The chapter concludes by reflecting on the desirability of employing "citizenship" as the central normative concept in political and social thought, including in the scholarship on women and work.

In chapter six, I return more directly to the legal status of alienage and to the troubled place of aliens in a society committed to liberal egalitarian citizenship values. My focus is the hard-on-the-outside, soft-on-the-inside conception of citizenship introduced earlier. This is a conception that Walzer powerfully (though indirectly) articulated and that often grounds—explicitly or not—liberal democratic arguments on behalf of rights for aliens. I consider the model's attractiveness to many theorists, and suggest that the idea represents an understandable effort to resolve the perennial tensions in liberal theory between norms of universalism and particularism by way of a strategy of splitting, with the conflicting norms assigned to interior and to border, respectively.

The splitting strategy ultimately fails, however, because the separation between these jurisdictional domains is unachievable. Border and interior are in fact inevitably interpenetrated—nowhere more clearly than in the case of alienage. The impossibility of splitting citizenship means that citizenship's contrasting normative impulses remain directly in contention *within* liberal democratic national societies. In this respect and in this context, citizenship stands against itself.

CHAPTER 2

Defining Citizenship: Substance, Locations, and Subjects

THE PAST TWO DECADES have seen a huge outpouring of scholarly interest in the subject of citizenship. Probably no subject commands more persistent attention across the disciplines: the idea of citizenship figures centrally in constitutional theory, in political philosophy, in social theory, in cultural studies, and in legal studies. Nor does any other concept better satisfy so many kinds of normative appetites at once. Citizenship is championed by civic republicans, participatory democrats, cultural radicals, communitarians, egalitarian liberals, and sometimes social conservatives, all of whom have claimed it as a fulfillment of their particular moral vision.

Any concept that can mean so much to so many is bound to be highly enigmatic. And citizenship surely is that. It is possible to argue that the idea is more symbol than substance and that in analytical terms, our understandings of citizenship are highly fragmented, if not incoherent. Judith Shklar was right when she observed that "there is no notion more central in politics than citizenship, [yet] none more variable in history nor contested in theory."[1]

This is not to say that citizenship is entirely indeterminate in scope and meaning. For one thing, its normative valence is almost never in question. Citizenship is a word of the greatest approbation. To designate institutions and practices and experiences in the language of citizenship is not merely to describe them, but also to accord them a kind of honor and political recognition. In fact, it is precisely because of the concept's immense emotional resonance and perceived value that people disagree so sharply over the conditions for its proper application.

Analytically, furthermore, there are common themes and common divides that have come to organize the citizenship discourse in legal and political thought. Broadly speaking, questions about citizenship can be divided into three (inevitably overlapping) categories: those that concern the substance of citizenship (what citizenship is), those that concern its domain of action or location (where citizenship takes place), and those that concern the class of citizenship's subjects (who is a citizen). Each of these questions, in turn, has met with a range of conventionally acceptable answers that have served to structure the citizenship debates.

In this chapter, I first introduce some of the main responses convention-ally offered to citizenship's "what," "where," and "who" questions. I then go on to show that pressure has been brought to bear recently by scholars across the disciplines on the prevailing approaches to each of these questions in ways that seek to significantly redefine citizenship's scope and meaning. Briefly, scholars have sought to take the concept of citizenship beyond the strictly political, beyond the nation-state, beyond the individual, and beyond the ethical particularist and even humanist commitments usually associated with the concept. These efforts at re-definition are often supported by way of an appeal to citizenship's own expansive logic and ethics; the challengers purport to capture the norma-tive heart of the citizenship idea better than prevailing approaches have thus far done.

In response, some have argued that acceptance of the kinds of argu-ments the challengers have made would amount to an abandonment of the idea of citizenship altogether. I propose, in contrast, that citizenship is a concept flexible enough to take on new meanings, even some that appear sharply in tension with earlier understandings. Some of these new meanings will be emancipatory: citizenship contains enough universalist normative content that it can plausibly (though perhaps paradoxically) be used as a resource for challenging narrower and more exclusive under-standings. Yet it is unlikely that the idea of citizenship will ever become fully severed from its association with community belonging, and hence from the particular (ethically speaking). This is the defining ambiguity at the heart of citizenship: citizenship represents both an engine of universal-ity and a brake or limit upon it.

CITIZENSHIP AS MEMBERSHIP: MULTIPLE UNDERSTANDINGS

Despite citizenship's intellectual currency, there is often little agreement among scholars as to precisely how to understand the term. At a fairly broad level of generality, the term possesses a common substantive core: most commentators approach citizenship as a concept that designates some form of community membership, either membership in a political community (political and constitutional theorists) or membership in a common society (the sociologists). However, this answer to citizenship's "what" question begs its own questions in turn, since the nature and char-acter of this membership still remain to be specified. The membership that citizenship is understood to represent has in fact been quite diversely conceived, from its earliest invocations to the present day.

A useful starting point is J.G.A. Pocock's account of citizenship's con-ceptual origins, which counterposes the early Athenian and Roman understandings. On one side, the Athenians approached the membership associated with citizenship as the practice of collective self-governance; this is the Aristotelian conception of citizenship as the process of ruling and being ruled. Early Roman thought, on the other hand, approached citizenship as an entitlement possessed by the individual to protection by the rulers themselves.[2]

This early division in prevailing conceptions of citizenship has in some respects carried forward to our own time. From the Roman model we have derived two contemporary conceptions of citizenship. We first of all understand citizenship to be a matter of formal legal standing: to be a citizen is to possess the legal status of citizenship, one that brings with it certain privileges and obligations. In this usage, citizenship designates formal, juridical membership in an organized political community. In today's world, the site of such membership is ordinarily the political community of the nation-state, although citizenship status is also sometimes possessed at the subnational and (now in Europe) at the supranational levels, as well.

The Roman legalist conception of citizenship gave us, in addition, our widely shared understanding of citizenship as entitlement to, and enjoyment of, rights. In this conception, the enjoyment of rights under law is the defining feature of social membership. Citizenship requires the possession of rights (to noninterference, originally, and now to other goods as well), and those who possess the rights are usually presumed thereby to enjoy citizenship. In this century, the tradition is closely associated with the work of British sociologist T. H. Marshall, who is best known for his characterization of contemporary citizenship as constituted by a tripartite structure of civil, political, and social rights,[3] but the tradition of citizenship as rights has been elaborated and extended as well by a range of contemporary constitutional and political theorists.[4]

The Aristotelian conception of active citizenship also continues to shape prevailing understandings. This conception was reclaimed by figures including Machiavelli and Rousseau, and played a critical role in shaping both United States and French revolutionary thought. This tradition of "high citizenship"[5] was revived again in the mid-twentieth century by Hannah Arendt, but on the whole it lay dormant during this period, having been supplanted by liberal conceptions largely concerned with the rights and status of individuals. During the past two decades, however, civic republican theory has made a comeback in the academy and brought with it a revitalized interest in citizenship's classically political dimension. Today, as political and constitutional theorists often use the term, citizenship denotes the process of democratic self-government, deliberative democracy, and the practice of active engagement in the life of the political community.

In addition to these liberal and republican-derived conceptions of citizenship, there is today a fourth cluster of understandings that broadly have to do with the way in which people experience themselves in collective terms. The term citizenship is here deployed to evoke the affective elements of identification and solidarity that people maintain with others in the wider world. It conveys the experience of belonging; at stake are the felt aspects of social membership.[6] This subjective conception of citizenship finds it roots in the Greeks as well, though not in Aristotle: the Stoics spoke of being "citizens of the world,"[7] and in so doing meant to convey the sense of psychological membership to which the term citizenship is sometimes applied. Today, the "politics of recognition" are often debated in the language of citizenship.[8] The experience of national identity and patriotism is likewise often described as integral to citizenship as well.

Thus, status, rights, political engagement, and identity together define the contours of our contemporary understandings of citizenship as membership. But how are we to understand the relationship *among* these conceptions? Some commentators describe them (or some similar set) as distinct, though overlapping, dimensions of a larger citizenship whole.[9] In this view, citizenship "encompasses a variety of elements, some legal, some psychological, some behavioral."[10] This reading is plausible in certain respects: it seems clear that we define ourselves at times along each of these parameters and that they are not mutually exclusive—indeed, each is sometimes intimately related to the others in ways that contribute to the broader constitution of political and social subjects.

There are times, however, when the social ontologies and normative commitments associated with these various dimensions of citizenship appear more incommensurable than complementary. In particular, the largely liberal tradition of citizenship as rights and the largely republican tradition of citizenship as politics might be said to be highly incompatible on some readings.[11] There are, in addition, distinct disciplinary divides in the uses of the term. As a general rule, social theorists tend to employ Marshallian rights-based conceptions of citizenship, while political theorists commonly invoke republican conceptions. Often these groups seem to be talking past one another entirely.

THE DOMAINS OF CITIZENSHIP: POLITICS AND BEYOND

Despite the significant variations in substantive approach, the major conceptions of citizenship have traditionally tended to converge on one point: they have assumed that the domain of citizenship—the sphere in which it is enacted, and to which it is relevant—is broadly *political* in nature.

Republican theorists have specifically treated citizenship as representing the process of political self-governance, while in liberal understandings, citizenship has been defined in relationship to the state, the entity that both guarantees rights and defines legal status. It is true that the jurisprudential, rights-based conception of citizenship is concerned, according to T. H. Marshall's well-known formulation, not only with the rights of political participation but also with civil rights (rights to legal personality, to "sue and be sued," as Pocock puts it)[12] and with social rights (rights to enjoyment of a minimum level of social welfare). But these rights are defined as broadly public in nature, and in any event they are understood as entirely creatures of positive, state law.

Specifically excluded from each of these conceptions of citizenship, by contrast, are the domains of social life traditionally defined as private in character, including, most significantly, the spheres of the market and the economy at large. Indeed, citizenship has been famously criticized as a formalist construct that purports to extend juridical equality in the public sphere but that simultaneously obscures relations of domination in the private economic realm. Marxist thought is especially well known for counterposing citizenship to economy by maintaining that the formal equality of citizenship status masks relations of drastic inequality prevailing in what Marx himself called the domain of "material life."[13]

Over the past several decades, however, the notion that a private domain exists distinct and insulated from state and law has itself been contested and discredited. It is now widely recognized that public power serves both to frame and to constitute relationships in these ostensibly private spheres.[14] At the same time, many scholars have sought to redefine the domain of the political itself to include sites that hitherto had been treated as private in nature. Coercive power, it has been argued, is exercised in the economy, the university, the workplace, the family, the media, and elsewhere, and all of the relationships that take place in these domains have consequently been redescribed as fundamentally political in both character and significance.[15]

It is in this intellectual environment—one involving a thoroughgoing "politicization of the social,"[16] as Iris Young puts it—that some scholars have begun to press against traditionally statist conceptions of citizenship. Theorists of both left and right have sought to reclaim spheres of social life that have often been excluded from conventional understandings of the political as sites of citizenship. This literature has two principal strands.

The first applies republican conceptions of active citizenship to new domains. Political and legal theorists urge recognition of citizenship practices in the workplace, in the marketplace, in the neighborhood, in unions, in political movements, in cultural arenas, and even in the family.[17] Some authors employ the concept of citizenship here largely descriptively, to refer to actual practices of self-government and community-mindedness in these spheres; others are particularly concerned with the fostering of necessary conditions for "good citizenship," or civic virtue, in these arenas. In either case, the practice of citizenship is held to be no longer limited to the confines of the demos as it has been traditionally conceived.

Significantly, this redeployment of the republican conception of citizenship to apply to various non-state domains is closely linked to the ongoing debate in political and social thought over the status of civil society. Many of the sites claimed as alternative domains of citizenship have been characterized as constituting aspects of the sphere of civil society. Though a contested concept itself, civil society is often described as the sphere of association or sociability, the sphere in which people engage with one another and forge relationships independent of the constraints or demands of state governance. (The question of whether the economy constitutes a part of civil society remains a contested question in the literature.[18]) Traditionally, citizenship and civil society have been treated as standing in opposition, with citizenship regarded as a practice that occurs only at the level of the political community and therefore outside of civil society. Nevertheless, a number of scholars have recently insisted that politics and/or citizenship are integral to, and inevitable in, the domain of civil society.[19] The new social movements are the paradigmatic example; they have been described as civil society citizenship in its purest form. Arguably, such activity fulfills the normative criteria of republican and participatory conceptions of citizenship very well: it is engaged and robust and reflects "a commitment to the common good and active participation in public affairs."[20]

In a second strand of literature, exponents of rights-based conceptions of citizenship have sought to extend their entitlement claims to arenas traditionally viewed as insulated from public intervention. Some scholars, including many in the law, have recently pressed for understandings of citizenship that would ensure a basic measure of economic well-being in society. "Economic citizenship," in the prevailing language, might encompass a "right to decent work,"[21] a right to a financial "stake" in society,[22] and a right to more complete and meaningful social welfare schemes.[23]

Feminist scholars have analogously sought to extend the claims of citizenship to intrafamily relations. Because, as Susan Moller Okin has written, "power (and therefore politics) exists in both domestic and non-domestic life,"[24] it follows that traditionally "private" matters, including childcare, housework, and family violence, are among the issues amenable to legitimate (public) citizenship claims. Another group of scholars, especially those concerned with rights of ethnic and sexual minorities, have urged attention to the idea of "cultural citizenship." Cultural citizenship is described as the assurance of community recognition despite difference, or as recognition of "the right to be different," without marginalization or subordination in the membership community at large.[25] A final group has pressed arguments on behalf of "multicultural citizenship," pursuant to which minority groups would be afforded social and cultural recognition of their group identities, and would sometimes obtain rights to political autonomy as well.[26] The multicultural citizenship literature, notably, posits the cultural group rather than the liberal individual as the central protagonist in the struggle for citizenship rights (although much of the most important recent literature is seeking a way to mediate between the needs and interests of individuals and cultural groups).[27]

In all of these strands of scholarship, the claims of citizenship have been transposed from the domains of state and politics to spheres that have traditionally been regarded as insulated from direct public concern. This is a far cry from the Aristotelian conception of citizenship, according to which citizenship is distinctly political by nature, and it departs from the traditional liberal rights-based conception as well to the degree that it insists on dramatically expanding the scope of legitimate state involvement to previously off-limit domains. Although some purists have objected to these recent efforts,[28] it seems fair to say that the innovators have been relatively successful: the conjoining of the idea of citizenship with economy, culture, corporation, university, workplace, and civil society more broadly no longer sounds as jarring and paradoxical as it must once have. It is common by now, even in colloquial discourse, to link the idea of citizenship with activities and spheres that once seemed remote from citizenly concern.

This development, notably, can be read as either a broadening of citizenship's range of application or an expansion of our understandings of what constitutes the domain of the political. In either reading, citizenship has clearly gained substantial release from its conventional association with the traditionally defined public sphere. In the process, the range of claims for rights and self-governance and solidarity that are regarded as worthy of political recognition has been substantially enlarged as well.

LOCATING CITIZENSHIP: THE NATION-STATE AND THE POSTNATIONAL CHALLENGE

While citizenship is now understood by many scholars to extend to new social domains, the nature and the parameters of the broader community in which citizenship is located are almost always treated as given. Citizenship is presumed, with little question, to be a national enterprise—a set of institutions and practices that necessarily take place within the political community, or the social world, of the nation-state. Of course, citizenship has an important history that predates the nation-state's development; the idea of citizenship originated as a concept linking membership to the city-state. However, citizenship's national character and national location are today treated as axiomatic, so much so that they are rarely specified, much less defended.[29]

In the past several years, however, the national assumption in the citizenship literature has come under increasing challenge. A growing number of scholars across the disciplines have begun to press for updated understandings of citizenship's location. They have coined new phrases— "transnational citizenship," "global citizenship," "postnational citizenship"—and have revived the classic notion of "cosmopolitan citizenship." For some, these terms represent empirical claims about the changing nature of citizenship in practice: citizenship, they maintain, is becoming increasingly decoupled from the nation-state as a matter of fact. Others contend that citizenship *ought* to be conceived in ways that are divorced or distanced from state-belonging. The particulars of each of these arguments vary, but the common theme is that exclusively state-centered conceptions of citizenship are unduly narrow or parochial in this age of intensive globalization. Citizenship is described as increasingly denationalized, with new forms of citizenship (both above and below the state) either actually or ideally displacing the old.[30]

Efforts by scholars across the disciplines to talk about citizenship in ways that decouple it from the nation-state have met, in turn, with substantial resistance among mainstream citizenship theorists. Many agree with the view articulated half a century ago by Hannah Arendt that a citizen "is *by definition* a citizen among citizens of a country among countries. His rights and duties must be defined and limited, not only by those of his fellow citizens, but also by the boundaries of a territory. . . ."[31] This view has been reaffirmed recently by a number of theorists, perhaps most succinctly by historian Gertrude Himmelfarb, who has written that citizenship "has little meaning except in the context of a state."[32]

This traditionalist view continues to dominate the debate concerning citizenship's actual and proper location, with those seeking to either describe or promote citizenship's denationalization remaining largely marginalized. Yet blanket rejection of their claims is overly facile.

To begin with, because citizenship possesses multiple understandings in substantive terms, the question whether citizenship is in fact taking non-national form is actually several questions, to which different responses may be required.[33] It is clearly the case that citizenship in the sense of formal legal status remains closely bound to nation-state membership. As a practical matter, citizenship status is almost always conferred by national states, and as a matter of international law, it is national citizenship that is recognized and honored.[34] The proliferation of dual and multiple citizenships around the world obviously subverts the conventional expectation of citizenship exclusivity, but nevertheless keeps citizenship firmly within a national framework, and illustrates not so much the post-nationalization as the multinationalization of citizenship status.[35]

Yet even with respect to status citizenship, the postnationality claim has some real descriptive purchase. The most significant example is the emerging status of European Union citizenship. EU citizenship represents a dramatic reconstitution of citizenship in Europe in some respects; for EU citizens, Europe's borders have been effectively removed with the guarantee of the right to free movement,[36] and EU citizens enjoy economic rights and some political rights at a supranational level.[37] Nevertheless, EU citizenship remains grounded in, and derivative of, the citizenships of the constituent national states, and that it is still subordinate to those citizenships in important respects.[38]

Where citizenship is understood as the enjoyment of basic rights and entitlements, the idea of transnational or global citizenship seems generally more plausible. This is because the various rights associated with citizenship in this tradition, including civil, political, social and cultural rights, are no longer exclusively guaranteed at the national level. While nation-states continue to define the nature and scope of most rights, as well as to enforce them, states can no longer be said to be the sole source of existing positive rights. As is well known, the international human rights regimes that developed in the post-World War II period were designed to implement supranational standards for the treatment of individuals by states. These standards, which encompass civil, social, and sometimes cultural rights, represent an alternative source of rights that transcends the jurisdiction of individual nation-states. There are real limits to the international human rights system, certainly, and people continue to face serious constraints in enforcing internationally guaranteed rights.[39] But there is no disputing that many of the rights commonly associated with citizenship are no longer entirely circumscribed by nation-state boundaries.[40] Although this incipient form of citizenship may often be more symbolic than real, the same has often been true of citizenship rights within national states as well.

To the extent, furthermore, that we approach citizenship in its republican sense as active political (and now civic) engagement, the claims of transnational citizenship seem more plausible still. There is today a burgeoning literature on the "new transnational forms of political organization, mobilization and practice" that have emerged in the wake of accelerating processes of globalization.[41] This literature highlights the proliferating political engagements (such as voting, campaigning, and office holding) that emigrants maintain with their states of origin, and the corresponding efforts of those states to retain political connections with their nationals residing abroad.[42] The idea of "transnational citizenship" also characterizes the increasing numbers of people who are engaged in democratic political practices across national borders in the form of transnational social movements, including those of labor rights activists, environmentalists, feminists, and human rights workers.[43] Describing this latter sort of activism as citizenship, as many scholars have done, clearly requires recognition of citizenship practices in the domain of civil society—a recognition that, as we have seen, many commentators have begun to extend. What is distinct, in this context, is that the civil society at issue is not nationally bounded but takes transnational form; its domain is the arena of what some have called "global civil society."[44]

Finally, when citizenship is approached psychologically, as an experience of identity and solidarity, anthropologists and others have shown that people increasingly maintain central identities and commitments that transcend or traverse national boundaries. These include the solidarities and identifications that may develop among members of transnational social movements and of transnational elites.[45] It includes, as well, the experiences of migrants who live in various diasporic and other cross-national communities. These individuals "lead dual lives," as sociologist Alejandro Portes observes. "Members are at least bilingual, move easily between different cultures, frequently maintain homes in two counties, and pursue economic, political and cultural interests that require a simultaneous presence in both."[46] The proliferation of transnational communities has resulted in the production of plural identities and solidarities among their members that are not reducible to unitary statist models of social belonging.[47]

A number of critics have responded to these various efforts to extend the idea of citizenship beyond the nation-state by contending that proponents are not describing citizenship at all but events and processes that either directly undermine citizenship or are, in any event, distinguishable from it. Sociologist David Jacobson, for example, maintains that the rise of international human rights law represents not a relocation of citizenship but rather citizenship's "devaluation" or displacement.[48] Political theorist David Miller has argued, correspondingly, that while Greenpeace activists may well be doing something laudable, they are not engaged in the practice of *citizenship*—among other reasons, because citizenship requires "rooted[ness] in a bounded political community."[49]

These responses, notably, begin with an a priori state-centered definition of citizenship, and then categorically rule out any institutions or practices that depart from this framework. A better approach, it seems to me, is to begin by treating citizenship as a core political idea that is conventionally used to designate a variety of different practices and experiences and institutions, and then to recognize that some of the practices and experiences and institutions described by the idea of citizenship have in fact begun (however, unevenly) to take transnational or non-national or extranational form or direction. In this approach, the concepts of postnational or transnational citizenship cannot be regarded as incoherent per se, and they are at least sometimes plausible in descriptive terms. As with the case of civil society citizenship, there seems to be no compelling logical or empirical reason to refuse to allow the term citizenship to evolve along with its referents.[50]

Perhaps the deeper debate goes to the normative question of where citizenship *should* be located. Much of this debate revolves around questions of citizenship understood as ethical identification and solidarity. A number of theorists have recently argued on behalf of cosmopolitan conceptions of citizenship solidarity, or "world citizenship." These are ethical universalist notions that are meant to express the fundamental moral duties we owe to humanity at large.[51] Others—including activists in the globalization protests in Seattle and elsewhere—have begun to argue for a cross-border, anticorporate, class-based solidarity of the marginalized, which they have characterized as a form of "global citizenship" or "globalization from below."[52] In each case, the claim is that citizenship solidarity, particularly in the domain of distributive justice, need not, and cannot legitimately, be constrained by national boundaries.

In response, critics have insisted that national conceptions of citizenship as solidarity must remain primary, for at least two reasons. First, liberal institutions and practices depend on it: redistribution has been and is likely to remain a national project, grounded in relations of mutual solidarity that cannot be developed on a global scale. As David Miller has written, "the welfare state—and indeed, programmes to protect minority rights—have always been *national* projects, justified on the basis that members of a community must protect one another and guarantee one another equal respect."[53]

Others have maintained that national conceptions of citizenship are not merely necessary but intrinsically desirable. The nation-state, they contend, is the only large-scale contemporary institutional setting in which people may develop the sense of "common good" or "shared fate" that is so vital to human flourishing.[54] In this fundamentally communitarian view, "having a secure sense of national identity is an important, indeed, a crucially important, element for the very possibility of a full human existence."[55]

Yet these arguments have, in turn, been subject to challenge, not least on grounds that they represent an unjustifiably parochial vision of ethical commitment. Normatively privileging identification with, and solidarity toward, compatriots presumes the existence of a class of non-national others who are necessarily excluded from the domain of normative concern. Some outsiders are located outside the national territory and are routinely denied access to it; others reside within the national territory as aliens or as perceived foreigners. In either case, the question arises as to why the people with whom we happen to share formal membership status and territory should be the objects of our identification and solidarity to a greater extent than others with whom we are joined by other kinds of status or affiliative ties. Why, in other words, should "compatriots take priority"?[56] Some scholars have argued that liberal-egalitarian principles themselves require abandonment of nationalist ethics in favor of ethical universalism or other forms of cross-national solidarity.[57]

In addition to the question of the scope of citizenship's ethical community, the national conception of citizenship raises important concerns of democratic political theory. Here, republican conceptions of citizenship as political engagement emerge as central. With the increasing globalization of social and economic life, the capacity of national states to regulate in ways that can effectively respond to many of today's most pressing policy problems has notoriously diminished. The enormous growth and influence of globalized corporate activity is of special concern. A growing number of democratic theorists have recently warned that "[s]ome of the most fundamental forces and processes which determine the nature of life-chances within and across political communities are now beyond the reach of nation states."[58] To the extent one supports development of institutions that permit people to have a meaningful voice in the process of democratic self-governance, establishing mechanisms of global democratic accountability, and cultivating forms of transnational participatory politics more generally, would seem to be essential.[59]

These debates—both ethical and institutional—between supporters of nationalism and forms of cosmopolitanism are complex and ongoing. For my purposes here, what is significant is that they have increasingly taken the form of debates over *citizenship*. At one level, this is a debate over definitions—over the question of when and how the idea of citizenship is properly applied. But it is also clear that given citizenship's power as a great honorific, both sides have had substantial incentive to claim the term as their own.

The Subjects of Citizenship

One of the perennial themes in the academic literature on citizenship concerns the question of how far citizenship extends in social terms; this is the question of *who* will constitute the class of citizenship's subjects. Because citizenship is conceived as representing political or social membership (almost always, as we have seen, in the context of the nation-state), the question of citizenship's subjects is consequently the question of who it is that will be counted as (usually national) political or social members.

But because membership is very differently conceived in different understandings of citizenship, the answer to citizenship's "who" question should arguably vary as well. The class of republican participatory citizens, for instance, will not necessarily correspond—and has not always corresponded—with the class of rights-bearing citizens more generally, nor with the class of legal status citizens, nor with the class of psychological citizens. In practice, the elements of citizenship are often disaggregated. For example, status noncitizens had the vote in some American states, while significant groups of formal status citizens have been denied effective voice and vote and civil recognition. Even rights-bearing citizens themselves are not a monolithic group: the class of persons enjoying what Marshall termed civil citizenship, for instance, is not always, and has not always been, the same as the class of people enjoying political or social or cultural citizenship. [60]

Most discussions of citizenship's subjects tend not to acknowledge such distinctions in the meanings of citizenship; the usual approach is to treat citizenship as an undifferentiated whole, and to assume that certain groups of people either enjoy it or do not. Scholars of citizenship do tend to diverge, on the other hand, in the way in which they approach citizenship's normative orientation. Some treat citizenship principally as a universalist project while others emphasize its exclusionary attributes. Much of the literature on citizenship's who question can be divided this way.

Universal Citizenship

On one side, the story of citizenship is often recounted as a tale of progressive incorporation, with new social classes increasingly demanding, and ultimately achieving, inclusion as citizens over time. T. H. Marshall expressly contemplated this kind of expansion in his work: He wrote that "[s]ocieties in which citizenship is a developing institution [have strived for] a fuller measure of equality, an enrichment of the stuff of which the status is made, *and* an increase in the number of those on whom the status is bestowed."[61] Likewise, Michael Walzer has written that "the number and range of people in [citizenship's] commonality grows by invasion and incorporation. Slaves, workers, new immigrants, Jews, Blacks, women— all of them move into the circle of the protected, even if the protection they actually get is still unequal or inadequate."[62] This is citizenship's "expanding . . . circle of belonging," in Kenneth Karst's phrase.[63]

These accounts of citizenship's progressive inclusiveness over time give voice to what Iris Marion Young has called "the ideal of universal citizenship." This ideal, she writes, has "driven the emancipatory momentum of modern political life." It stands for "the inclusion and participation of everyone."[64] And indeed, the claim of "citizenship for all" has been a very powerful normative touchstone in most liberal democratic societies in the modern period. But it is an aspirational value, and tells only part of the story.

As a historical matter, for one thing, the progressive trajectory has been interlaced with other, more regressive social narratives. In the United States context, the liberal universalist citizenship story has always been accompanied by a regressive strand—one that Rogers Smith calls "ascriptive Americanism"—which has served to justify the exclusion of African Americans, women, and other racial, ethnic, and religious minorities from recognition as full citizens.[65] Beyond histories of overt exclusion, furthermore, critics have charged that even where citizenship has been made available to ever-widening groups of people, the citizenship they enjoy in substantive terms is often strikingly narrow. Some critics characterize this as citizenship formalism: although citizenship has been extended horizontally to increasing numbers of social groups, the citizenship they enjoy in substance is often illusory. The best-known version of this claim is the Marxist and neo-Marxist contention that the grossly unequal distribution of resources in capitalist societies renders many formal citizenship rights largely empty, since most citizens are not in a position to avail themselves of those rights in any meaningful way.[66]

Other critics have emphasized existing inequalities in the enjoyment of citizenship rights among formally equal citizens. This claim lies at the heart of the well-known and rhetorically powerful critique of "second-class citizenship:"[67] The argument is that certain marginalized social groups may now enjoy nominal citizenship status, but their members are, in fact, afforded less in the way of substantive citizenship than others in society, either because they suffer directly unequal treatment (for example, gays and lesbians in the United States) or because the legal system treats certain social domains where de facto inequality prevails (for example, the ostensibly private spheres of economy, culture, and family) as falling beyond the constraints of citizenship altogether.

There is, additionally, the charge that despite the increasingly widespread extension of citizenship to community residents, levels of civic and political engagement are exceptionally low. From a civic republican perspective, the universal availability of citizenship rights means little in the context of a society of citizens who live pervasively passive and privatized lives, with little engagement in community and the process of self-government.[68] Finally, critics have emphasized that possession of formal citizenship status often fails to protect people from exclusion and violence directed at those perceived to be "foreign" in character, habit, or appearance.[69]

Each of these critiques makes clear that even when citizenship is formally extended to ever-broader groups of subjects, the widespread enjoyment or practice of citizenship is not thereby guaranteed. Rather, there is often a gap between possession of citizenship status and the enjoyment or performance of citizenship in substantive terms. Indeed, each of these critiques suggests that expansion in the class of citizenship's subjects has more or less outrun the expansion and deepening of its substance.

Nevertheless, in political and legal theory on citizenship, universalism remains the defining normative touchstone. It is no longer disputed that citizenship—meaningful, substantive citizenship—should be available to "everyone." As always, however, the notion of universality is itself subject to pressure and renegotiation. Recently, for instance, some advocates and commentators have pressed for recognition of the citizenship of nonhuman animals and of members of future generations, often under the rubric of ecological citizenship.[70] Others have sought to extend the recognition and protections imparted by citizenship to fetuses or the "unborn."[71] While relatively marginal formulations, the entry of these claims into the discourse attests to power, and the perceived expansiveness of citizenship's universalist ethic.

Bounded Citizenship

Universalism is the prevailing ethic within a political community whose boundaries and identity are taken as given. And most legal and political theorists do take these boundaries as given: they presume a fixed national citizenry and devote themselves to inquiring about the nature of the relations that do or ought to prevail among its members. Yet the study of citizenship is not confined to these internal questions, and universalism does not exhaust citizenship's fundamental commitments. For a different group of legal and political scholars—usually scholars of immigration and nationality—citizenship is the core analytical concept for thinking about the way in which the community's membership and boundaries are constituted in the first instance. And in the context of this scholarly enterprise, citizenship stands not for universalism but for closure.

Citizenship in this latter understanding is concerned not with the interior life of the political community but with its threshold. And in most versions, the community threshold with which citizenship is concerned is that of the national state. Citizenship is a status that assigns persons to membership in specific nation-states. At the same time, citizenship status in any given nation is almost always restricted, available only to those who are recognized as its members.

Different states, of course, have different policies regarding admission to citizenship. Virtually all states assign citizenship to children born of the state's nationals (*jus sanguinis*), while only some—though increasing numbers—grant citizenship to children born within the state's territory (*jus soli*). Most states, furthermore, make provision for naturalization by foreigners into citizenship after birth. In each case, however, citizenship status is not automatically granted either to anyone who seeks it or, necessarily, to anyone who enters into or resides within state territory, but is instead subject to rationing by the state. This kind of rationing is accepted as a matter of international law: states are deemed fully sovereign with respect to decisions about whom to admit to membership (although there are some constraints on forcible expatriation).[72]

Legal scholars have devoted much attention to questions concerning acquisition and loss of citizenship. The debate over the propriety of *jus soli* assignment of citizenship has garnered particular attention in recent years. In the U.S. context, some prominent scholars urged in the 1980s that birthright citizenship should no longer be accorded to children born in the United States of undocumented immigrant parents.[73] This proposal was highly controversial, partly in light of the nation's history of denying citizenship to blacks through the Civil War and the specific repudiation of that exclusion through the Fourteenth Amendment of the U.S. Constitution. Most commentators agree that a state's denial of citizenship to persons born and raised within its territory presents significant problems of political legitimacy, though again, not all states have embraced this principle.

Dual or multiple nationality has been another subject of intense scholarly interest.[74] In recent years, more people than ever hold citizenship in more than one nation. This is the result, in part, of recent liberalization of different national rules on naturalization, expatriation and assignment of citizenship at birth, which together make multiple citizenship legally possible and often routine. It is also due to the availability of dramatically improved transportation and communications technologies, which make the pursuit of life in more than one nation-state increasingly possible in practical terms. This increase in the incidence of dual nationality has led to widespread debate: whereas some critics have insisted that national citizenship must remain a unique commitment,[75] others have increasingly celebrated the rise in cases of plural allegiances and identities that multiple citizenships often entail.[76]

In addition to issues involving the allocation and distribution of status citizenship, scholars have devoted substantial attention to questions about the legal significance of the status. The inquiry here is what, exactly, possession or lack of possession of citizenship status should rightfully entail within a national society. Because citizenship is an exclusive status, and because in most states foreigners enter the territory in some status short of citizenship, the question arises as to how those without citizenship status should be treated. To what extent should enjoyment of basic rights depend on being a status citizen, and to what extent should it depend on the fact of personhood and territorial presence alone? Legal theorist Alexander Bickel famously launched the modern version of this debate in the United States by arguing that possession of citizenship status has long been, and should remain, fundamentally insignificant in the American constitutional order. The American Constitution, he wrote, presents "the edifying picture of a government that bestow[s] rights on people and persons, and [holds] itself out as bound by certain standards of conduct in its relations with people and persons, not with some legal construct called citizen."[77] Others, by contrast, have disputed this account in historical terms and have urged, in any event, that the status of citizenship has been wrongly "devalued" and deserves constitutional prominence and honor.[78] This debate has enormous practical implications for the treatment and condition of aliens in the national society in which they reside.

There is, finally, a vast scholarship in law and policy on the regulation of the border itself. The concern here is national immigration policies in all their dimensions: those pertaining to substantive admission, exclusion, and deportation criteria, those concerned with procedures at the border, and those concerned with refugee and asylum policy. Although these subjects do not involve citizenship directly, they are the indispensable backdrop and corollary to any study of citizenship in its threshold dimension. The regulation of immigration presumes the noncitizenship of national outsiders; it is their lack of citizenship that allows the state to limit and otherwise place conditions on their territorial ingress and membership. Immigration control is thus the policy expression of bounded citizenship in its purest form.

The great majority of commentators endorse the right of nation-states to restrict their membership: communitarians maintain that such a right is an essential part of a community's process of self-definition,[79] while liberal theorists tend to endorse restrictions at least to the extent necessary to preserve the liberal order.[80] But state control of access to territory and to national membership status is not entirely uncontroversial at the level of normative theory; a few commentators have challenged the prevailing commitment to closure. Joseph Carens in particular has argued that a commitment to liberal principles necessarily entails support for a policy of relatively open borders.[81] Carens's position still represents an outlying view, however, and in most legal and political theory, the legitimacy of barriers to territorial entry and to national citizenship is not even on the table.

The Citizenship of Aliens

The question of who it is that constitutes citizenship's subjects thus has two kinds of answers: a universalist answer (everybody) and a nationally particularist answer (members of the nation). In most circumstances, the radical divergence between these two answers is hardly noticed, because each answer is viewed as relevant to a different domain: Universality is understood to govern life within the community, while exclusivity is assumed to govern the community at its threshold.[82] This account is mostly accurate; yet, there is one significant context in which the two commitments are not divided jurisdictionally but in fact occupy the same terrain.

This context involves the condition of noncitizens who reside within a national political community. On the one hand, the status of noncitizens, or aliens, is a product of citizenship's exclusionary regime: these are people who are legally defined as lacking in full national membership, and who are subject to certain disabilities, including lack of political rights and potential deportation as a result. In the case of alienage, citizenship's exclusionary threshold shifts inside to operate directly within the territory of the national society.

On the other hand, the status of aliens in liberal democratic societies is, in many respects, hardly distinguishable from that of citizens.[83] By virtue of their territorial presence and their personhood, aliens in most such societies are routinely entitled to a broad range of important civil and social rights—rights of a kind that are commonly described in the language of citizenship. These are rights that are distributed according to citizenship's internally universalist logic, which means their extension (no doubt paradoxically) to noncitizens as well. In most liberal democratic societies, many noncitizens are entitled, among other things, to full due process rights in criminal proceedings, to expressive, associational, and religious freedom rights, to the protections of the state's labor and employment laws, and to the right to education and other social benefits. And although they always remain subject to potential deportation, noncitizens are often entitled to important procedural rights that serve to constrain state power over them in the expulsion process as well. [84]

Aliens can thus be described as both outsiders to, and subjects of, citizenship simultaneously. This dual location can make for legal uncertainty and sometimes conflict, because in any given case it is not always clear which regime—exclusive national citizenship or universal internal citizenship—should and will prevail. Whereas immigration protectionists invoke the national interest to justify use of citizenship as an "instrument of social closure,"[85] immigrants rights advocates press to extend citizenship's universalist promises beyond the class of nationals to further protect aliens—or noncitizens—themselves.[86]

What is significant for analytical purposes is that alien status represents an arena in which both the universalist and particularist commitments of citizenship are relevant and determinative. The condition of aliens makes clear that citizenship at the border and citizenship within the community are not always jurisdictionally separate projects but are instead sometimes deeply imbricated with one another. And it is not always clear where the boundary lies between them.

The case of alienage is also significant for a different, conceptual reason: it highlights the segmented, even fractured, quality of conventional understandings of citizenship. To the extent that noncitizens can, comprehensibly, be described as governed by the norms of universal citizenship—to the extent that saying that one is making *citizenship* claims on behalf of aliens is not entirely incoherent—it becomes clear that the class of citizenship's subjects and the domain of citizenship's substance are not always in alignment. Just as there are some status citizens who are denied important aspects of rights citizenship (and are thereby understood to be second-class citizens), a person need not possess status citizenship in order to enjoy many of the incidents of rights citizenship. Citizenship, in this respect, is not a unified condition but a set of different institutions and practices that converge in some respects but are relatively autonomous in others. Any answer to the question, "who is a citizen?" will depend, in large part, on which particular institutions and practices are under discussion.

CITIZENSHIP'S FUTURES

If so many aspects and concerns of our collective lives can be articulated in the language of citizenship, how useful can the term really be in scholarly discourse, including legal studies? In one view, the concept is simply too multivalent to play the kind of central analytical and aspirational role that it has come to play in the work of many contemporary scholars. Citizenship too often seems to represent all things to all people; in the process it is often hard to know what is at stake and how the concept advances discussion at all.

Yet it is also true that citizenship's meaning is not entirely indeterminate. Status, rights, political participation, and identity represent the core of its analytical concerns. Moreover, citizenship's long association with egalitarian and democratic ideals in at least some of its understandings make it a powerful term of progressive political rhetoric. It is this aspect of citizenship that has led to the many ongoing efforts to reshape and extend the term to new subjects and new domains. Cultural citizenship, economic citizenship, minority group citizenship, postnational/global citizenship, citizenship of nonhuman animals, ecological citizenship, alien citizenship: these all represent efforts to press the idea of universality beyond its currently given boundaries. But while these attempts generally reflect the concerns of the political left, there is nothing intrinsically emancipatory about this process, as current efforts to recognize and protect "fetal citizenship," among other things, make clear.

It is not yet certain which of these new formulations will become part of our conventional understandings of citizenship. Those that seek to sever citizenship from its presumed association with the nation-state and national forms of belonging represent among the deepest challenges to conventional understandings today, and will face especially strenuous resistance. Still, citizenship is nothing if not a pliable concept. And in its universalist aspect, it may contain the seeds of its own transformation.

CHAPTER 3

The Difference That Alienage Makes

IN MOST COUNTRIES, some set of rights and benefits are reserved to people who possess that country's citizenship status. This means that individuals who lack citizenship status—who are designated by law as "aliens"—are denied the full enjoyment of social, political, and civil rights in the receiving society, at least for some period. People differ on the question of how accessible citizenship status should be in the first instance, but most agree that, once acquired, possession of citizenship status should be legally consequential for some purposes.[1]

But for which purposes, and when? Citizenship distinctions have often been controversial in particular contexts and applications. These are, after all, measures that discriminate; they distribute rights and benefits differentially in a variety of social spheres based on state-assigned status. Especially where alienage is a long-term, even potentially permanent condition, the privileging of citizens over noncitizens would seem to depend on, and to reinforce, caste-like stratification among societal groups. On this reading, government policies that disadvantage noncitizens directly contravene the egalitarian norms to which liberal democratic national societies claim to adhere.

Yet this is hardly the consensus view. Many otherwise staunch egalitarians defend citizenship preferences as an unavoidable and even desirable feature of national membership communities. The fact is that in liberal democratic societies, discrimination can be deemed impermissible or justifiable, depending on the circumstances. And discrimination on account of alienage has often been a difficult call.

In the United States in particular, the law has been chronically ambivalent about the significance of alienage for the allocation of rights and benefits. At times the law treats alienage as an irrelevant and illegitimate basis on which to justify the less favorable treatment of persons. The Supreme Court has characterized alienage as a legal status that, "like . . . nationality or race," is a presumptively illegitimate basis for discriminatory treatment.[2] It is "[h]abit, rather than analysis," one justice has written, that "makes it seem acceptable and natural to distinguish between . . . alien and citizen."[3] At other times, though, the law treats alienage as an eminently appropriate basis for differential treatment of persons. The very existence of the status of alienage presupposes a national state with boundaries and the sovereign authority to maintain those boundaries against outsiders. As part of that sovereign authority, the government has provided an "ascending scale of rights [to the alien] as he increases his identity with our society."[4] In this view, alienage matters because citizenship matters; citizens are full members of the national community, while aliens "are by definition those outside of this community."[5]

American law is, in short, deeply divided about the significance of the status of alienage for the allocation of rights and benefits. In some contexts, alienage matters a great deal; in others, it matters very little or not at all. But to characterize the law this way is actually to beg the question. What accounts for the stark division in the doctrine? How can we understand the law's ambivalent approach to alienage as a category of difference?

The answer, I will argue, resides in another question, one that plagues the law of alien status at every turn, and it is this: What legitimate bearing should the government's claimed interest in regulating the ingress of foreigners have on its general treatment of noncitizens who are present in our society? To what extent do national concerns with protecting the boundaries of territory and membership properly structure the status of noncitizens currently residing in the national territory and participating in national life? What, in short, is the proper relationship between *immigration* law and policy, on the one hand, and *alienage* law and policy, on the other?

In this chapter, I analyze the conflicting normative commitments American law brings to bear in its treatment of discrimination on account of alienage. I argue that the law has constructed alienage as a hybrid legal status category that lies at the nexus of two legal and moral worlds. On the one hand, it lies within the world of borders, sovereignty and national community membership. This is the world of the government's immigration power, which regulates decisions about the admission and exclusion of outsiders and places conditions on their entry and residence. The very existence of alienage is a product of this world because the government designates aliens as such in the course of exercising its immigration power. In the broader landscape of American public law, this power remains exceptionally unconstrained.

Yet alienage as a legal category also lies in the world of social relationships among territorially present persons. In this world, government power to impose disabilities on people based on their status is substantially constrained. Formal commitments to norms of equal treatment and to the elimination of caste-like status have shaped American public law in important ways over the past several decades. In this world, aliens appear to be at once indistinguishable from citizens and precisely the sort of social group that requires the law's protection.

Because alienage lies at the nexus of these two legal worlds—because it is a hybrid legal status that is the creature of both—the question of when and whether a person's status as an alien, or noncitizen, legitimately matters in determining the allocation of rights and benefits in our society tends to take the form of what can best be described as a jurisdictional dispute in the law. This dispute concerns the question of which of the two worlds, or regulatory domains, defining alienage properly controls in any given case—or, assuming the relevance of both, how they are to be accommodated. To what extent is discrimination between citizens and aliens a legitimate expression of the government's power to regulate the border and to control the composition of membership of the national community? On the other hand, how far does sovereignty reach before it must give way to equality; when, that is, does discrimination against aliens implicate a different kind of government power, subject to far more rigorous constraints? These questions shape the law's conflicted understandings of the difference that alienage makes.

To develop my argument, I begin by examining the treatment of alien status in the work of political theorist Michael Walzer.[6] Walzer's analysis of the normative dimensions of a country's "admissions policy" in *Spheres of Justice* is well-known to immigration analysts, yet as part of his broader treatment of what he calls the "membership" sphere, Walzer also examines the status of immigrants who reside within the territory of a democratic national community. This latter aspect of Walzer's work has been far less influential in the immigration literature, but it is of substantial utility in thinking about the law's approach to alienage discrimination. It is useful, however, not so much as a normative theory of alien status but as a framework for thinking analytically about the structure of the alien/citizen divide in the law. It is especially helpful because he recognizes that the difference that alienage makes in a particular society is shaped by that society's conception of the proper boundaries of what he calls its "membership sphere." Walzer's analytical account of membership as a distinct regulatory domain with contested boundaries provides a useful conceptual framework for understanding the law's approach to alienage as a legal status category.

The chapter then goes on to analyze, in some detail, the American constitutional law of alien status in light of this reading of Walzer. I show how the case law is currently structured by a tension between two broad normative paradigms, each of which represents a distinct approach to what I have called the jurisdictional question. The first emphasizes the fundamental irrelevance of membership concerns in the shaping of the status of noncitizens in the economic and social spheres of national life, and the need for strict boundaries between the domain of membership and that of equal personhood. The second stresses the rightful place of membership concerns in shaping the status of noncitizens in all spheres of national life, notwithstanding our commitments to equal personhood.

NATIONAL MEMBERSHIP AND ITS BOUNDARIES

Walzer and Membership

Michael Walzer's concept of membership, elaborated twenty years ago in *Spheres of Justice* and elsewhere,[7] made an enormous contribution to theoretical debates on immigration across the disciplines. Walzer's membership concept is most widely invoked by immigration scholars for the proposition that nation-states are normatively justified in seeking closure against outsiders, or "strangers," to the national community. According to Walzer, a country is a membership community, a "world of common meanings" and shared "ways of life," which its members are entitled to preserve. Because the unimpeded entry of strangers would render such preservation impossible, the members of a national community must have the right "to make [their] own admissions policy, to control and sometimes restrain the flow of immigrants."[8]

Walzer's defense of the right of states to enforce boundaries against strangers is grounded in his broader theory of distributive justice. For Walzer, "[t]he primary good that we distribute to one another is membership" in a national political community, and membership "is a good that can only be distributed by taking people in" or refusing to take them.[9] Walzer argues that the members of a community have a right to shape their membership community according to their own preferences: a community's admissions policy is, for him, an eminently political decision. Walzer presumes that "we who are already members do the choosing, in accordance with our own understanding of what membership means in our community and of what sort of community we want to have."[10] And in the current international context, some states will be faced with difficult choices.

> Affluent and free countries are, like elite universities, besieged by applicants. They have to decide on their own size and character. More precisely, as citizens of such a country, we have to decide: Whom should we admit? Ought we to have open admissions? Can we choose among applicants? What are the appropriate criteria for distributing membership?[11]

Although Walzer insists that the legitimate authority to resolve these questions lies with the members of each community, he also argues that open admissions will rarely be desirable because communities, by their nature, "depend[ ] upon closure" in order to maintain their cultural distinctiveness and in order to protect "the sense of relatedness and mutuality" that membership communities, by their nature, require. In this respect,

Walzer regards "[t]he community . . . itself [as] a good—conceivably the most important good—that gets distributed." He consequently views national control over admissions as an inherent and precious value, one that he forcefully affirms.[12]

Most immigration analysts, quite rightly, read Walzer as articulating a normative justification for national immigration restriction.[13] Yet Walzer's treatment of countries' admissions policies in *Spheres of Justice* does not represent the whole of his immigration analysis. His work has another dimension, one that has received far less attention in the immigration literature despite its centrality to his overall treatment of membership. This dimension of his work addresses the status of aliens already residing inside the national political society. According to Walzer, once immigrants reside within a political community and labor there, they must be treated as members of that community.[14] If they are not yet full members, they must be on a swift track to citizenship, or full membership. Justice requires that "every immigrant and every resident [be] a citizen too or at least a potential citizen." To the extent that immigrants who live and work within a national community are not recognized as members, they are subject to nothing short of "tyranny."[15]

The paradigmatic example of this sort of tyranny, Walzer maintains, was the status of metics in the ancient Athenian polis. Metics were resident aliens in Athens who "could not hope to become citizens." They lived and worked in the city, but they possessed neither political rights nor "welfare rights." While citizens transmitted their status through birth and blood, metic status was passed down through the generations so that the children of metics were likewise metics rather than citizens. Lacking citizenship, metics were treated with contempt; they were "the subjects of a band of citizen tyrants, governed without consent."[16]

Walzer acknowledges that the ancient Greeks viewed the metic system as legitimate, but he maintains that any like system cannot be deemed acceptable in the context of the "shared understandings" of "contemporary democratic communities:" democracy, he insists, cannot abide caste-like status.[17] Nevertheless, the contemporary world of democratic states has fashioned its own metic caste-system, Walzer contends, in the form of the system of guest worker immigration that existed in several European countries until the early 1980s (and whose effects still linger today). Guest workers are brought in to do a country's undesirable work, the dangerous and dirty labor none of the citizens want to do at the offered rate. They come, in theory, temporarily, though they often remain indefinitely. They have no political rights and few, if any, welfare rights. They are expressly denied civil liberties, or they are unwilling to exercise rights that they have for fear of job loss and deportation. By law, they have no prospect of political or legal incorporation into the national community; they are not eligible for naturalization.

At an instrumental economic level, Walzer allows, the guest worker system "works" because it apparently advantages everyone. The host country gets its undesirable labor done at a desirable price, while the laborers get better paying jobs than they could obtain at home. But the system does not work politically, for while the workers are guests, "they are also subjects. They are ruled, like the Athenian metics, by a band of citizen-tyrants." And whereas it might formally appear that they have "agree[d] to be ruled," the consent implied in their willingly coming "is not sufficient for democratic politics."[18] These workers do socially necessary labor, they live among the citizens, and they are subject to the nation's laws. In Walzer's view, "political justice" requires that

> the processes of self-determination through which a democratic state shapes its internal life, must be open, and equally open, to all those men and women who live within its territory, work in the local economy, and are subject to local law. . . . Men and women are either subject to the state's authority, or they are not; and if they are subject they must be given a say, and ultimately an equal say, in what that authority does.[19]

Thus, for Walzer, while decisions regarding the admission and exclusion of strangers are fundamentally political decisions, subject only narrowly to the "constraints of justice," decisions regarding the status of immigrants in the national community's interior are "entirely constrained."[20] Once residing and laboring here, immigrants are no longer strangers, Walzer argues, and to treat them as if they were violates the fundamental moral commitments of democratic community life.

Separate Spheres and "Illegitimate Conversion Patterns"

There are several possible reasons why Walzer's metic analysis has received relatively little attention in the scholarly immigration literature, and why it has received so much less attention than his analysis of states' admissions policies. In the first place, immigration analysts have tended to focus more on matters of entry and exclusion than on the general status of aliens who are already present because, at least until the mid-1990s, admission and exclusion issues were at the heart of the policy debates about immigration in this country. It could also be that since Walzer has little to say about the status of aliens other than guest workers, the relevance of his work to the condition of aliens in the United States is not immediately apparent to many analysts of the American scene. The United States currently hosts only a small class of guest workers,[21] and most aliens here do not precisely match Walzer's profile of contemporary metics. Lawful permanent resident aliens are not barred from naturalizing as the European guest workers were, and undocumented immigrants have not been formally admitted to residence, as those guest workers had been. Perhaps because of Walzer's European focus, it has seemed difficult to transpose the metic principle to the dilemmas of alien status in this country.[22]

Yet whatever accounts for the disparate attention the two parts of his membership analysis have received, for Walzer they are fundamentally and inextricably linked. Walzer emphasizes their mutual dependence: "The theory of distributive justice," he writes, "must vindicate *at one and the same time* the (limited) right of closure and the political inclusiveness of the existing communities."[23]

The linkage of the metic and admissions principles is of the utmost significance to Walzer for two reasons. The first derives from his broader methodological commitments in *Spheres of Justice* and elsewhere.[24] Justice, for Walzer, consists in the shared understandings of a particular community about what is just. There are no absolute or universal standards of justice, only the local standards shared by members of a particular community. The social critic (in this case, Walzer himself) is engaged in neither "discovery" nor revelation of divinely ordained principle but in a social, interpretive practice—the practice of interpreting "to one's fellow citizens the world of meanings that we share."[25] In his role as interpreter of our conventional moral understandings, Walzer insists on both the admissions and metic principles because he finds both to be actual expressions of our common understandings of legitimate social practice. As a matter of fact, he asserts, we do conventionally agree *both* that a core element of national self-determination lies in our collective control over the community's admission process *and* that once immigrants live and work among us, they should not be relegated to second-class status but should be fully embraced as members. Our moral tradition simultaneously embraces external boundedness and internal inclusive equality.

The second reason that Walzer insists on the complementarity of the admissions and metic principles is analytically more fundamental. Their linkage is significant for him because it both illustrates and instantiates the broader structural theory of "complex equality" that he elaborates in *Spheres of Justice*. Walzer's principle of complex equality, briefly stated, is that "no citizen's standing in one sphere or with regard to one social good can be undercut by his standing in some other sphere, with regard to some other good."[26] To understand the significance of this principle for Walzer's analysis of membership, we need to pause and examine its elements.

Walzer seeks to set out a moral theory, grounded in the "shared understandings" of our community, concerning the just distribution of social goods. By social goods, Walzer means everything, both material and intangible, that human beings "share, divide and exchange."[27] Social goods, in turn, are distributed according to procedures, agents and criteria that vary depending on the social good; these sites and systems of distribution Walzer calls distributive spheres. Once again, Walzer views membership as a social good, and its system of distribution constitutes one of the many distributive spheres that make up our social lives.[28]

In elaborating his theory of just distributions, Walzer rejects the notion—common, he says, among moral philosophers—that justice consists in the equal distribution of goods within spheres. Such an ideal, which he calls the ideal of "simple equality," is problematic, first because it is impracticable—Walzer maintains that "monopoly" is a natural condition of distributive spheres, one that is nearly inevitable absent continual state intervention—but, more important, because monopoly within spheres is not always and necessarily unjust. Justice, for Walzer, is not a fixed and invariant quality but is instead intelligible only by reference to the rules of distribution internal to the various distributive spheres. Each distributive sphere, that is, has its own criteria of justice; "there are standards (roughly knowable even when they are also controversial) for every social good and every distributive sphere in every particular society."[29] And the criteria of justice in most spheres allow for monopoly. For example, within the distributive frame of the market, concentrated economic power is not necessarily unjust; nor is concentrated political power considered inappropriate in the political arena.

Yet while Walzer is not much concerned about monopoly, he is exceptionally concerned about a state of affairs he calls "dominance." Dominance is advantage obtained *across* sphere boundaries. It occurs when the fact of possession of goods in one distributive sphere entitles the possessor to goods in other spheres.[30] Dominance reflects "illegitimate conversion patterns" among the spheres; they are illegitimate not on any absolute or universal grounds but because "social meanings call for the autonomy, or the relative autonomy, of distributive spheres."[31]

Thus, Walzer argues, while "[t]here is nothing wrong . . . with the grip that persuasive and helpful men and women (politicians) establish on political power . . . [t]he use of political power to gain access to other goods is a tyrannical use."[32] Likewise, the possession of disproportionate financial power in the market is one thing, and arguably legitimate of itself. But a person's financial power should not, consistent with justice, translate into political power—or into educational power, or power in the sphere of love and affection. It is the "[d]ominance of capital outside the market [that] makes capitalism unjust,"[33]—that makes it, in Walzer's terms, a form of "tyranny."[34]

If dominance were eliminated, Walzer argues, a regime of "complex equality" would prevail. A society is characterized by complex equality to the extent that it "distribut[es] goods for internal reasons."[35] Internal distributions would still allow for many "small inequalities," but "inequality [would] not be multiplied through the conversion process,"[36] leading to the compound forms of power and powerlessness characteristic of dominance regimes.

In short, according to Walzer, "[e]very social good or set of goods constitutes, as it were, a distributive sphere within which only certain criteria and arrangements are appropriate."[37] Dominance results when power in one sphere entitles a person to power in another, when power is illegitimately "converted" from one sphere to another. To the extent power crosses the perimeters of distributive spheres, this is, in his view, "a violation of boundaries,"[38] and the hallmark of distributive *injustice*. In contrast, "different outcomes for different people in different spheres make for a just society."[39]

Significantly, although Walzer emphasizes that the possession of power in one sphere should not give purchase to power in another, he also signals the converse: that the lack of power in one sphere should not be transposable into lack of power in another. In other words, powerlessness should be no more convertible than power among spheres. For Walzer, a good is "dominant" "if the individuals who have it, because they have it, can command a wide range of other goods."[40] Correspondingly, he suggests, a good is negatively dominant if the individuals who do not have it are deprived of other goods in other spheres.[41]

Here we return to Walzer's treatment of membership, for the inverse statement of his basic principle of sphere separability is precisely what Walzer objects to about the status of contemporary metics. The denial of basic civil liberties to these aliens, he argues, exemplifies an exercise of power outside its proper domain. When aliens are denied basic civil and social rights by virtue of their alienage, principles endemic to the membership sphere have exceeded their proper bounds, resulting in a kind of imperialism by the membership domain. Unless aliens are "possessed of those basic civil liberties whose exercise is so much preparation for voting and office holding," they are subject to domination of the membership sphere.

Likewise, Walzer argues that an illegitimate conversion problem results when aliens inside the political community find themselves subject to the "everpresent threat of deportation."[42] The perennial threat of deportation, in his view, is an indirect means of keeping the alien from exercising any civil rights she might formally be permitted. Again, Walzer condemns the persistent threat of deportation faced by aliens as a kind of membership imperialism that entails an overreaching of power outside its rightful sphere.

Walzer insists, in short, that the admissions principle be read in light of the metic principle, and that the latter signals the need for ensuring limits

on the former. National communities may legitimately exercise their prerogatives to define the community's membership—indeed, they must—
but that prerogative must be exercised *within its own domain*. What is
wrong with the status of metics, he argues, is precisely that membership
principles have exceeded their legitimate bounds. The status of metics
represents a paradigm case of the need for the defense of boundaries between spheres.

Separation, Conversion, and Ambiguity

Or perhaps I should say that status of metics represents *almost* a paradigm
case of the need for boundary defense. For although metic status is presented by Walzer as an object lesson in the dangers of "illegitimate conversion patterns," Walzer's critique does not, in fact, demand complete
sphere autonomy. A strict interpretation of the nonconvertibility thesis
would appear to allow no membership-related regulation of a noncitizen
immigrant in the interior of a country. Once a person lives and labors
here, in this view, she would have to be treated indistinguishably from
any other member.[43] Walzer's account, however, does not require this.
While he emphasizes that the principles of justice demand that every resident alien be a citizen or potential citizen, the word *potential* is critical:
he allows that there "can be stages in the transition" from stranger to full
member,[44] and that during the transition, the alien may be denied political
(but not other) rights. To this extent, Walzer suggests—without arguing
the case directly—that the distributive principles of the membership
sphere may legitimately shape, if only temporarily and somewhat narrowly, the distribution of goods in another sphere.[45]

How might we account for this apparent exception within the terms of
Walzer's own theory on sphere separability? Perhaps this way: In one of
his many iterations of the principle of complex equality, Walzer states that
no power endemic to one sphere should be wielded in another "where
there is no intrinsic connection between the two" spheres.[46] Perhaps he
allows for this (limited) exception to strict separation during the alien's
transition to citizenship because he believes that there is, in fact, an intrinsic connection between admission at the border and full incorporation
into the life of the political community. He asserts as much when he writes
that the political community "is a good that can only be distributed by
taking people in, where all the senses of that latter phrase are relevant:
they must be physically admitted *and* politically received."[47]

Whatever the substantive merits of this view, this response is inadequate
as a formal matter because it begs the question. It fails to explain what it
is about the connection between membership and the sphere of politics
that is so intrinsic that it permits the abrogation of the fundamental re-

quirement of complex equality—"different goods to different companies of men and women for different reasons and in accordance with different procedures."[48] On what justification may membership principles and political principles occupy the same terrain? Walzer does not say.[49]

Walzer's sphere separation principle also gives rise to ambiguities beyond those associated with naturalization. Perhaps most important, there is the matter of a government's power to deport aliens who live and work within the national society. We have seen that Walzer views the "everpresent threat of deportation" as an example of membership principles operating outside their own sphere because, he asserts, the fact of this threat serves to deter aliens from exercising the civil and social rights they might otherwise formally enjoy.[50] As a descriptive matter, this is an important insight, as I will argue below. But the relationship between this critique and Walzer's broader normative position on membership is less than clear. While Walzer assails the repressive effect that the specter of deportation can have on aliens who reside within the political community, can he be arguing that any and all deportations of resident aliens are illegitimate?

One wonders, for example, about the deportation of aliens who violate the nation's criminal laws—an issue that Walzer does not address. A strict interpretation of Walzer's autonomy principle would seem to hold that the deportation of aliens on criminal grounds is unacceptable: a criminal should pay for her misconduct by going to prison, not by being expelled from the country.[51] Yet it seems unlikely that Walzer is arguing that national governments must abandon their deportation power altogether, since we know that he thoroughly endorses the right of a national society to regulate the composition of its own membership. Such authority would presumably include the decision to preclude those less than full members who have committed certain crimes from continued community residence. Precisely how we are to accommodate the demands of the admissions and metic principles in this context Walzer does not say.

Membership, Boundary Conflict, and Law

Walzer's treatment of metic status does not (and was never meant to) represent a complete theory of alienage and citizenship with direct relevance and applicability to the American legal system. His account contains certain ambiguities and leaves important questions about alien status unanswered. Yet when read in the context of his broader theory of complex equality, Walzer's metic analysis is of great utility in thinking about the complexities of alien status in American law. The value of this analysis does not, however, lie directly in his normative claim on behalf of sphere separation in the membership context. In fact, whatever its substantive merits, Walzer's normative argument has a fundamental methodological problem. Although Walzer purports to ground his theory of alien status in the "shared understandings" of our political culture, our shared understandings, at least as reflected in law,[52] do not entirely support what he claims for them. Contrary to Walzer's representation, we do *not* all agree on separation of spheres when it comes to the status of aliens. The lawmakers and activists who have agitated, often successfully, to deny aliens access to various rights and benefits in this country seek not sphere separation but an increasing *convergence* of spheres. Membership concerns, in their view, rightfully and necessarily structure the status of aliens within the national community. Alienage matters not merely at the border but for the allocation of rights and benefits in the interior as well.

The point is that the rightful boundaries of the membership domain are subject to substantial contestation in the "shared understandings" of our political and legal culture, and Walzer's metic principle captures only one among the competing strands of legal and political thought on the subject of alienage. Given his methodological commitments, Walzer's "correspondence" problem would seem to detract, at least to some degree, from the value of his analysis.

Still, these limitations do not undermine the value of his analysis entirely, for two reasons. First, the fact that there is sharp debate on the appropriate boundaries of the membership sphere would not necessarily surprise Walzer, at least not in principle. He acknowledges as a general matter that the question of where, exactly, the boundaries of any distributive sphere should legitimately be drawn is going to be subject to dispute in practice. Upon introducing his theory of complex equality, he writes:

> No account of the meaning of a social good, or of the boundaries of the sphere within which it legitimately operates, will be uncontroversial. At best, the arguments will be rough, reflecting the diverse and conflict-ridden character of the social life that we seek simultaneously to understand and to regulate.[53]

Elsewhere, he asserts that "boundary conflict is endemic" among the distributive spheres. He seems to mean, among other things, that the nature of a sphere's relationship with other spheres is always contested. "[T]he principles appropriate to the different spheres are not harmonious with one another," he recognizes; the relationship between spheres often entails "deep strains and odd juxtapositions."[54]

While Walzer is speaking generically, these observations are particularly germane in the membership context. As I argue below, matters of alien status in the law are both plagued and structured by boundary conflict. Although Walzer's treatment of alienage does not expressly acknowledge the conflict, his broader theory of complex equality recognizes that such conflict might well arise, and his treatment of alienage should, I think, be read in light of these more general caveats.

The second reason that the correspondence problem does not entirely undermine the value of Walzer's metic analysis is related to the first, and is especially important for my analysis here. Although Walzer may be wrong about what we agree about, he has managed to highlight the defining issue about which we *disagree* when it comes to the status of aliens. The issue is this: What is the legitimate scope, or jurisdiction, of what Walzer has called the membership sphere? When do membership principles appropriately shape the status of noncitizens residing within the nation and when are they insulated from membership's reach? Having analyzed the status of aliens in this way, Walzer's contribution is vital, because knowing what it is that divides us is the key to understanding the nature of the chronic ambivalence that characterizes the law's approach to alien status.

ALIENAGE, LAW, AND THE BOUNDARIES OF MEMBERSHIP

At first glance, American law governing the treatment of aliens in the United States is striking in its apparent capriciousness. Justifications for different classes of cases, particularly in constitutional law, are difficult to discern. All noncitizens, for example, are entitled to full due process protections in criminal proceedings,[55] and resident aliens are entitled to "freedom of speech and of press."[56] Yet a lawful permanent resident alien may be denied Medicare benefits that are available to a citizen so long as the denial is not "wholly irrational,"[57] even though she may not be denied state welfare benefits without a showing by the state of a compelling governmental interest.[58] Further, a noncitizen may be excluded from the jobs of parole officer and public school teacher on account of her alienage,[59] although she may not, for the same reason, be prohibited from taking the bar examination or serving as a notary public.[60]

A closer look at the constitutional jurisprudence of alienage, not surprisingly, reveals underlying patterns that apparently account for these anomalies. The courts have developed doctrines and drawn lines that distinguish between state- and federally sponsored alienage discrimination,[61] between deprivations of constitutional and subconstitutional rights,[62] between the rights afforded to permanent resident aliens and those afforded to undocumented and other nonresident aliens,[63] between economic and political forms of alienage discrimination,[64] and between discriminatory action taken by different branches or agencies of the federal government.[65] To the extent one becomes familiar with this tangled complex of rules, one can begin to "understand" the constitutional alienage cases.

But the understanding these rules provide is rather thin. They permit us to make ballpark predictions as to how the courts will come out in a given case, and to that extent the apparent capriciousness is greatly diminished. But if the rules help us anticipate results, they do not help us comprehend what is at stake. In fact, by focusing on these doctrinal distinctions, they tend to obscure what it is that the cases all have in common.

There is, I believe, another level of available understanding of the constitutional law concerning the status of aliens within the United States, one that goes not to the cases' outcomes but to the structure of the disputes themselves. The law is driven by perennial uncertainty, and sometimes conflict, over the proper scope of the government's immigration-regulating authority—over the proper scope, that is, of what Walzer calls the nation's membership sphere. The chronic question that drives the doctrine is when and to what degree membership regulation properly subsumes matters of alien status beyond the regulatory domain of the border.

Membership and the Government's Immigration Power

Walzer's sphere of membership broadly corresponds to that body of American law that regulates both the admission and exclusion of aliens, and the terms of their residence once here. This is the domain of what we traditionally regard as the government's immigration power. Territorially, the government exercises its immigration power at the national border, where, in determining whom to admit and exclude, it undertakes a literal gatekeeping function.[66] But the immigration power also reaches into the territorial interior. The government's deportation power permits it to pursue, arrest, and expel aliens who reside here, and its immigration power provides the basis for its prohibition of employer hiring of undocumented aliens. Moreover, an integral part of the government's membership authority is the power to set the terms of and procedures for the naturalization of aliens. Thus, in addition to literal border regulation, the immigration power entails regulation of both the border's "equivalents" in the interior,[67] and of internal "borders" to full membership, or citizenship.

The single most salient feature of the government's immigration power is the fact that it is substantially unconstrained as a constitutional matter. American courts describe the immigration power as "plenary" in character, by which they mean that the judiciary has virtually no authority to scrutinize what the political branches do in this domain. As the Supreme Court has often, and notoriously, reiterated, "over no conceivable subject is the legislative power of Congress more complete than it is over" the regulation of immigration and naturalization.[68]

Many commentators have observed that the plenary power doctrine is an extraordinary doctrine of judicial abdication that has few, if any, analogues in other fields of public law.[69] The reasons for this uncommon deference have been variously articulated over the years. Ordinarily, courts have invoked the foreign affairs power and the government's interest in national sovereignty and self-defense as rationales for the doctrine. In recent years, however, courts have often declined to justify the doctrine, perhaps because it seems increasingly difficult to do, and have tended simply to invoke the early cases as unquestioned authority.[70]

Whatever rationales support it, the plenary power doctrine has often had distressing real-life consequences. Plenary power was invoked to justify the exclusion of Chinese nationals in the late nineteenth century[71] and the exclusion and deportation of political radicals and homosexuals in the twentieth.[72] More recently, plenary power has been invoked in support of a policy that has provided for interdiction on the high seas and the forcible return of Haitian and other nationals seeking to apply for political asylum in the United States.[73] In the wake of 9–11, it was cited as grounds for justifying the indefinite detention of many aliens.[74] For years, scholars have characterized the doctrine as a national embarrassment and have called for its abandonment by the courts.[75]

On the other hand, and despite the judiciary's substantial abdication in the immigration field, the government's immigration power is not entirely unconstrained. To begin with, courts have not absolutely foreclosed the possibility of judicial review of the government's substantive immigration decisions. The Supreme Court has signaled that, in the event of a particularly egregious misuse of government power in this area, the courts would not stand by.[76] Far more significantly, courts have treated the procedures pursuant to which the government's immigration power is exercised as fair game for often rigorous scrutiny, at least under some circumstances. A century ago the Supreme Court established that aliens, including undocumented aliens, were entitled to due process in deportation proceedings,[77] and since then, deportation procedures have been substantially constitutionalized.[78] In addition, courts have sometimes been willing to interpret the immigration statute broadly enough to confer substantial procedural and substantive rights on aliens undergoing exclusion and deportation (now "removal" proceedings), as well as naturalization.[79] While conceding that the political branches possess plenary constitutional power with regard to substantive immigration decision making, the courts have fashioned, as Hiroshi Motomura has shown, both "procedural surrogates," and "phantom constitutional norms"[80] through statutory interpretation, to make real inroads into the formally unconstrained federal power to regulate immigration.

Now, all of the forgoing issues—the substance of government regulation of the border and its equivalent, the plenary power doctrine and its justifications, the disputes over the procedural constraints on the government's exercise of the immigration power—together constitute the warp and woof of the field of immigration law as it is usually defined. These are the issues addressed by the immigration statute and regulations, and by courts in their interpretation. Until recently, these were also the issues covered by courses in immigration law in the law school curriculum.

Yet whether these issues in fact exhaust the field, or the domain, of immigration regulation is less than clear. Is government treatment of aliens in arenas *beyond* the border, broadly construed—beyond, that is, questions of admission, exclusion, deportation, and perhaps naturalization—itself to be viewed as an incident, or an extension, of the immigration power? To the extent the immigration power is understood to represent the power to define membership in the national community, how far does that power extend? Does it extend to regulate the status of aliens in the various economic, social, and political domains of life within our society? Briefly stated, the power to define membership in the national community begins at the nation's border, but where exactly does it end?

These are, of course, the questions that Walzer himself addresses in his examination of the status of metics, both ancient and contemporary. In light of his commitment to complex equality, he asks, What are the proper boundaries of the sphere of membership? Where and when are its distributive principles rightfully exercised, and where and when not? As we have seen, Walzer's own answer to the question calls for stringent limits on the reach of membership principles. He urges a strict separation between the sphere of membership and the various economic and social and political spheres internal to the national society in which aliens conduct their lives.

However, as I argued earlier, although Walzer's answer captures an important strand of thought on the rightful scope of membership principles in the law's understanding of alienage, it is only one strand. The rightful parameters of the membership domain are often deeply uncertain and highly contested in American law. In fact, the separation thesis that Walzer embraces competes with a different vision, one that treats membership principles as appropriately structuring the lives of aliens who live and work within the national society. In this latter view, membership concerns are not separable from the concerns of aliens' general status in the United States but rather inevitably and rightfully converge with them.

The question of just how far into the life of the alien the government's membership authority legitimately extends thus lies at the core of the dilemmas and complexities associated with the legal treatment of alienage. The effort to answer it, directly or indirectly, has structured virtually all judicial and scholarly treatments of alienage discrimination, and virtually all public debate about the difference that alienage makes as well.

The Core Separation

In 1886, the federal government argued before the Supreme Court that the Court had, in the words of Justice Field, the "right . . . to deny to the [alien] accused the full protection of the law and Constitution against every form of oppression and cruelty to them" by virtue of their status as aliens.[81] The case was *Wong Wing v. United States,* and the question was whether the government could punish aliens with imprisonment at hard labor for violation of the immigration law without affording them a trial by jury. For the government, the answer was clearly yes. Aliens in this country cannot be said "under all circumstances, and especially in a procedure which grows out of a political regulation, [to be] entitled to the protection of the Constitution of the United States."[82] Any alien who was present in the country without government consent could not reasonably invoke the constitution in an effort to defend himself from "the express will of the sovereign."[83] The government cannot be

> cribbed, cabined and confined in imposing punishment as an accessory to effectuate its will by the limitations of a Constitution which was not made nor intended for all humanity, nor to operate as a restriction on the Government to protect foreigners against its action in political matters, but was ordained and established by the people of the United States for their own benefit and the benefit of those lawfully within their Territory.[84]

For the government, in short, the fact that the petitioners were deportable aliens placed them outside the protective sphere of the Constitution, whose provisions were available only to citizens and those foreigners who were present by consent.

In what remains a keystone decision in the field,[85] the Supreme Court rejected the government's argument. While the Court took pains to reaffirm its previous holdings that the government possesses plenary power to protect "the country from the advent of aliens whose race or habits render them undesirable as citizens, or to expel such if they have already found their way into our land and unlawfully remain there,"[86] the Court concluded that what was at stake in this case was *not* immigration regulation but criminal punishment, and that invocation of the government's plenary power in the immigration sphere was therefore off the mark. As Justice Shiras wrote for the Court, "to declare unlawful residence within the country to be an infamous crime, punishable by deprivation of liberty and property, would be to pass out of the sphere of constitutional legislation, unless provision were made that the fact of guilt should first be established by a judicial trial."[87] Criminal trials are necessary, even in the case of aliens threatened with punishment for violations of the immigration law, because, in the words of the Court, "all persons within the territory of the United States are entitled to the protection guaranteed" by the Fifth and Sixth Amendments.[88] In other words, the fact of the alien's personhood, combined with her territorial presence, serves to protect her against the unconstrained power of government, so long as the matter at hand is not a matter of *immigration*—by which the Court meant matters of admission, exclusion, or deportation.[89]

In effect, *Wong Wing* stands for the following proposition: Just because the object of government power is an alien does not mean that the government is exercising its immigration power. The proper domain of immigration regulation has limits. There is immigration power, there is governmental power in spheres not directly connected with admission and exclusion, and the two are not coextensive but must be kept apart. As Justice Field wrote in concurrence, "[i]t does not follow that, because the Government may expel aliens or exclude them from coming to this country, it can confine them at hard labor in a penitentiary before deportation, or subject them to any harsh and cruel punishment."[90] Power in one sphere does not necessarily entail power in the other.

This is a profound and not immediately intuitive holding. A person, after all, is an alien only by virtue of an exercise of the federal government's immigration power which defines her as such; as a result, the immigration power might seem, of necessity, to follow the alien wherever she goes. But in *Wong Wing*, the Supreme Court concluded that although the immigration power is extraordinarily broad, it must be exercised *within its own domain*. That domain governs matters of admission, exclusion, and deportation; beyond it, the alien inhabits the domain of territorially present persons, where different and more protective rules against government power apply.

Wong Wing was not the first Supreme Court case to recognize a sphere of constitutional protection for aliens beyond the domain of immigration regulation. Several years earlier, the Court issued the famous *Yick Wo* decision,[91] whose legacy has since come to be associated with noncitizens' rights.[92] Two Chinese noncitizens, Yick Wo and Wo Lee, had been prosecuted for violating a San Francisco ordinance which, although neutral on its face, was enforced in a way to preclude Chinese laundry owners in San Francisco from pursuing their businesses.[93] Because they challenged their prosecution under the equal protection clause of the Fourteenth Amendment, the threshold question in the case was whether the petitioners, as aliens, could invoke the equal protection clause *at all* in their challenges to the race-based application of the law. The Supreme Court, in response, held that notwithstanding their alienage, resident aliens enjoy the protections of the Fourteenth Amendment. Specifically, the Court declared that the terms of the Fourteenth Amendment are

> not confined to the protection of citizens. . . . These provisions are universal in their application, to all persons within the territorial jurisdiction, without regard to any differences of race, of color, or of nationality. . . . The questions we have to consider and decide in these cases, therefore, are to be treated as involving the rights of every citizen of the United States equally with those of the strangers and aliens who now invoke the jurisdiction of the court.[94]

This same principle was reasserted ninety years later in a case involving the constitutional rights of undocumented aliens. In *Plyler v. Doe*, the state of Texas had argued that undocumented aliens—children, in this case—could not invoke the protections of the Fourteenth Amendment to challenge their exclusion from access to state-provided public education. The state's theory was that the children could not be deemed to be "within the jurisdiction" of any state, as the Fourteenth Amendment requires, because of their irregular immigration status. The Court rejected the argument:

> [T]he protection of the Fourteenth Amendment extends to anyone, citizen or stranger, who is subject to the laws of a State, and reaches into every corner of a State's territory. That a person's initial entry into a State, or into the United States, was unlawful, and that he may for that reason be expelled, cannot negate the simple fact of his presence within the state's territorial perimeter. . . . [U]ntil he leaves the jurisdiction—either voluntarily, or involuntarily in accordance with the Constitution and laws of the United States—he is entitled to the equal protection of the laws that a State may choose to establish.[95]

In effect, the Court held that even though an undocumented alien is subject to the government's immigration authority—pursuant to which she might well be deportable—the fact of being so subject does not define her entire relationship with government power. As in *Wong Wing* and *Yick Wo*, the *Plyler* Court insisted upon a separate sphere of constitutional rights and obligations available to all persons who are present within United States territory, or some part thereof.[96]

In sum, *Wong Wing*, *Yick Wo*, and more recently *Plyler* stand for the proposition that when it comes to the alien's relationship with the government, the government's immigration power does not occupy the entire terrain. While noncitizens, by virtue of their alienage, are subject to the government's membership-regulating power, they also inhabit a sphere of territorial personhood that remains insulated from the action of membership principles.

These core constitutional cases, of course, precisely embody Walzer's metic principle. They assert that membership principles, while largely unfettered within their own domain, must nevertheless be confined to that domain. They stand against the convertibility of power from one sphere to another.

This separation of spheres model has served as a crucial baseline paradigm for the status of noncitizens in the United States, and much has followed from it. Aliens' common law rights to sue in tort and contract or for other redress of grievances have been uniformly recognized by the courts, both state and federal.[97] Most federal antidiscrimination statutes have been interpreted to protect aliens, including the undocumented.[98] Furthermore, Supreme Court decisions following *Wong Wing* and *Yick Wo* have extended the separation principle to other parts of the federal Constitution. In *Bridges v. Wixon*,[99] the Court held that aliens who reside in the United States are protected by the provisions of the First Amendment. And the Court has held that aliens are protected by the Fourth Amendment, and may suppress illegally seized evidence in criminal proceedings.[100]

Important as this baseline of legal personhood for territorially present aliens is, however, it only begins the inquiry,[101] and beyond it, things get more complex. For recognizing that aliens enjoy the status of persons for constitutional purposes does not, by itself, preclude many forms of differential treatment based on alienage. In constitutional law, the government is not precluded from discriminating against aliens—or anyone else—simply because they are constitutionally recognized persons. Assuming core constitutional protections are not denied, the government can discriminate so long as it possesses a sufficient justification for doing so. The question therefore becomes, what constitutes a sufficient justification for discrimination in this context? When does the fact of alienage legitimately matter? When may an alien properly be subject to less favorable treatment than a citizen simply on account of her lack of citizenship?

Separation and Convergence: Constitutional Approaches to Alienage Discrimination

The answer the law gives to this question almost invariably depends on the way it responds to another question, which is this: What relevance does the government's power to regulate immigration have for the treatment of the alien in the economic, political, and social spheres in our society? What effect, that is, should the government's membership-defining concerns have on the general status of the alien within the national society? The law's response to this question varies according to context. In some circumstances, the government's membership power is understood to properly shape the status of aliens across the domains of national life; here, membership concerns and internal status concerns are treated as largely coextensive and convergent. In other contexts, aliens are understood to require insulation from the operation of the membership sphere; here, membership concerns and internal status concerns are treated as largely distinct and separate.

EQUALITY AND NATIONAL MEMBERSHIP

The contrast between the convergence and separation models is starkly exemplified by two of the best-known constitutional alienage discrimination cases, both of which concerned the exclusion of aliens from eligibility for government benefits. In the first case, *Graham v. Richardson*, the Supreme Court was presented with challenges to two state laws that limited welfare benefits to citizens or intending citizens. In a unanimous opinion issued in 1971, the Court rejected prior precedent, which had permitted discrimination against aliens in the allocation of state benefits, and held that "[a]liens as a class are a prime example of a 'discrete and insular minority,' for whom . . . heightened judicial solicitude is appropriate."[102] Applying strict scrutiny, the Court found the states' articulated rationales for the welfare laws—to preserve state resources for the states' members—to be inadequate, and affirmed the lower court rulings that had struck down the laws.

As part of its analysis, the *Graham* Court emphasized that although the cases at issue concerned governmental treatment of *aliens*, the cases had nothing whatsoever to do with *immigration*. The Court pointed out that it is the national government that regulates immigration; for state governments, therefore, immigration concerns are necessarily entirely irrelevant. Indeed, Justice Blackmun wrote, "[s]tate laws that restrict the eligibility of aliens for welfare benefits merely because of their alienage conflict with these overriding national policies in an area constitutionally entrusted to the Federal government."[103] In short, the *Graham* Court treated membership concerns and status concerns as separate and distinct in the context of state-sponsored alienage discrimination, in large part due to the supremacy of federal power in the immigration sphere.

In the second case, *Mathews v. Diaz*,[104] the Court was faced with a challenge to a federal Social Security Act provision that excluded aliens from coverage for Medicare unless they had resided in this country as lawful permanent residents for at least five years. In this case, decided five years after *Graham*, the Court rejected the plaintiffs' challenge. Writing for a unanimous Court, Justice Stevens refused to treat the case as one involving a burden imposed upon a suspect class, arguing instead that "[t]he fact that an Act of Congress treats aliens differently from citizens does not in itself imply that such disparate treatment is invidious."[105] Applying a highly deferential form of rational basis scrutiny, the Court concluded that the classification was not "wholly irrational."[106]

The reason the Social Security provision was not wholly irrational, in the Court's view, was that as a sovereign state, the United States extends its "bounty" to foreigners as a matter of grace, and "[t]he decision to share that bounty with our guests may take into account the character of the relationship between the alien and this country."[107] Significantly, the "character of the relationship" between alien and nation to which the Court refers is the relationship established in the *immigration sphere*. For the *Mathews* Court, the immigration sphere is determinative here because Congress has been constitutionally conferred with the authority to establish the terms and conditions of aliens' membership in the national community. Since it was Congress that enacted the Social Security statute at issue in this case, Congress is to be understood, by so doing, as exercising its constitutionally conferred prerogative to regulate immigration. And since, under the plenary power doctrine, the judiciary is bound to defer to the political branches when a matter of immigration is at stake, the exclusion of aliens from eligibility for Medicare benefits need only be reasonably related to a legitimate governmental interest—a burden that the Court believed the government had more than satisfied.[108]

Thus, while in *Graham*, the Court stressed the irrelevance of immigration principles to the discrimination at hand, in *Mathews* immigration concerns structured the analysis. Because of its treatment of alienage discrimination as an incident, or an extension, of the government's immigration power, *Mathews* illustrates the convergence paradigm in its purest form.

Commentators have made a great deal of the contrast between *Graham* and *Mathews*. After *Mathews* was decided, some questioned the radical difference in outcome between the cases, especially given their analogous facts. Gerald Rosberg, for instance, asked, "[I]f alienage is a suspect classification when made on the basis of state legislation, should it not remain suspect when it is used by the federal government?"[109] After all, the Supreme Court has rarely made "suspectness" depend on who is discriminating rather than on the nature of the object group or of the substantive interest at stake. Indeed, the Court has more recently rejected such bifurcated standards in the affirmative action context.[110] There is presumably nothing to distinguish noncitizens' powerlessness in relation to Congress from their powerlessness in relation to the states, at least with respect to social benefits disbursement,[111] and the discrimination against noncitizens by the federal government is presumably equally stigmatizing.[112]

Over time, however, the distinction between the two cases has come to be treated as largely self-evident. Commentators today tend to characterize the contrast as the inevitable result of the division of labor between the states and the federal government. Since (the argument goes) the federal government is constitutionally understood to possess the power to regulate matters of immigration and naturalization, courts must yield to its decisions regarding the treatment of noncitizens. States, on the other hand, enjoy no such constitutional power; when states discriminate against aliens, therefore, courts must apply equal protection analysis full force.[113]

Ironically, it was the *Graham* Court that supplied the preemption theory that makes the distinction now seem so inevitable. By stressing that the individual states are not empowered to engage in immigration regulation, the Court assumed that federal discrimination against aliens *would* constitute, or at least implicate, an exercise of the immigration power. The *Graham* Court invalidated the state alienage discrimination at issue in that case at least in part on the basis of a premise—that alienage discrimination is a form, or an expression, of the exercise of the immigration power—that has served to insulate most federal alienage discrimination from judicial scrutiny. Indeed, the Court in *Mathews* relied directly on *Graham* for this proposition. As Justice Stevens wrote, *Graham*

> actually supports our holding today that it is the business of the political branches of the Federal Government, rather than that of . . . the States . . . to regulate the conditions of entry and residence of aliens. . . . [A] division by a State of the category of persons who are not citizens of the State into subcategories of United States citizens and aliens has no apparent justification, whereas a comparable classification by the Federal Government is a routine and normally legitimate part of its business.[114]

This is not to say that the *Graham* Court's holding was exclusively a product of preemption analysis. The decision in *Graham* spoke forcefully of the conditions of aliens as a vulnerable group in need of and entitled to special solicitude under the equal protection clause. And in subsequent cases involving state alienage discrimination, the Court reaffirmed the equality analysis without recourse to the supremacy clause argument.[115] This sort of analysis, obviously, depends not on institutional process concerns—concerns about who decides—but on substantive commitments to equality, and on a vision of noncitizens as the rightful subjects of equality.

But several other cases have since emphasized supremacy concerns,[116] and much of the commentary on the issue of discrimination has tended to emphasize the preemption question as well. In fact, some commentators have asserted that the only defensible basis for judicial invalidation of state discrimination against aliens is a process-based preemption theory. As Michael J. Perry has argued,

> constitutional doctrine regarding alienage-based classifications is better understood in terms, not of equal protection, but of federalism: Congress may . . . distinguish among persons on the basis of alienage—so long as it has a rational

basis for doing so; and state government may treat aliens differently from citizens so long as in doing so the state is acting consistently with federal policy regarding aliens.[117]

Under this analysis, where federal policy specifically authorizes states to discriminate against aliens, states would be entirely free to do so, without any equal protection constraint.[118]

Thus, the Supreme Court's decisions in *Graham* and *Mathews* may be read as at once antagonistic and perfectly compatible. The antagonism derives from their differing approaches to the equal protection question. *Graham* is fundamentally an equality case: it emphasizes noncitizens' personhood, their powerlessness as a class, and yet (implicitly) their functional identity with citizens in virtually all areas of state life. On this basis *Graham* imposes a substantial burden of justification on states that choose to discriminate against them. *Mathews*, in contrast, bypasses the issue of noncitizens' equal personhood entirely and focuses instead on the nation's interest in regulating national community membership. For *Graham*, the membership status of aliens is irrelevant when it comes to their treatment in the economic and social spheres of American society, whereas in *Mathews*, membership concerns are absolutely determinative of how they may be treated. In this respect, the holding in *Graham* embodies a vision of alien status that resembles Walzer's call for separation of spheres in the treatment of aliens, while the *Mathews* holding looks strikingly like the "tyrannical" sphere conversion that Walzer assails.

But while *Graham* and *Mathews* part company on the equal protection question, they do so in large part for compatible reasons. Both cases assume that federal discrimination on the basis of alienage is a form of regulation of immigration—or regulation of the nation's membership sphere. In this respect, both embrace the convergence model, at least with respect to the federal government. Both presume that membership concerns are always relevant for the treatment of aliens in the federal domain, even if they are not in the states.

EQUALITY AND STATE MEMBERSHIP

In the years since *Graham*, the constitutional jurisprudence of state discrimination against aliens has developed its own internal tension between separation and convergence. While *Graham* held membership considerations to be irrelevant with respect to the status of aliens in the state context, the Court later inaugurated another line of doctrine that places membership concerns front and center. The doctrine is known as the "political function exception" to the strict scrutiny requirement first established in *Graham*.[119]

In *Sugarman v. Dougall*, one of the earliest state alienage discrimination cases following *Graham*, the Supreme Court suggested in dictum that although most forms of state alienage discrimination should be subjected to strict scrutiny, if a case involves "matters resting firmly within a State's constitutional prerogative" to "defin[e] [its] 'political community,' " a lesser standard of scrutiny might apply.[120] This language lay briefly dormant, and the strict scrutiny model prevailed until 1978, when, in a case involving a citizenship requirement for the job of police officer, the Court held that state discrimination against aliens requires only rational justification where the discrimination involves " 'participation in [our] democratic political institutions.' "[121] Several years later, the political function exception garnered a full theoretical exposition by the Court in the case *Cabell v. Chavez-Salido*, [122] which involved the denial to three aliens of positions as Spanish-speaking deputy probation officers in the County of Los Angeles. The denial was made pursuant to a California statute that excluded noncitizens from positions as "peace officers," an occupational category defined to include the desired post.[123] Rejecting an equal protection challenge brought by the aliens against the state statute, the Supreme Court concluded that probation officers "exercise and, therefore, symbolize [the] power of the political community over those who fall within its jurisdiction."[124] So concluding, the Court upheld the statute under rational basis review.

In elaborating its reasons for this holding, the Court stated that prior cases had established that "although citizenship is not a relevant ground for the distribution of economic benefits, it is a relevant ground for determining membership in the political community."[125] When the restriction at hand implicates the state's definition of its political community, distinctions between citizens and aliens are not necessarily to be discouraged; indeed,

> [t]he exclusion of aliens from basic governmental processes is not a deficiency in the democratic system but a necessary consequence of the community's process of political self-definition. Self-government, whether direct or through representatives, begins by defining the scope of the community of the governed and thus of the governors as well. Aliens are by definition those outside of this community. Judicial incursions in this area may interfere with those aspects of democratic self-government that are most essential to it.[126]

The Court thus concluded that strict scrutiny is inappropriate where the restriction against aliens "primarily serves a political function."[127]

What is striking about the political function exception is that through it, the Court expressly reintroduced membership interests into the state alienage jurisprudence. While *Graham* and its progeny established that the equality interests of aliens drive the equal protection analysis in state cases,[128] and futher emphasized the need to separate alienage from membership concerns, *Cabell* and the other political function cases have articulated an alternative vision, one in which aliens' rights of equal personhood give way to the interests and prerogatives of the membership community of the state.

Of course, the membership interest at stake in this context is in some respects dissimilar to those we have seen so far because it is not embodied in the federal immigration power. The community's concern here is not to regulate admission to the national territory or to formal citizenship status, but rather to regulate political—and perhaps, one senses, spiritual—admission to the "community of the governed and thus of the governors as well."[129] Having affirmed states' authority to regulate such admission, the Court effectively treats membership questions as extending beyond matters of national immigration control and policy to include states' rights to ensure a "fundamental . . . identity between a government and the members, or citizens, of the state."[130]

Interestingly, the subordination of aliens' individual rights to state community interests under the political function exception seems to have occurred without much of a battle, at least at the level of the Supreme Court. All of the justices have agreed, at least from *Sugarman* forward, that alienage, or citizenship status, cannot reasonably be deemed irrelevant for all purposes, and they have nearly all agreed that it is the political domain where such status is relevant. The Court in *Sugarman* made clear that *Graham* would not compel states to permit aliens to vote or to hold high public office, for these are matters, according to Justice Blackmun, that "rest[ ] firmly within a State's constitutional prerogatives."[131] (The *Sugarman* language, notably, is reflected in Walzer's argument that during the transition to full membership, an alien may be denied political, but not other rights.)

The battle, instead, has raged over the question of how broadly or narrowly to interpret the domain of the political. The conservative Justices have tended to urge the broadest possible interpretation of "political": for them, the exercise of "judgment and discretion" by state troopers,[132] the role played by public school teachers "in developing students' attitude toward government and understanding of the role of citizens in our society,"[133] and the deputy parole officer's "exercise [of] coercive force over the individual"[134] were all intimately linked with citizens' "right to govern."[135] The more liberal justices, in contrast, have urged both a narrow reading of "political" and a separation of political interests from other sorts of state interests, particularly where economic interests are arguably at issue. They have emphasized that the *Sugarman* dictum had provided for the exclusion of aliens from positions whose holders "participate directly in the formulation, execution, or review of broad public policy"[136] but had precluded "blanket exclusion of aliens from state jobs."[137] State troopers, school teachers, and deputy probation officers, they argued, cannot reasonably be understood to make policy; rather, they "implement [ ] the basic policies formulated directly or indirectly by the citizenry."[138]

On balance, the expansive reading of the "political function" exception seems to have prevailed. Given the broad construction the Court has afforded the notion of the political, the political function exception more or less "swallow[ed] up the entire proposition that alienage classifications are suspect."[139] Still, the Supreme Court's last word on the subject was somewhat cautionary. Eight justices described the political function exception as a "narrow exception," applicable only to "laws that exclude aliens from positions *intimately* related to the process of democratic self-government," and refused to apply it to the position of notary public, even though the state's constitution had expressly designated notaries as public officers.[140]

What seems most striking about the development of the political function exception in the state alienage cases is how readily the structure of tensions characterizing the law of alien status in the federal cases was transposed to the state context. In both *Graham* and *Mathews*, the states were portrayed as the site of pure personhood, in contrast to the federal domain, where, according to both cases, membership concerns were weighty and should legitimately prevail. With the advent of the political function exception, state cases have come to resemble the federal cases more closely; they are now structured around the question of the proper scope or jurisdiction of the government's membership-defining authority.

DISCRIMINATION AND THE UNDOCUMENTED ALIEN

It may be that the tensions between separation and convergence are at their most acute when it comes to the status of aliens who reside in this country without authorization. Although Walzer does not directly address the status of these aliens, they would seem to present an interesting—and difficult—case for him. On the one hand, undocumented immigrants live among the nation's formal members, often perform their menial labor, and are subject to local law, but ordinarily have no prospects for acquiring legal status or citizenship. In this respect, they are a quintessential metic class. On the other hand, these immigrants have bypassed or violated formal admissions mechanisms and are present in the United States without formal community consent, thereby violating the community's right to define its own membership.

The following question therefore arises: What bearing should the logic or imperatives of the membership sphere have on the lives of undocumented immigrants residing within the community's borders? Should the fact of undocumented immigrants' violation of the nation's border laws be deemed relevant in determining how they should be treated beyond the border? Is this a context in which the separation principle begins to break down?[141]

The law has been of two (or more) minds about these questions. At one level, the answer is clearly no; separation holds here, as elsewhere. We have already seen that the Supreme Court has rejected the proposition that a person's unlawful immigration law status places her beyond the protective bounds of the Constitution. A century ago *Wong Wing* established that even aliens who are in the country illegally enjoy the protections of the Fifth and Sixth Amendments, and in *Plyler*, nine Justices agreed that undocumented aliens are to be considered "persons" for Fourteenth Amendment purposes, notwithstanding their status under the immigration laws.[142] In these cases, the Court carved out for all aliens a zone of protected personhood, where the nation's membership interests are of no consequence at all.[143]

These "core separation" decisions have, in turn, provided the foundation for a broad line of cases that treat the fact of an alien's unauthorized status as entirely irrelevant in determining her standing in various spheres of public and private life in our society.[144] For instance, undocumented aliens may sue in tort and contract; as one court put it, "[e]ven assuming that violations of the immigration laws by the [plaintiffs] occurred, the remedy for these violations is . . . criminal sanctions, not denial of access to court. We seriously doubt whether illegal entry, standing alone, makes outlaws of individuals, permitting their contracts to be breached without legal accountability."[145] The undocumented have also been held to be protected employees under the National Labor Relations Act, Title VII, and other protective employment statutes[146] (although their access to compensatory remedies for violations has been constrained).[147]

Yet the fact that the courts have deemed the immigration status of undocumented aliens to be irrelevant in many contexts does not mean that such status may never be considered pertinent to determining the allocation of rights and benefits. After the Court's threshold holding in *Plyler* that plaintiffs could invoke the equal protection clause, there still remained the "more difficult question" of whether, by effectively denying undocumented children access to the public schools, the state of Texas had violated their equal protection rights.[148] Here, the significance of the aliens' immigration law violation became the focal issue of debate.

That violation of law was, not surprisingly, the dominant concern of the four-member dissent in *Plyler*. The dissent, first of all, urged rational basis review, invoking *Mathews* for the proposition that "in allocating governmental benefits to a given class of aliens, one 'may take into account the character of the relationship between the alien and this country.' "[149] Because the "character of the relationship" between the undocumented alien and this country is a "federally prohibited one," the exclusion of these aliens from the benefits of state membership cannot reasonably be treated as a form of "invidious discrimination stemming from prejudice and hostility" that would require heightened scrutiny.[150] According to the dissent, the equal protection clause would not be offended so long as the classification is not "arbitrary and irrational."[151] Furthermore, the dissent concluded, the state's legitimate concern about the aliens' unauthorized immigration status itself provided the rational basis necessary for upholding the challenged statute. "Without laboring what will undoubtedly seem obvious to many," Justice Burger wrote,

> it simply is not "irrational" for a state to conclude that it does not have the same responsibility to provide benefits for persons whose very presence in the state and this country is illegal as it does to provide for persons lawfully present. By definition, illegal aliens have no right whatsoever to be here, and the state may reasonably, and constitutionally, elect not to provide them with governmental services at the expense of those who are lawfully in the state.[152]

As is well known, the majority in *Plyler* rejected this analysis. Although the justices refused to treat undocumented aliens as a suspect class,[153] they nevertheless employed a heightened standard of scrutiny in evaluating the challenged law and struck it down on the grounds that the state had failed to show that denial of an education to these children advanced "some substantial state interest."[154] The Court concluded, among other things, that while a state might well have a permissible interest in "mitigating the potentially harsh economic effects of sudden shifts in population, . . . [t]here is no evidence in the record suggesting that illegal entrants impose any significant burden on the State's economy,"[155] or that the provision at issue would serve to deter the influx of undocumented aliens into the state.[156] The Court also emphasized the injurious consequences of the Texas statute for the individual immigrant and for the national society, arguing that "[t]he inability to read and write will handicap the individual deprived of a basic education each and every day of his life,"[157] and warning that "[w]e cannot ignore the significant social costs borne by our Nation when select groups are denied the means to absorb the values and skills upon which our social order rests."[158]

Plyler has been both widely celebrated and castigated for its reading of the equal protection clause. For some, the case is exemplary of the worst sort of judicial activism,[159] while for others, it has become a powerful symbol of a jurisprudence committed, in Kenneth Karst's phrase, to "the demise of 'caste legislation' in America."[160] In either case it tends to be viewed as the ultimate aliens' rights decision—which is why immigration restrictionists have long been eager to be rid of it.[161]

Still, as much as *Plyler* may be said to express a powerfully egalitarian vision of the Constitution, and as much as it has served to protect the interests of an exceptionally marginalized class of people, the decision itself is far more equivocal in its vision of undocumented aliens than these characterizations would suggest. In fact, the majority opinion is shot through with tensions over the rightful status of undocumented aliens in the United States, and, in particular, over the relevance of their unlawful immigration status in spheres of national life typically understood to lie outside the domain of the immigration law.

First, while Justice Brennan showed enormous compassion for the alien children who are the direct targets of the state's challenged law, his solicitude did not extend nearly so far when it came to the children's parents. In fact, the Court structured much of its opinion around an opposition between the "innocent children" and their culpable parents, attributing sharply contrasting degrees of deservingness to each.[162] The parents are persons, Justice Brennan writes, "who elect to enter our territory by stealth and in violation of our law," and who, as a result, "should be prepared to bear the consequences, including, but not limited, to deportation." The children, by contrast,

> "can affect neither their parents' conduct nor their own status." Even if the State found it expedient to control the conduct of adults by action against their children, legislation directing the onus of a parent's misconduct against his children does not comport with fundamental conceptions of justice.[163]

In other words, undocumented status should be treated as substantially irrelevant here because the undocumented status of these children was acquired involuntarily, and its consequences cannot, therefore, fairly be visited upon them. Had the case involved denial of state benefits to undocumented adults (whose undocumented status, it is assumed, would be the result of their own, voluntary, action),[164] and had the case not specifically involved educational rights (which the Court treats as fundamentally important in this case),[165] the outcome might well have differed very little from the one urged by the dissent. As Justice Brennan put it, "[p]ersuasive arguments support the view that a State may withhold its beneficence from those whose very presence within the United States is the product of their own unlawful conduct."[166]

The Court's stern portrayal of the adult undocumented alien presents a picture of *Plyler* different from the one to which most of us are accustomed. In this *Plyler*, the alien's status in the immigration domain is not at all irrelevant to her rights beyond the border. Instead, an individual's unauthorized immigration status may rightfully structure her treatment inside the national community, so long as that status was acquired through purposeful action. A convergence of spheres, in this view, is not only permissible but eminently just as proper retribution for transgression of national legal norms.

The innocent child/culpable adult opposition is not the only tension in the majority opinion. Equally prominent is a persistent uncertainty about who really is at fault when it comes to undocumented immigration, and who should properly bear its associated costs. For even though the majority (in dictum) attributed culpability to undocumented alien adults and endorsed the denial of certain rights and benefits to them as appropriate "consequences" for their wrongdoing, it simultaneously insisted that it is unfair to penalize these aliens for conduct that our own government has often encouraged and that, at the time of the decision, it had not effectively sought to curtail by law. As Justice Brennan wrote,

> Sheer incapability or lax enforcement of the laws barring entry into this country, coupled with the failure to establish an effective bar to the employment of undocumented aliens, has resulted in the creation of a substantial "shadow population" of illegal migrants—numbering in the millions—within our borders. This situation raises the specter of a permanent caste of undocumented resident aliens, encouraged by some to remain here as a source of cheap labor, but nevertheless denied the benefits that our society makes available to citizens and lawful permanent residents.[167]

In this latter account, undocumented aliens, whatever their age, are not so much predatory lawbreakers as quintessential victims, even dupes; their " 'presence is tolerated, [their] employment is perhaps even welcomed,' " yet they are " 'virtually defenseless against any abuse, exploitation, or callous neglect to which the state or the state's natural citizens and business organizations may wish to subject them.' "[168] To visit the effects of their undocumented status on these aliens in spheres beyond the border would be to make them pay for the government's own ineptitude and, perhaps, our own selfishness and bad faith. The status of these aliens within the national community, in this view, must be insulated from the effects of their unlawful immigration status, at least so long as we do not get serious about controlling the borders.

Plyler's contending visions of undocumented aliens—as blameworthy lawbreakers and as hapless victims—each undoubtedly served the majority's strategic purposes. The prominence of the guilty, undeserving adult alien in the opinion served as a kind of insurance that the Court was neither condoning undocumented immigration nor declaring undocumented status irrelevant per se in the allocation of rights and benefits in the states; it thus represented a figurative brake on the holding, allowing a decision that might otherwise have seemed beyond the pale to appear more palatable. At the same time, the Court's repeated references to the government's own enforcement failures, and its suggestion that government and citizens had long tolerated and perhaps encouraged the process of undocumented immigration, signaled that the aliens did not bear true responsibility for the problem. Thus, imposing burdens on aliens merely because of their status would violate our conventional understanding that, as Walzer has put it, "punishment . . . ought to go to people who are judged to deserve it."[169]

Yet successful as these rhetorical strategies were for the immigrant children in *Plyler*, the decision set up a structure for thinking about when and whether undocumented alienage matters that bodes ill for undocumented aliens in future constitutional cases. As we have seen, *Plyler* is not likely to be very helpful in a case in which state benefits or rights are denied to undocumented aliens over the age of eighteen; this is especially true given that Congress has since enacted employer sanctions legislation and has otherwise attempted to upgrade border enforcement.[170] Accusations of lax enforcement on the part of the government will no longer easily serve as a formal counterweight to the aliens' perceived culpability.[171]

What is clear is that the law is sharply divided over the difference that *undocumented* alienage makes. On one hand, we find it makes very little difference; the law regulating membership status has no bearing at all on aliens' status as persons in a variety of spheres of national life. On the other hand, unauthorized status seems to make a great deal of difference, and the difference that it makes is integrally related to the perception that these aliens have willfully flouted the nation's prerogative to define its own membership. It is the absence of consent—at least formal consent—that seems to stick in the craw, and that serves to make membership regulation appear both legitimate and necessary, not merely at the border but also in the national community's interior.

Aliens, Rights, and the Specter of Deportability

In arguing against the convertibility of power that characterizes the status of contemporary metics, Walzer complains, among other things, that they are subject to "the everpresent threat of deportation."[172] Civil liberties are "commonly denied" to noncitizens, not merely explicitly but also "implicitly by the threat of . . . deportation."[173] He considers the effects of this threat an unjustifiable incursion by the membership sphere into the various other domains that constitute the national society.

Of course, status noncitizens are potentially deportable by definition. An alien is a person who is present in a state's territory only conditionally. So long as a state claims the power to control the composition of the national community's membership, an alien's potential vulnerability to deportation in some circumstances is probably an inescapable fact.[174] In the United States, the Immigration and Nationality Act contains dozens of grounds for possible removal, which are, in principle, applicable to any noncitizen who is present within the national territory.[175] Whatever rights noncitizens enjoy in the civil, social, and economic spheres of our society, the imperatives of the membership domain will always circumscribe their lives, [176] making absolute sphere separation, at least to this extent, a practical impossibility.

But Walzer's concern about "the everpresent threat" of deportation usefully points to the fact that conflicts over the proper boundaries of the membership domain can take more than one form. So far, I have examined conflicts over the degree to which membership principles may directly affect the allocation of rights and benefits to noncitizens; I have examined courts' and commentators' consideration of the question of whether the fact of a person's alienage should formally constrain her rights in spheres other than the immigration sphere, and if so, to what degree. However, Walzer's everpresent threat critique highlights another way in which the debate over boundaries can arise; at issue here is the legitimacy of the *indirect* effects that membership regulation can have on noncitizens' lives in the national community. Specifically, the question is when and whether the de facto inhibiting effects of possible deportability on the lives of noncitizens in our society illegitimately interfere with the rights they are formally understood to hold as equal persons.

A noncitizen may be subject to deportation (or "removal," under the current statutory language) for a variety of reasons. Some deportation provisions make noncitizens deportable for having violated one or more of the nation's immigration laws (for having entered without inspection and formal permission, for having overstayed a visa, for having obtained a visa fraudulently, and so forth). Other provisions make noncitizens deportable for behavior that itself has no bearing on immigration regulation but that has been deemed by lawmakers to be undesirable and a basis for removal. The indirect effects of the everpresent threat of deportation operate somewhat differently with respect to each of these categories.

IN THE SHADOW OF IMMIGRATION LAW

The provisions that make violation of the immigration laws a basis for deportation apply to all noncitizens; any noncitizen can be deported for having violated these provisions at any point. However, they weigh most heavily on undocumented or unauthorized immigrants, whose status *as* undocumented means that their very presence contravenes the nation's immigration laws in some way.[177] This illegality under the immigration laws, in turn, very often makes them unwilling to avail themselves of the various non-immigration-related civil and economic rights that they *have* been accorded out of fear that, by doing so, they may precipitate an inquiry into their immigration status.[178]

The result is that the rights undocumented immigrants formally enjoy in the sphere of territorial personhood are often rendered irrelevant, as a practical matter, by operation of the nation's border-regulatory authority. This is a consequence of a de facto—though not a formal—conversion of power between spheres. While the deportation provisions penalize aliens for violations of the country's membership rules and thus arguably act "within their own sphere," they also have substantial collateral effects for undocumented immigrants in the domains of territorial personhood—domains that are, in formal terms, insulated from membership regulation.[179]

The collateral effects of these deportation provisions on undocumented immigrants arguably structure their experience in this country more than any other single factor. It is widely recognized that the vulnerability of the undocumented to deportation makes them highly exploitable in various domains within the society, especially the workplace. Yet these effects are rarely subject to direct judicial attention or constraint.[180] Courts and administrators tend to treat these immigrants' perpetual vulnerability to deportation as an inevitable product of the country's immigration-control authority and of the immigrant's original immigration law violation. The rebound effect that the threat of border enforcement has on immigrants' rights outside immigration law proper is generally ignored.

To give just one example, in the United States, undocumented immigrants are formally protected by the nation's employment laws; they have been deemed to be "covered employees" under the wage and hour, anti-discrimination, and collective bargaining laws.[181] This means that it is a violation of federal law for an employer to, among other things, contact the immigration authorities in response to the efforts of an undocumented employee to organize a union; technically, this constitutes an unfair labor practice.[182] Yet even if it is determined that the employer acted unlawfully, the immigrant is not insulated from the deportation process that may well have been triggered by the employer's original phone call.[183] The fact that engaging in ostensibly protected organizing efforts may lead to deportation obviously serves as a huge disincentive for those immigrants who might otherwise wish to participate. As a practical matter, the rights they technically enjoy are rendered ineffective or meaningless.

The point is that the government's deportation power substantially constrains undocumented aliens' sometimes acknowledged rights as territorial persons. Given current commitments to the plenary power doctrine and the conception of territorial sovereignty that underlies it, it is generally assumed and accepted that, whatever rights undocumented aliens enjoy inside the national society, these are enjoyed in the shadow of, and subject to defeasance by, federal immigration control authority.

IMPOSING MEMBERSHIP PENALTIES ON RECOGNIZED RIGHTS

A second category of deportation provisions in U.S. law makes noncitizens deportable for conduct that itself has no bearing on immigration regulation proper. Some of this conduct is otherwise deemed illegal; for example, noncitizens are deportable for committing a variety of acts defined as violations of federal or state criminal laws. In this context, the individual is subject both to the political community's criminal justice system and, simultaneously or subsequently, to the community's border regulatory regime, which attaches immigration consequences to the underlying behavior.[184]

However, some non-immigration-related behavior that triggers deportation is not otherwise illegal; such behavior does not violate any law outside the immigration sphere. It is this latter category of deportation ground that interests me here. The principal provisions of this kind in American law are those that render a noncitizen deportable for engaging in forms of political advocacy that are otherwise protected under the First Amendment.[185] These provisions entail imposition of what Walzer might call a "membership" penalty on conduct that is otherwise deemed to be within the constitutionally protected sphere of territorial personhood.

These "ideological deportation" provisions became the subject of judicial controversy during the 1980s and 1990s. One case, which concerned several members of the American Arab Anti-Discrimination Committee, crystalized the controversy. Beginning in 1987, a group of eight noncitizens, including seven Palestinians, were charged as deportable under several of the McCarran-Walter provisions of the then-current immigration law, which treated as deportable acts (among other things) membership in, or affiliation with, organizations advocating world communism, and advocacy on behalf of, or affiliation with, any organization that itself advocated the unlawful destruction of property.[186] In response, the individuals involved and several ethnic and religious organizations brought suit against the government, charging that these provisions were overbroad in violation of the First Amendment.

The plaintiffs' argument to the court was relatively simple. In a decision falling squarely within the territorial personhood tradition, the Supreme Court had held years before that resident aliens were protected by the provisions of the First Amendment.[187] As a result, the plaintiffs argued, aliens should not be criminally or civilly penalized for expressive activity unless such activity fails the prevailing First Amendment test for expression, which today only proscribes speech "directed to inciting or producing imminent lawless action and . . . likely to incite or produce such action."[188] Because any governmental effort to penalize the expressive conduct at issue would fail this constitutional test as a general matter, such an effort should be deemed similarly unconstitutional in the deportation context. Aliens must not be provided a " 'different' Bill of Rights" in the deportation setting, both because the Supreme Court has never provided for such a distinction[189] and because this distinction would render meaningless aliens' rights *outside* the deportation context.[190]

This last point represented the heart of the plaintiffs' argument, and it is of critical interest here. As the plaintiff described it, to subject an alien to deportation for forms of advocacy otherwise constitutionally protected is to chill irrevocably the alien's exercise of these same constitutional rights.[191] In essence, the plaintiffs contended that the principles of the membership sphere—here, the substantive grounds of deportation—had impermissibly penetrated their sphere of protected territorial personhood—here, their right to engage in expressive conduct. The plaintiffs did not dispute the government's power to deport aliens in principle; they simply challenged the government's authority to exercise the deportation power against aliens in such a way as to invade the sphere of their rights as territorial persons.[192] This argument, of course, is a quintessential "separation" argument: Membership regulation within its own domain is fine, but to the extent that it interferes with the action of other spheres, it is illegitimate and must be struck down.

Notably, the government's argument in the case was the mirror image of that of the plaintiffs. According to the government, although aliens may well be constitutionally protected against the imposition of criminal or civil sanctions for most expressive conduct, "aliens do not enjoy First Amendment rights in the deportation context."[193] As justification, the government cited Congress's plenary power over immigration, which affords it "virtually absolute and unchecked power over immigration matters."[194] The government argued that if Congress had chosen to make aliens deportable for conduct that would not otherwise support government interference, such an action is within Congress's prerogative, and the courts are compelled to abide by Congress's determination.

What is intriguing about the government's argument is that, like the plaintiffs', it took the form of a separation argument. But unlike the plaintiffs, who were attempting to guard the realm of territorial personhood against incursion and distortion by membership principles, the government sought the converse. It sought to insulate the government's membership domain—its domain of immigration-regulatory authority—against encroachment by the logic of territorial personhood.[195] In the government's view, the plenary power doctrine serves to insulate the deportation sphere from the penetration of equality-based norms that have come (at least formally) to characterize contemporary public law more generally. The government maintained, in short, that the courts were bound to protect Congress's distinct prerogatives in this area.

The court in *ADC* was therefore faced with two radically opposed constructions of the question at hand. The plaintiffs defined the issue as one in which immigration law had improperly invaded the sphere of territorial personhood, whereas the government viewed the issue as one in which immigration law required insulation from the onslaught of equality demands.

To many observers, the case's outcome seemed preordained. However compelling the plaintiffs' position might be, no federal court had ever struck down a substantive deportation provision on constitutional grounds,[196] and it seemed unlikely that this case would be an exception. Remarkably, however, the district opted for the plaintiffs' position. Although the court recognized that Congress enjoys extraordinary authority in the immigration domain, the judges in the case nevertheless concluded that under Supreme Court precedent "we are not relieved of our duty to ensure that Congress exercises its power within constitutional limits."[197] Moreover, the court reasoned, nothing in prior Supreme Court case law served to condone the congressional policy challenged in this case. In its only decision addressing the First Amendment rights of aliens in the deportation setting, the Supreme Court had presumed that the same First Amendment standards would apply within the deportation context as outside it;[198] in that decision, the Court had "refused to recognize an alien-citizen distinction among speech and speakers in this country."[199] The district court pointed out that the Court's refusal to tolerate such a distinction made sense, given that the Court has elsewhere determined that " '[t]he constitutional guarantee of free speech 'serves significant societal interests' wholly apart from the speaker's interest in self-expression. . . . The identity of the speaker is not decisive in determining whether speech is protected.' "[200] For this reason, the court concluded that it was appropriate to apply current First Amendment standards to the challenged McCarran-Walter provisions, and, upon conducting such an analysis, determined that the provisions were facially overbroad, and struck them down.[201]

What was notable about this decision was not merely that a court invalidated a substantive immigration law provision on constitutional grounds, but also that the plaintiffs managed to convince a federal court that what appeared to be an issue lying "inside" immigration law—and thereby off-limits to the courts—was in fact a question intimately linked to the general status of aliens in our society beyond the immigration domain. As Judge Wilson wrote for the district court:

> [I]t is impossible to adopt for aliens a lower degree of First Amendment protection solely in the deportation setting without seriously affecting their First Amendment rights outside that setting. Under a lower First Amendment stan-

dard, and without the constitutional protection against ex-post facto laws,[202] the Government could conceivably pass a law allowing for the deportation of aliens for statements made several decades earlier. An alien would have no way of knowing whether his or her speech would someday become a ground for deportation and consequently, would be chilled from speaking at all.[203]

For the court, in short, denial of rights to aliens in the immigration context served to deprive them of the enjoyment of rights elsewhere;[204] and given the Constitution's commitment to protecting the rights of aliens as territorially present persons, the court concluded the judiciary could not tolerate such an outcome.[205]

ADC's constitutional holding was later vacated on appeal on unrelated grounds,[206] and Congress has since repealed the specific McCarran-Walter provisions at issue in the case (although it has since enacted new antiterrorist provisions that allow the government to deport aliens for associative activity that is otherwise protected under the first amendment). Nevertheless, the broader conceptual and political questions raised by the case, remain pressing. What are we to do when the operation of the government's immigration power functions to curtail fundamental rights noncitizens enjoy as persons outside the immigration arena? Should we regard this as an exercise of immigration power outside its rightful sphere? (What, exactly, *is* immigration law's proper sphere?) Conversely, how far into the domain of immigration regulation can equality norms legitimately extend? May equality norms trump membership norms in the deportation arena itself? The district court's decision in *ADC* remains significant today because it so explicitly wrestled with these questions.

The Boundaries of Membership Regulation

Conflicts in American law over the legitimacy of government discrimination against noncitizens, I have argued, tend to take the form of a dispute over boundaries. The dispute concerns the question whether discriminatory treatment of aliens is to be understood as a legitimate exercise of the government's power to regulate membership or as an illegitimate violation of their rights as persons. This is a dispute over boundaries because in our legal system, noncitizens are subject, broadly speaking, to two distinct regimes of regulation and relationship: the first governs admission to community membership, and the second governs the general status of territorially present persons. The question in the cases is always which regime controls; and in so asking, the law seeks to establish the legitimate boundaries—or jurisdiction—of each regime.

I have also argued that the law has developed two broad paradigm responses to this boundary question. One supports a minimalist understanding of the scope of the government's authority to regulate membership and urges a relatively strict separation between the membership domain and the domains of territorial personhood. The other supports an expansive understanding of the legitimate sphere of membership regulation and argues that membership concerns are rightfully part of the regulation of social relationships among all territorially present persons. Drawing on Walzer's analysis of complex equality, I have called these the separation and convergence models, respectively.

These models could be said to reflect competing strands of normative political sentiment in our society about the nature of the relationship between the individual and the political community. The separation model stresses both limits on government law enforcement power and the equal rights of persons. It tends to presume the membership of territorially present persons, and devotes itself to thinking about the nature of the relationships that should prevail among them. The convergence model, in contrast, treats community affiliation as the fundamental source of standing in any national society. It envisions status in the national community as structured by a series of concentric circles of belonging, with those individuals in the innermost circle enjoying the full benefits and burdens of membership and those farther from the center possessing progressively few claims on the community.[207]

Expressed in these terms, the tension between separation and convergence might seem to represent a version of the liberal/communitarian divide that structures so much of our contemporary political thought.[208] Yet this characterization itself has its limits. The fact is that *both* models treat the nation state's authority to regulate the admission of outsiders to the national society as a paramount normative value, and to this extent, both fall on the communitarian side of the line. Whatever else it stands for, the *Plyler* decision is a ringing affirmation of this principle.[209] Walzer, of course, regards the political community's right to admit and exclude strangers as fundamental. The separation model is, in this respect, not strictly "liberal," despite its emphasis on individual rights and constraints on government power, since it does not endorse the end of national border enforcement or the free movement of individuals across borders.[210] The separation model shares a nationalist-communitarian foundation with the convergence model, one in which exclusion of persons on purely national grounds is both necessary and legitimate.[211]

The difference between the models lies, rather, in what each believes follows from this initial normative baseline. The convergence model stresses the intimate linkage between the government's authority to regulate admission to membership and the status of persons who reside within the territorial community. The national community's interest in membership regulation dictates the nature of legal and social relations not merely at the territorial border but in the interior as well. As constitutional scholar Michael Perry has written,

> [The] proposition that the members of a political community may appropriately decide whether, to what extent, and under what conditions persons who are not members may enter the territory of the political community and share its resources and largesse [ ] . . . *necessarily entails* the view that a person, in some respects at least, is more deserving by virtue of his status as a citizen than a person who is not a citizen.[212]

This means, for Perry, that alienage cannot be considered a "morally irrelevant status, because to say that a trait or status . . . is morally irrelevant is to say that a person is *not* less deserving by virtue of the status."[213] And if alienage is not a morally irrelevant status, undocumented alienage surely is not. In Perry's view, "a person's status . . . as one who is illegally present in the territorial jurisdiction in question—indicating as it does that particular acts, acts contrary to law, have been committed" cannot reasonably be deemed "a problematic basis for differential treatment."[214] A person's status under the community's border laws, in short, rightfully and necessarily shapes her status beyond the literal border.

The separation model, in contrast, treats the community's claimed right to control the composition of national community membership as a distinct and delimited moment in the ongoing relationship between individual and political community.[215] Important as the right to control membership is, the state's jurisdiction to do so is circumscribed. As Walzer insists, membership principles must be confined to their own sphere. This means that while a person's alienage may be legitimately taken into account for purposes of determining admission to membership, alienage is not a morally relevant status for purposes of determining the civil, social, and economic rights of individuals who reside within the membership community—or, in the case of undocumented aliens, its moral relevance is minimal at best.[216]

In characterizing the legal debate over alienage discrimination as a dispute over the legitimate boundaries of regulatory spheres, and in characterizing separation and convergence as the two principal competing approaches to this boundary dispute in the law, I do not mean to claim that there is anything necessary or inevitable about the structure of these arguments.[217] Things could be—and have been—otherwise. For both conceptual and political reasons, however, it is useful to understand the current shape of the debate. Our arguments about the status of noncitizens tend to be organized around this recurrent question: Where does the regulatory regime of the border legitimately begin and end?

CHAPTER 4

Constitutional Citizenship through the Prism of Alienage

NOTWITHSTANDING Alexander Bickel's declaration a generation ago that the concept of citizenship is of little significance in American constitutional law,[1] the idea of citizenship has enjoyed a huge resurgence of interest in constitutional law scholarship in recent years. Much of the literature concerned with citizenship today deploys the concept in the mode of normative political theory, with scholars embracing it as an aspirational ideal for our national political life. Citizenship is portrayed in this literature as embodying the highest political values: democracy, egalitarianism, pluralism, civic virtue, community—and sometimes all of these at once.

Constitutional theorists' decidedly romantic preoccupation with citizenship in recent years echoes the work of theorists in neighboring disciplines for whom the concept of citizenship has likewise become a central normative benchmark. Yet the work of many constitutional scholars goes beyond normative theory per se; increasingly, many have sought to attach the commitments they ascribe to the idea of citizenship to constitutional text. In particular, many have urged that the concept of constitutional citizenship should be read to encompass and ground our most basic individual rights. There is today a burgeoning movement in American constitutional theory to recast our constitutional rights framework in the language and structures of citizenship.

In their efforts to reorient constitutional rights discourse around the idea of citizenship, scholars have pursued a variety of textual strategies. Some invoke the privileges or immunities clause of the Fourteenth Amendment, urging interpretive restoration of this long dormant provision to Fourteenth Amendment jurisprudence.[2] Others have seized on the amendment's citizenship clause. Despite its usual interpretation as a definitional provision,[3] these commentators argue that the clause should be understood to guarantee basic substantive rights as well.[4] Still others have located the idea of constitutional citizenship in the equal protection clause. In this reading, the clause's core animating principle is the principle of "equal citizenship."[5]

The citizenship turn in American constitutional theory has important virtues. Among other things, reincorporating Fourteenth Amendment citi-

zenship into our national rights discourse could arguably provide the
foundation for a more coherent rights jurisprudence. Those seeking a revival of the privileges or immunities clause, in particular, regard the effective disabling of the clause (both in the *Slaughter-House Cases*[6] and
through the subsequent development of individual rights jurisprudence
under the aegis of the due process and equal protection clauses) as having
produced deep irrationalities in the doctrine.[7] It might well be true that
the revitalization of the privileges or immunities clause would help to
rationalize and perhaps even to deepen the various doctrines of substantive, fundamental rights.[8]

It is also true that the idea of citizenship as an organizing value possesses substantial normative and rhetorical power.[9] The concept of citizenship is particularly resonant in its evocation of a mutual and engaged
relationship between the political community and its members. This is a
relationship that some traditional rights theory has, arguably, sometimes
obscured or ignored, to its detriment.

Despite its potential benefits, however, this turn to the idea of citizenship as a foundation for constitutional rights is not without its costs.[10]
Perhaps the principal one has to do with its implications for the status of
aliens. If rights are defined as an attribute of citizenship, what then of
those who lack citizenship by legal definition? Those formally lacking in
citizenship would seem to fall, at least arguably, outside the scope of this
normative discourse. Bickel himself warned thirty years ago that aliens
would suffer under a citizenship-centered constitutional regime,[11] and this
concern remains pressing today. Notwithstanding the common criticism
that the idea of rights grounded in the status of personhood is excessively
thin,[12] I believe that a constitutional system that treats noncitizens as entitled to a significant measure of community recognition and protection
represents a substantial accomplishment in human rights terms.[13]
Whether such recognition and protection would withstand adoption of a
rights regime organized around the idea of constitutional citizenship remains an open question.

Nevertheless, these implications for the status of aliens represented by
the turn to citizenship are most often ignored by constitutional scholars.
Even among progressive scholars, who by vocation are concerned with
the condition of the marginalized and subordinated, the subject is rarely
on the radar screen. Progressive constitutional scholars have recently
urged the recognition of the citizenship of gays and lesbians[14] and of the
economically marginalized,[15] along with racial minorities, women, and
others, without, in most cases, acknowledging the potential doctrinal and
rhetorical costs that doing so might pose to noncitizens.[16]

Among those scholars who *have* addressed the question, the conventional view is that the grounding of constitutional rights in the idea of

citizenship does indeed run the risk of excluding aliens. Laurence Tribe, for instance, has recently noted that a revival of the privileges or immunities clause may ultimately result in the denial to aliens of the constitutional protection they now enjoy under substantive due process. "There may be no convincing escape," he writes, "from the conclusion that the Privileges or Immunities Clause, while providing a sounder basis than the Due Process Clause for the protection of substantive rights, protects only a limited group of persons—United States citizens."[17] Similarly, John Ely wrote a generation ago that, in light of the express terms of the privileges or immunities clause, most commentators see themselves as "stuck with the conclusion that only citizens are protected."[18]

For some commentators, such an outcome is not particularly troubling. Their view is that citizenship is a constitutional value too long ignored in this country and that, once revived, citizenship rights belong, quite naturally and rightfully, to those who possess citizenship status.[19] For those concerned with the condition and well-being of noncitizens, however, their exclusion from this potential new domain of rights is worrisome. Charles Black, for example, noted in the course of outlining his structural argument for grounding constitutional rights in the citizenship clause that he used the word *citizen* hesitatingly, because the "inference of rights from citizenship" might be regarded as excluding or otherwise disadvantaging aliens.[20] In earlier work, I myself questioned the turn to citizenship as a basis for rights for precisely the same reason: I argued that grounding rights in the concept of citizenship is problematic because doing so would likely redound against those individuals who lack citizenship status by legal definition.[21]

But would it, necessarily? No doubt there is reason for discomfort as a rhetorical matter: to speak of rights in the language of citizenship certainly *sounds like* it entails an exclusion of aliens. But as an analytical matter, I now think things are more complicated. What I want to argue in this chapter is that the premise that a return to citizenship as the basis for rights necessarily entails the exclusion of, or disadvantage to, noncitizens is less secure than we might presume. Within the logic of constitutional citizenship theory itself, citizenship is not just for citizens.

My argument is prompted, in part, by a reading of constitutional theory of the 1970s and 1980s on the subjects of citizenship and alienage. Although citizenship was not then the fashionable concept it has since become, some scholars at the time argued that a reorientation of constitutional rights discourse around the concept of citizenship would serve as an antidote to the peculiarities of the substantive due process doctrine and, in the view of some, would serve as a response to the chronic legal marginalization and subordination of African Americans in American life. Thus, Charles Black, Philip Bobbitt, John Ely, Kenneth Karst, Philip

Kurland, and others each defended a return to citizenship as a basis for rights in constitutional law (though by way of several different doctrinal routes). In so doing, each of these scholars recognized the potential cost of doing so to noncitizens. Yet each sought to mitigate this effect by employing one of two main arguments. First, some argued, restoration of citizenship does not necessarily entail the elimination of rights grounded in personhood, but can serve instead to supplement them.[22] In essence, this is an argument that constitutional rights doctrine can hereafter proceed on a double track, with the law of personhood not displaced but augmented by the law of citizenship. Philip Kurland, for example, wrote of the possible revival of the privileges or immunities clause: "there the clause is, an empty and unused vessel which affords the Court full opportunity to determine its contents without even the need for pouring out the precedents that already clog the due process and equal protection clauses."[23] And indeed, he and others have argued that the precedents on alienage discrimination under the equal protection clause could presumably be invoked to diminish most differences in the treatment of aliens that might result from reliance on citizenship-related provisions as a source of rights.[24]

A second mitigating argument found in the literature—though it has been in most cases more a suggestion than an elaborated argument—is that a return to constitutional citizenship as the basis for individual rights is not, in fact, inherently exclusionary toward aliens. Rather, the suggestion is that aliens can be incorporated into the turn to constitutional citizenship along with everybody else. Ely proposed a textual argument to this effect: instead of concluding that "the privileges or immunities *of* citizens"[25] are available only *to* citizens, he maintained that "one may plausibly read the Privileges or Immunities Clause [to provide] that there is a set of entitlements, 'the privileges and immunities of citizens of the United States,' which states are not to deny to anyone [including aliens]. In other words, the reference to citizens may define the class of rights rather than limit the class of beneficiaries."[26]

Similarly, though in a broader vein, Philip Bobbitt suggested that reconceptualizing constitutional rights as flowing from a structural principle of citizenship (such as that proposed by Charles Black) need not be read as inherently exclusionary toward aliens. Bobbitt specifically rejected the view that there exists an "antinomy between citizen and alien"; he instead proposed that "for constitutional purposes," the alien "be analogized to the citizen, with only such exceptions—voting and office-holding—as the Constitution itself provides."[27]

Crucially, neither Ely nor Bobbitt maintained that aliens can escape marginalization under a revived citizenship regime by *becoming* citizens via naturalization. Rather, their argument was that aliens, while they are aliens—*qua* aliens—can be said to enjoy citizenship, or should not be precluded from enjoying citizenship, in at least some respects.

It is this second effort to ameliorate constitutional citizenship's alienage problem that interests me here. The notion that a return to constitutional citizenship as the conceptual anchor for individual rights need not leave aliens behind is fascinating because it leads to the apparently paradoxical idea that aliens can enjoy, or partake in, some aspects of citizenship. It points to the prospect, in other words, of "alien citizenship"[28] under the U.S. Constitution.

At first glance, the notion of alien citizenship may seem impossible—baldly contradictory by its terms.[29] Yet it has not seemed so to all observers. And the fact that this idea has not seemed impossible—including to several of constitutional law scholarship's most eminent commentators—is itself quite striking. These scholars' conviction that a (re)turn to citizenship as a basis for constitutional rights need not imply the exclusion of aliens—and indeed might well bring them along—casts important light on the idea of constitutional citizenship. What it suggests, in essence, is that American understandings of constitutional citizenship are segmented and divided in nature. As an analytical matter, citizenship references both formal membership of the national political community and the state of enjoyment of rights and recognition within that community. In normative terms, citizenship comprises both universalist and exclusionary commitments. It is these divisions, and especially their interplay, that make the idea of alien citizenship paradoxically possible.

My reading of citizenship as a divided construct bears close affinity with other recent work on the nature and history of citizenship in the United States, particularly that of constitutional historians, who have pointed out that the rights that comprise the enjoyment of citizenship in this country have never been cut from a single cloth but entail a range of entirely distinguishable sorts of entitlements and protections.[30] This work, which focuses on the distinctions between civil, political, social, and (more recently) economic conceptions and practices of citizenship, is useful not merely because it allows us to think about the enjoyment of (and the exclusion from) citizenship in more complex terms than we are accustomed to doing, but because it raises the possibility that citizenship is not an all-or-nothing affair; it is, instead, a construct that is internally complex and segmented. Historian Nancy Cott for example, has shown that although white women in nineteenth century America enjoyed citizenship in "nominal" terms, they were nevertheless denied many of the rights we now consider fundamental to citizenship in its fullest sense.[31] In the course of the study, she observes that "citizenship can be delivered in different degrees of permanence or strength. . . . Citizenship is not a definitive either/or proposition—you are or you are not—but a compromisable one."[32]

This notion of citizenship as divisible, compromisable—indeed, fragmented—helps to capture the relationship aliens maintain to constitutional citizenship. The fragmentation of citizenship results in diverse sorts of partial citizenship identities, including the anomalous identity of the alien citizen. What is distinctive about the case of alienage is that it introduces into the mix an aspect of citizenship that most constitutional theorists who focus on rights tend to ignore—citizenship as formal national membership status. It is the uneasy relationship between citizenship as rights and citizenship as status, as well as between the universalist and particularist commitments embodied in the idea of rights citizenship itself, that is the focus of this chapter.

CITIZENSHIP'S SUBJECTS AND CITIZENSHIP'S SUBSTANCE

Interpreters of the Constitution have long been uncertain about precisely what the Fourteenth Amendment has to say about citizenship. Everyone, of course, acknowledges that passage of the amendment radically altered American constitutional understandings of citizenship. We recognize, first of all, that the Fourteenth Amendment made citizenship a matter of national law and national concern. Whereas prior to its passage, the meaning and regulation of citizenship were understood to be matters reserved to the states, the new amendment "decisively repudiate[d] state sovereignty"[33] and signaled a fundamental realignment of the relationship between the state and federal governments.

Everyone, furthermore, recognizes that the amendment's citizenship clause served to reverse the Supreme Court decision in *Dred Scott*, which held that persons of African descent did not and could not possess citizenship.[34] In so doing, the amendment provided "a definition of citizenship in which race played no part."[35] Most commentators read the Fourteenth Amendment as defining the criteria for citizenship in more general terms as well;[36] the amendment "tells us who are citizens of the United States,"[37] thereby designating the class of formal members of the nation.[38]

Yet while most commentators agree on these fundamentals, there looms beyond them a host of uncertainties about the Fourteenth Amendment's vision of, and mandate concerning, citizenship. In recent years, divisions around these questions have mostly found expression in two broad debates. The first concerns the question of citizenship's substantive meaning and scope. While scholars increasingly concur that constitutional citizenship has been wrongfully neglected, if not repressed, for too long, the literature is replete with heated exchanges over precisely what effect the return to citizenship would or will have on constitutional jurisprudence—on the constitutional jurisprudence of rights, especially. Scholars have debated, among other things, whether the privileges or immunities clause, the citizenship clause, or both should be read to incorporate the federal Bill of Rights or a much narrower set of rights;[39] whether the protections of citizenship are confined to antidiscrimination guarantees or embody protection of those fundamental rights now guaranteed under substantive due process theory—and perhaps other unenumerated rights as well;[40] and whether the enjoyment of citizenship necessarily entails social and economic, as well as political and civil, rights for society's members.[41]

A second major debate on the subject is a debate over the significance of citizenship in our constitutional system. Alexander Bickel famously launched the modern version of this debate by espousing the view that possession of citizenship status has been, and should remain, fundamentally insignificant in the American constitutional order.[42] Many scholars have since attempted in a variety of ways to contest this view; some dispute the historical account,[43] and others have urged that the status of citizenship has, in any event, wrongly been "devalued" and deserves constitutional prominence and honor.[44] Still others, however, continue to characterize the Constitution as centrally committed to the rights of persons, and to normatively defend such a commitment.

On the face of it, these two debates are intimately related. At the most obvious level, it will be worthwhile to engage in protracted debates about the meaning of citizenship only to the extent that we regard citizenship as legally and politically significant. Yet the debates are also distinguishable in ways that are conceptually important. For one thing, the precise object of their concern—the "citizenship" that they address—is not identical in each case. Those engaged in the debate over the meaning of citizenship treat citizenship as an ensemble of rights enjoyed, and practices undertaken (as well, sometimes, as responsibilities borne), by community members, the nature and scope of which require specification. Those involved in the debate over the significance of citizenship, in contrast, approach citizenship as a formal legal status and ask what that status means, and what it ought to mean, in our constitutional system. The two debates also have radically different starting points with respect to the class of persons deemed to constitute citizenship's subjects. Those engaged in the meaning-of-citizenship debate presume at the outset that everyone in the community enjoys the formal status of citizenship and focus on the nature and distribution of the substantive rights to which these citizens are entitled. In contrast, those addressing the significance of citizenship begin by recognizing that *not* everyone is a formal citizen, and then go on to examine the implications of possessing or not possessing citizenship status.

These differences in baseline and focus set the debates apart from one another in conceptual terms, but the distinctions are not merely conceptual. As it happens, something of a professional divide has developed as well between those engaged in the two citizenship debates. Whereas the meaning-of-citizenship debate is central fare in mainstream constitutional theory (in theory concerning both rights and democratic self-governance), the significance-of-citizenship issue has been of special interest to immigration scholars and those concerned with the status of aliens. Only rarely do scholars involved in one of these two debates cross the line to engage with the other.

This seems to me to be an unfortunate divide. While the two debates do indeed address different sorts of questions, these are questions that inevitably bear very closely on one another. Simply stated we cannot think productively about the substance of constitutional citizenship without addressing the question of who it is that constitutes citizenship's formal subjects. Futhermore, the question remains as to precisely *how* rights and status bear on one another. What exactly is the nature of the relationship between citizenship's subjects and citizenship's substance, between the who and the what of constitutional citizenship?

This relationship has been extremely complex and uncertain in constitutional thought. For one thing, it is not always clear on the face of it which of these aspects of citizenship commentators are addressing in any given context. The two are often conflated, and they can be hard to distinguish in any event.[45] At the same time, because constitutional law and commentary on citizenship often treat substance and subjects as distinct legal concerns that employ different analytical and even normative vocabularies, the relationship between them is rarely directly considered.

One context in which the two debates naturally and necessarily do converge, however, is in relation to the legal status category of alienage. At first glance, alienage might seem to be a subject wholly encompassed within the significance-of-citizenship debate, for inquiring about the legal and social differences that citizenship status makes necessarily entails an inquiry about the difference that alienage makes, as well.[46] But alienage, as it happens, is also significantly implicated in the meaning-of-citizenship debate. To the extent that the idea of citizenship is imbued with greater constitutional meaning—to the extent that increasing numbers of rights and responsibilities and practices are expressed in the vocabulary of citizenship—we inevitably face the question whether aliens—who are *noncitizens*, by legal definition—will find themselves excluded from the scope of many of the Constitution's protections altogether.

Although this risk, as I have said, is most often ignored in the literature, some constitutional commentators have recognized exclusion of aliens as a real possibility. Of these, most have assumed that rights grounded in citizenship will necessarily extend to status citizens only, and that status noncitizens will thereby be negatively affected. However, a handful of commentators have contested this view, seeking to argue that exclusion of aliens is not a strictly necessary outcome of the revival of constitutional citizenship. They have done so by positing, in Philip Bobbitt's terms, that there is no necessary "antinomy between citizen and alien,"[47] and by suggesting that, as a matter both of constitutional text and theory, aliens might themselves be understood to enjoy some aspects of constitutional citizenship.[48] What is so striking about this proposal is that it implicitly relies on a conception of citizenship in which citizenship's subjects and citizenship's substance are not necessarily co-extensive but are instead relatively autonomous. This is a conception in which a person need not be a citizen in order to enjoy citizenship.

Citizenship Minimalism and Its Critics

The Fourteenth Amendment tells us who the nation's citizens are. Yet beyond designating the class of national citizens, it remains uncertain what more the Fourteenth Amendment has to say about citizenship. One reading, which has long dominated American jurisprudence and constitutional thought, is that it says very little else. In this minimalist reading,[49] the effect of the amendment's citizenship clause is almost entirely definitional.[50] The clause designates a class of national citizens who owe allegiance to the polity and are in turn guaranteed its protection in the international sphere.[51] And while the amendment contains the privileges or immunities clause as well, the longtime interpretation of this clause by the Supreme Court has regarded it as guaranteeing very little by way of substance to those defined as Fourteenth Amendment citizens. In an 1873 decision not yet overruled, a majority of the Court held that the privileges or immunities guaranteed in the amendment's first clause guaranteed virtually nothing beyond a set of minimal rights already guaranteed or implicit elsewhere in the Constitution.[52] Until fairly recently, most scholars have taken largely for granted both the *Slaughter-House* Court's evisceration of the clause and the development of the jurisprudence of individual rights under the aegis of personhood by way of the equal protection and due process clauses.[53]

On this traditional account, then, the Fourteenth Amendment does no more than specify who is a citizen, and offers an exceptionally thin conception of what citizenship is. Citizenship, in this understanding, is "membership of a nation,"[54] and not a great deal more.[55] As Bickel put it, "[w]hile we now have a definition of citizenship in the Constitution, we . . . set very little store by it."[56]

Against this minimalist reading, contemporary scholars urging the revival of the idea of constitutional citizenship have protested that the Fourteenth Amendment has much more to say about citizenship than this account acknowledges. Specifically, they argue that beyond defining the class of citizenship's subjects, the idea of citizenship carries with it substantive rights that are far more elaborate and robust than the minimalist reading allows. Some would locate these in the citizenship clause itself; they argue that implicit in the constitutional definition of citizenship's subjects is a commitment to provide fundamental rights to citizens.[57] Others maintain that the constitution's framers entrusted citizenship's substance to the privileges or immunities clause,[58] while others still read a commitment to substantive citizenship values in the equal protection clause by way of the principle of equal citizenship.[59] Some would confine the rights of citizenship to civil or political rights, while others insist that constitutional citizenship entails commitments to economic and social equality, as well.[60]

In each case, though, revivalists want to press beyond the minimalist reading of Fourteenth Amendment citizenship in two respects. First, they maintain that the Fourteenth Amendment should be read not merely to designate citizenship's subjects but also to provide substantive guarantees associated with citizenship. Second, they contend that these guarantees are thicker and more meaningful than the traditional minimalist account allows.

As to why constitutional citizenship should be understood more thickly and substantively, scholars' rationales have varied. Some analysts regard the minimalist account as simply mistaken as a historical matter; in their view, citizenship minimalism ignores the intent of the Framers and the original meaning of the Fourteenth Amendment.[61] Others contend that, beyond history and text, citizenship minimalism obscures the meaning of the Constitution in a deeper sense. Whether animated by an anti-caste vision of the Constitution or by principles of republican self-government,[62] the ideal of citizenship is understood to represent a core source of rights and responsibilities in our constitutional nomos.

As a purely interpretive matter, I have some sympathy with the view, espoused by critics of citizenship minimalism, that the idea of constitutional citizenship can fairly be read to possess a meaning that goes beyond providing for the sheer delineation of national status. Notice, however, that to the extent we adopt a more robust reading of constitutional citizenship, we are presuming a dual conception of Fourteenth Amendment citizenship. Under this dual conception, the amendment's provisions work *both* to designate the class of persons entitled to citizenship *and* to set out a substantive vision of citizenship rights. This conception may represent a more complete accounting of citizenship's meaning under the

Constitution, but it introduces complexities as well. Specifically, it opens up a variety of analytical and normative questions concerning the nature of the relationship between status citizenship and rights citizenship in the first instance.

"Mere Status" and "Equal Citizenship": The Second-Class Citizenship Critique

In discussions of citizenship in political and social theory, it is common for scholars to distinguish between "thin" and "thick" versions of citizenship. Thin citizenship is citizenship-as-status—"mere status," in the disparaging phrase of some commentators.[63] This thin version of citizenship is contrasted with more robust, substantive conceptions. These thicker conceptions vary in kind: some scholars focus on citizenship as the meaningful enjoyment of rights, while others, in a more civic republican vein, approach citizenship as a mode of democratic engagement and self-governance. In either case, a hierarchy is posited: to possess the legal status of citizenship is to enjoy citizenship only in the most formal and nominal sense. The true and full enjoyment of citizenship requires much more.[64]

In the constitutional literature, some accounts of the relationship between citizenship status and citizenship rights employ a similar hierarchical framework, with rights the superior and status the inferior term. The work of Kenneth Karst is especially illustrative. Karst describes the Fourteenth Amendment as containing two conceptions of citizenship: a "narrow" conception, pursuant to which citizenship constitutes legal status, and a "broader conception" that embodies, in his argument, the principle of "equal citizenship."[65] For Karst, citizenship status is a "simple idea,"[66] a "constitutional trifle,"[67] whereas the broader conception of equal citizenship entails "the dignity of full membership in the society,"[68] and constitutes, for this reason, the fundamental normative value of our national life.[69]

There are good reasons for approaching citizenship in this hierarchical fashion. Doing so represents a response to the history of discrimination in this country and elsewhere, pursuant to which the formal citizenship status of subordinated groups has been recognized while these groups have, nevertheless, remained excluded and marginalized in many significant respects. Scholars' normative prioritization of rights citizenship over status citizenship can be read, in other words, as part of a critique of legal arrangements whereby individuals possess formal citizenship status but experience de facto exclusion and powerlessness. Such a critique is often articulated as the critique of "second-class citizenship."

Second-class citizenship is a concept that has been normatively powerful in American political and legal discourse in recent decades. In rhetorical terms, it has been extremely effective in conveying the idea that the
extension of the formal status of citizenship alone can mask real oppression and thereby represents a largely empty husk.[70] Much of the history
of citizenship in this country can be, and has been, recounted in these
terms.[71] After the passage of the Fourteenth Amendment, African Americans possessed formal citizenship but remained subordinated in virtually
every sphere. Likewise, for many years women were recognized as possessing the nominal status of citizenship, yet they were denied the franchise and other fundamental incidents of membership. Sometimes, the
denial of rights to citizens was overtly defended; the citizenship of some
groups was simply deemed to be less complete than that of others. Increasingly, however, rights that we now regard as integral to citizenship were
denied to status citizens through court decisions maintaining that these
rights fell outside the core substantive requirements of citizenship. The
classic example is the decision in the 1875 case of *Minor v. Happersett*,
in which the Supreme Court concluded that voting was not a "privilege
or immunity of citizenship."[72]

The critique of second-class citizenship is thus a critique of citizenship
formalism—a condition in which nominal membership serves to mask the
continued exclusion and social domination of historically marginalized
groups. It is a critique of citizenship minimalism as well: It rejects the
notion that the class of citizens can be defined as pure status holders without being acknowledged and empowered as active community participants, and it demands recognition and effectuation of rights and protections that make community membership meaningful.[73]

While the second-class citizenship critique is an indispensable form of
political and legal criticism, it also suffers from certain limitations. One
problem is that the focus on the denial of rights to status citizens often
renders the critique insensitive to the history of systematic denial of citizenship status itself to members of subordinated groups in this country.
Important recent scholarship on Asian and other nonwhite exclusion
from naturalization eligibility, and on the history of married women's
nationality laws—which, among other things, denationalized American
women who married foreigners—makes the point vividly.[74] So too does
the growing literature on the exclusion of Puerto Ricans from constitutional citizenship status.[75] Possession of the "mere status" of citizenship
does not appear so trivial a matter when approached in the context of
these struggles.[76] This account, furthermore, obscures the ways in which
a *lack* of the status of citizenship itself, in the form of alienage, sometimes
serves as a basis for caste-like treatment and discrimination.[77]

But beyond this insensitivity to the continuing significance and intractability of citizenship status questions, there lies another, more conceptual difficulty with the second-class citizenship critique. I have said that commentators often treat citizenship status and citizenship rights as elements in a hierarchy, with status the lesser of the two values. Yet the hierarchy posited is usually not one of otherwise independent variables. Instead, the possession of citizenship status is often regarded as logically prior to—as a necessary but insufficient condition for—the enjoyment of citizenship rights. In this account, citizenship status is assumed to be an embryonic form of citizenship, an indispensable antecedent to citizenship in its more substantive mode.

However, conceiving of the relationship between status and rights this way can be misleading. Citizenship status is not, in fact, always an antecedent to citizenship rights. While the status of citizenship is a condition precedent for the enjoyment of some rights in the United States, there are many rights that many citizenship revivalists have wanted to characterize as rights of citizenship—expressive and associational rights, for instance, or procedural rights in the criminal context, or the right to attend public schools with other children, or property-related rights—for which citizenship status is not a prerequisite at all. Such rights have been regarded instead as attaching to persons—territorially present persons, usually by reference to the constitutional values of equal protection and due process. It is true that the right most closely associated with citizenship in both popular understandings and in political theory—the right to vote[78]—has in recent decades been confined to people who possess citizenship status. But the franchise was not limited to status citizens historically; as a number of scholars have chronicled in recent years, aliens possessed the right to vote in many states through the late nineteenth century, and even today they vote in a handful of local elections.[79]

The point is that citizenship status does not always serve as the ground floor in the larger edifice of constitutional citizenship. Instead, we find that, just as citizenship status has not always entailed citizenship rights, the possession of rights doesn't always require prior possession of citizenship status. Rights and status, in short, are relatively autonomous.[80]

ALIENAGE AND THE CITIZENSHIP REVIVAL

This relative autonomy as between citizenship status and citizenship rights goes a long way toward explaining the proposition that the revival of constitutional citizenship need not undercut aliens' rights. Aliens can enjoy much in the way of rights citizenship, even if they lack status citizenship by definition. Citizenship, in other words, is a divided condition.

It is this conception of citizenship as divided that enabled Charles Black to write that "filling with content the concept of citizenship need not result in neglect of the rights of aliens among us."[81] Rather, Black argues, the grounding of rights in citizenship should result in the further protection of aliens—"lawfully resident aliens," he qualifies—"for their position is in many respects and for many purposes soundly to be analogized to that of citizens."[82] Likewise, it is this sort of disjuncture between status and rights that John Ely invoked when he suggested that the privileges or immunities clause need not be read to protect citizens only; instead, he maintains, it can plausibly be read to mean that "there is a set of entitlements, 'the privileges and immunities of citizens of the United States,' which states are not to deny to *anyone*,"[83] aliens included. The phrase "privileges or immunities of citizens," he writes, "define[s] the class of rights rather than limit[s] the class of beneficiaries."[84]

And it is with this conception of the relative autonomy of citizenship's subjects and substance implicitly in mind that Philip Bobbitt could criticize the assumption "that 'alien' and 'citizen' are opposites sharing no characteristics, defined as negations of one another."[85] Bobbitt would presumably concur that alien and citizen are to some degree opposing categories in the domain of formal citizenship status, since our statutory immigration law defines the category alien precisely as "any person not a citizen" of the United States.[86] But with regard to substantive citizenship—understood here as enjoyment of rights—the relationship, he suggests, is far more subtle and complex.[87]

Kenneth Karst's discussion of the alienage question in his early work is a notable example of constitutional theory employing a divided conception of citizenship. Karst is a longtime proponent of revitalizing the normative ideal of citizenship as a basis for constitutional rights, although unlike many other scholars, he has argued that the principle of equal citizenship is best housed not in the citizenship clause or the privileges or immunities clause but in the equal protection clause.[88] He acknowledges that this may seem counterintuitive; after all, he notes, it is the former clauses that expressly address the subject of citizenship.[89] Yet Karst endorses the equal protection clause as a textual foundation for equal citizenship for several reasons.

First, he notes that there is value and safety in precedent: "we already have a store of well-developed equal protection doctrine embodying the principle of equal citizenship. . . . It seems sensible to leave the principle where it took root."[90] Moreover, he contends (contrary to the weight of more recent opinion on the matter) that the equal protection clause "shows every sign of being able to bear the full meaning of the equal citizenship principle."[91] There is, in other words, no intrinsic reason of doctrinal integrity or coherence to depart from our recent interpretive practice.

However, for Karst, the most important reason for sticking with the equal protection clause is that it extends its protection "not only to 'citizens' but to every 'person.' "[92] This is, for him, a signal virtue. It is a virtue because it means the clause is maximally inclusive, as the equal citizenship principle ought to be. It is a virtue, in particular, precisely because the equal protection clause does not confine its protections to citizens—and Karst maintains, "it is important to extend most of the content of the equal citizenship principle to aliens."[93]

Now this is a very striking position: Karst urges retention of the equal protection clause as the textual site of the equal citizenship principle precisely because the equal protection clause does not limit its protective scope to citizens. Karst himself acknowledges the apparent paradox; on introducing the argument, he requests of his readers "the suspension of incredulity."[94] He goes on to explain his view that, "for most purposes aliens are entitled to be regarded as respected participants in our national society, even though they lack citizenship in the narrow sense. The broader principle of equal citizenship extends its core values to noncitizens because for most purposes they are members of our society."[95]

Karst thus employs his preference for substantive over formal citizenship to urge inclusion of formal noncitizens within citizenship's substantive scope. Aliens' lack of the "narrow" citizenship of status does not require them to be denied the "broader" citizenship of membership because status citizenship, in his formulation, is not a precondition for equal citizenship.

What each of these scholars shares in common is the conviction that locating the idea of citizenship at the center of the constitutional discourse of rights need not entail the wholesale exclusion of aliens. This conviction presupposes that citizenship is not a monolithic whole but rather a compound and ultimately severable concept: citizenship's subjects and its substance—its "beneficiaries" and its "rights," in Ely's terms[96]—are treated as discontinuous. Just as being a citizen does not guarantee (although it should, all agree) any particular citizenship substance, *enjoying* citizenship does not require *being* a citizen in any formal sense.[97] In this understanding, citizenship status and citizenship rights are simply nonconvergent.

THE PREVAILING VIEW: CITIZENSHIP FOR CITIZENS

The reading these scholars give to the status of alienage under an enhanced citizenship rights regime in constitutional law is not, to be sure, the prevailing understanding. Most scholars seem to take it for granted that the enjoyment of citizenship rights requires possession of citizenship status. This is made clear in many contemporary discussions of the revival of the constitutional concept of citizenship as a basis for rights. Scholars most often read the privileges or immunities clause, for example, as ensuring citizenship rights only for people who possess citizenship status. As Michael Kent Curtis has written, "the rights possessed by virtue of the Privileges or Immunities Clause of the Fourteenth Amendment are held by those with the status of citizens of the United States."[98] This is, he says, "a simple and direct reading" of the textual language.[99] Likewise, Akhil Amar specifically rejects Ely's bifurcated reading of the clause, maintaining that the clause is best read as "defining the rights *of* Americans *as* Americans."[100]

The assumption that citizenship is the preserve of citizens has also been voiced by some scholars who have criticized the citizenship revival in constitutional and political discourse. Scholars have argued, on that basis, that a revitalization of citizenship will almost certainly work to the detriment of aliens. In earlier work, I warned of such a consequence, contending that, as a rhetorical and practical matter, treating "citizenship" as the measure of full political and social inclusion may implicitly work to exclude persons who lack citizenship by legal definition.[101] Once again, the operant assumption here is that the status and substance of citizenship necessarily converge. If rights are conceived as a kind of citizenship, in this view, then aliens will be unjustly disadvantaged.

On its face, the notion that citizenship is the exclusive preserve of citizens is hardly a surprising proposition. Commonsense understandings tend to regard the term *citizenship* as the state of being a citizen[102] and *citizen* as the identity of one who enjoys citizenship. This reciprocal and mutually referential sort of definition is reflected in much of the theoretical scholarship about citizenship. In political and legal theory, citizenship's subjects are often defined entirely derivatively, by reference to their possession of substantive citizenship, and citizenship's substance is likewise defined in relation to what the subjects of citizenship possess or enjoy or do. Civic republicans, for example, approach citizenship as a state of purposeful engagement in the life of the political community; for them, active self-governance is citizenship's substance. And in this tradition, when a person exercises or enjoys or enacts such citizenship, she becomes a citizen by definition. Conversely, a citizen in the republican sense is understood to be a person who is actively engaged in the process of the political community's process of self-government; and when a person is a citizen, she or he is, by definition, practicing citizenship.[103]

In the prevailing view, then, a subject of citizenship is simply one who enjoys citizenship in substantive terms, and substantive citizenship is simply what citizens have or do. Substance and subjects are not independent attributes of citizenship; they are merely different ways of expressing the same citizenship-related condition.

Yet as we have seen, this is not the only way that the relationship between the subjects and the substance of citizenship is conventionally understood. Indeed, in American constitutional discourse, the relationship between these attributes of citizenship is often regarded as distinctly fractured. The second-class citizenship critique specifically recognizes that the subjects and substance of citizenship do not always converge; people not infrequently possess citizenship status without enjoying much in the way of what we consider to be the substance of citizenship.

The status of aliens presents another possibility of disjuncture between citizenship's subjects and its substance. Immigration commentators have often noted that today, lawful permanent resident aliens "live lives largely indistinguishable from those of most U.S. citizens . . . exercis[ing] most constitutional rights on the same terms as native-born and naturalized citizens."[104] To the extent the exercise of such rights is characterized as the enjoyment of "citizenship"—and describing rights in the language of citizenship is increasingly common—we face the prospect of what we can only call "alien citizenship"—or, more to the point, "noncitizen citizenship." While apparently paradoxical, such neologisms make clear that the American conception of constitutional citizenship is partially split, with the who and the what of citizenship not always neatly lined up.

Is Citizenship for Aliens Unjust?

Most constitutional scholars today criticize this lack of alignment when it takes the form of second-class citizenship. Most assume, in other words, that if a person possesses the status of citizenship, she ought to fully possess the substance of citizenship as well. As we have seen, this is a critically important staple of progressive constitutional thought. To grant membership in formal terms while denying protections and privileges enjoyed by other members is simply unjust exclusion. To use the fact of a person's nominal membership as a smokescreen for their de facto exclusion is rank hypocrisy. This seems clear.

But does the converse argument hold as well? Is bifurcated citizenship in the other direction—the enjoyment of citizenship rights without the possession of citizenship status—similarly objectionable?

One response to this question would be that such a divide is indeed objectionable, and that citizenship status should be a prerequisite for citizenship rights. The strongest versions of this argument rely on a heavy dose of symbolic nationalism, espousing the claim that formal citizenship is an essential status for marking who belongs to "we the people." In this perspective, citizenship status is significant precisely because it separates members from outsiders. Anti-immigrant activists and commentators defend views of this sort,[105] but constitutional analysts have as well. Jeffrey Rosen, for instance, has argued that the Supreme Court should "resurrect [ ] the distinction between citizens and aliens . . . [and thereby] resurrect the meaning of citizenship itself as something more than a pale and disembodied legalism."[106]

Such views have also been expressed by more progressive scholars. William Eskridge, for instance, has recently defended the "proposition that the 'privileges or immunities of citizens of the United States' are those entailing obligations as well as rights that set apart the full membership in the political community from the outsider, or alien."[107] This is not merely an interpretive statement about the meaning of the privileges or immunities clause; it is an affirmative claim, as well, about the proper relationship between citizenship rights and citizenship status, a claim that important citizenship rights are properly confined to those possessing the status.

Despite the somewhat inflammatory phrasing, Eskridge's is not entirely an outlying view. Many people assume that citizenship status "has to count for something,"[108] that it must be consequential,[109] and they assume that its consequentiality resides, in part, in assured and exclusive access to certain rights (and the bearing of certain responsibilities). Indeed, the notion that citizenship status ought to be a prerequisite for the enjoyment of at least some citizenship rights is presupposed by anyone who supports continued denial to aliens of the right to vote—a near universally accepted feature of even the most liberal democratic states today.[110] The citizen voting rule represents a rather weak version of the principle that citizenship status should be necessary for citizenship rights in that it confines itself to only one right rather than many. Nevertheless, the principle is widely accepted in this context.

On the other hand, it is striking to note the degree to which the "citizenship for citizens" principle does not much characterize the state of the law in the United States, at least beyond the franchise. As we have seen, most aliens, including undocumented aliens, are afforded a broad range of constitutional (as well as statutory) rights which in some respects render them indistinguishable from citizens.[111] This is a function of the American constitutional system's guarantee of rights to persons rather than citizens in most cases—a state of affairs that has been forcefully defended by many scholars over the years. Their basic argument is that personhood embodies a powerful ideal of universality, one that represents a core commitment of our constitutional system.[112]

Precisely because of this universalist commitment, most of those who defend the personhood model would not regard the extension of citizenship rights to those without citizenship status as morally reprehensible;

indeed, they regard it as entirely necessary. From their perspective, the two sorts of citizenship misalignment discussed here—rights without status and status without rights—cannot be regarded as moral equivalents. As a supporter of personhood-based conceptions of rights,[113] I believe they are clearly right about this. So long as citizenship status is made available to noncitizens on liberal terms,[114] granting what we often call citizenship rights to status noncitizens is not a constitutional wrong but instead gives appropriate expression to the Constitution's universalist commitments.

UNIVERSAL CITIZENSHIP AND BOUNDED CITIZENSHIP

But even if citizenship for aliens is not normatively objectionable in the way that second-class citizenship is, there remains the question of whether the notion of "alien citizenship" is coherent by its own terms. Can Ely, Bobbit, Karst, and the others persuasively maintain that persons constitute the rightful subjects of most constitutional rights, while at the same time characterizing the substance of those rights as a form of citizenship?[115]

At one level, answering this question is a matter of constitutional interpretation. Certainly, the scholars I have focused on see themselves as making interpretive arguments about the meaning of the Fourteenth Amendment; they are interested precisely in how that amendment accommodates (or fails to accommodate) the mandates of personhood rights and citizenship. Should the Constitution, after the Fourteenth Amendment's passage, be read as "now identif[ying] personhood with United States citizenship,"[116] or did the Amendment intend a sharp divide between them?

There are various aspects to the debate in the constitutional literature. Much of the debate has taken the form of a dispute over the relationship between the equal protection and due process clauses (which speak of persons), on the one hand, and the privileges or immunities clause (referencing citizens), on the other. Scholars have asked, among other things, Are these clauses to be read as overlapping in meaning?[117] If so, is the privileges or immunities clause redundant? If not, what does its reference to "the rights of citizens" add to the mix (read both in light of and in spite of *Slaughter-House*)?[118] Are the rights referred to narrower than the rights guaranteed to persons in the other clauses?[119] Much ink has been spilled on these and related questions in the constitutional commentary, and scholars remain widely divided on these issues.

But assessing the coherence of the idea of alien citizenship is a matter that requires going beyond a parsing of constitutional history and text. It requires us to consider, as well, questions of normative constitutional theory. As Karst has written, citizenship—equal citizenship—is not merely a technical constitutional concept; it is also "an ideal, a cluster of value premises."[120] To evaluate the plausibility of the concept of alien citizenship, therefore, we need to consider it in these terms.

The pressing question thus becomes whether the constitutional commitments of rights to persons, on the one hand, and of citizenship as rights, on the other, can actually function as complementary. To what extent are they normatively and practically compatible? The answer, I want to suggest, is that their compatibility only goes so far.

On first reading, the ideal of equal citizenship does appear to be inextricably linked to an ethic of rights based on personhood. As many commentators have argued, the principle of equal citizenship embodies a commitment to universality. Kenneth Karst writes that under this principle, "[e]very individual is . . . presumptively entitled to treatment in our public life as a person . . . deserv[ing of] respect."[121] The ideal of equal citizenship is grounded in a commitment to justice and recognition "for all."[122] It is this grand universalism, which accords rights to persons by virtue of their common humanity, that accounts for much of the concept's powerful political resonance.

Yet on further review it becomes clear that "everyone" does not quite mean *everyone*. For despite equal citizenship's professed commitment to universality, the universality championed is, in fact, a circumscribed one. The constraints on universality's scope are the result of the other core animating ideal of the equal citizenship principle—that of community membership, or "belonging," in Karst's term. The notion of belonging is insistently inclusive within the community, yet it also presupposes community boundaries—boundaries that ultimately divide insiders from outsiders.[123] "By drawing a circle and designating those within the circle as sovereign and equal," Alex Aleinikoff has written, "the concept of citizenship perforce treats those outside the circle . . . as less than full members."[124]

Most theorists of equal citizenship have tended to disregard citizenship's exclusionary aspect in their work. Like many social and political theorists, they "tend[ ] to take the existence of a bounded national 'society' for granted and to focus on institutions and processes internal to that society."[125] Their focus on citizenship within the national community, in turn, allows them to treat citizenship as a universalist ideal with an inherently expansive logic. Karst, for instance, writes of equal citizenship's "expanding . . . circle of belonging"—though he has always acknowledged that the process of inclusion remains incomplete. This expansive conception of citizenship was expressed by Walzer, who similarly posits a citizenship that progressively incorporates outsider groups. He writes, "Slaves, workers, new immigrants, Jews, Blacks, women—all of them move into the circle of the protected, even if the protection they actually get is still unequal or inadequate."[126]

This statement captures the predominant conception of citizenship among mainstream constitutional scholars. Focusing on the nation's interior, they approach citizenship—at least ideally—as a source of progressively inclusive and egalitarian values.[127] As we have seen, it has fallen to those scholars specifically concerned with the community's threshold to attend to citizenship's nationally exclusionary dimension.[128]

Yet while most scholars who champion the concept of equal citizenship tend to ignore citizenship's exclusionary face, it is ultimately presupposed in their project. First of all, as I have said, constitutional scholars often characterize equal citizenship not merely as the universal enjoyment of rights but also as the experience of community belonging or membership. Membership communities, of course, have insides and outsides which are constituted by some sort of boundary, however permeable it may be.

Furthermore, many constitutional theorists make their case on behalf of equal citizenship by linking it to a particular form of community belonging, which they express through the concept of "national union" or "national unity."[129] Karst, for instance, writes that "[t]he union of the American people is a constitutional value of the first importance."[130] And it is a value that is inextricably linked with the value of equal citizenship. National unity is seen as a precondition for the practice of equal citizenship, and equal citizenship, in turn, is viewed as a necessary condition for the continued well-being of the community.[131] In Karst's view, "constitutional equality can be seen as part of the social cement that holds our nation together,"[132] while the "interdependence of citizens that is the foundation for the national union" likewise serves to "strengthen the material and moral foundations of equal citizenship."[133] A number of other constitutional scholars have similarly linked equal citizenship with a normative conception of "national unity."[134]

None of these scholars appears to see any inherent tension between the normative commitments associated with national unity and equal citizenship's universalist commitments. On the contrary, they regard equal citizenship and national unity as mutually necessary and mutually reinforcing parts of a whole. And they are surely right that these dual commitments are often productively complementary within the ambit of the nation. It seems indisputable that schisms internal to the national society along class or caste or state lines have thwarted struggles for universal and equal rights within the nation; and conversely, it is clear that a sense of national identification and community solidarity has animated many efforts to give content and effect to the equal citizenship principle in this country.

Yet while the ideal of national unity may sometimes serve as an antidote to divisiveness and fragmentation *internal* to the nation,[135] the practice of ensuring the "belonging" and "unity" of the nation's members simultaneously and inevitably signals the existence of a sharp divide between insiders and outsiders to the nation. The very rhetoric of "national unity," for one thing, is uncomfortably linked with the specter of foreign threat. Its invocations are often specifically meant to evoke a defensive posture in relation to a danger posed by non-national outsiders, at least as often as (and since September 11, far more than) to reference a domestic campaign against internal fragmentation and divisiveness.[136] Even where scholars who link equal citizenship with the ideal of national unity have no intention of conveying any such defensive and nationalist message, the term's reverberations are hard to deny.

The problem is not, moreover, merely rhetorical. The ideal of national unity remains, at its heart, an intrinsically nationalist construct in ethical terms. Describing national unity as a foundation of the equal citizenship principle at the very least conveys the message that we maintain a special commitment to the well-being of members of our own national community, that we feel a kinship with them and maintain moral obligations to them above all others.[137] In this ethical-nationalist formulation, we still presume a class of foreigners—outsiders, whose existence defines a national "we"; and while they may not be constructed as overtly dangerous, their experiences and interests are nevertheless assumed to be of lesser significance to us than those of our compatriots.[138]

The point is that while constitutional scholars tend to avoid paying direct attention to citizenship in its bounded aspect and focus instead on the community's interior, their substantive accounts of equal citizenship within the nation often presuppose such boundaries. The universality of citizenship that they champion is a circumscribed universalism, constrained by a concurrent commitment to ethical nationalism.

That the normative ideal of equal citizenship in constitutional thought is, in the end, a nationally bounded universalist project obviously poses important questions at the level of political theory, including questions about the moral justifiability of preferring the interests of national insiders over national outsiders in a world characterized by vastly unequal life chances.[139] Although these are pressing matters, I am concerned for the moment not so much with the legitimacy of nationalism per se as with the nature of the relationship between citizenship's nationalist and universalist commitments in the first instance. How can citizenship be both universalist and bounded simultaneously?

To the extent that the division between citizenship's dual commitments is acknowledged by scholars at all, the usual assumption, as we have seen, is that each applies to a different jurisdictional sphere or domain.[140] It is presumed, as a rule, that citizenship's nationalist commitments are relevant at the borders, facing outward, and that citizenship's universalist commitments are relevant within the community, facing in. It is presumed, in other words, that citizenship is *hard on the outside* and *soft on the inside*: whereas citizenship embodies a universalist ethic within the community, it is exclusionary at the community's edges.[141]

This Janus-like image of citizenship can be useful as a depiction of contemporary understandings of citizenship, including constitutional understandings, but it has significant limits. The basic problem is that the presumed divide between the community's inside and its edges often does not hold in factual terms. Citizenship's universalist commitments are, first of all, sometimes brought to bear at the nation's borders: humanitarian admissions policies and rules requiring due process in deportation proceedings are powerful examples. More significant here, citizenship's exclusionary commitments are not always confined to the state's territorial perimeter but are often brought to bear even *within* the nation's territory. When this happens, principles of universal citizenship and bounded citizenship occupy the same (internal) terrain.[142]

It is precisely this process of overlapping jurisdictions that defines the category of alienage. On the one hand, the equal citizenship principle regards aliens as entitled to equal regard and recognition as persons residing in our community. Karst argues that "it is important to extend most of the content of the equal citizenship principle to aliens . . . because for most purposes [aliens] are members of our society."[143] This is the universalist strand of the equal citizenship principle at work, and it has been highly influential, for aliens do enjoy many fundamental rights as members. At the same time, however, Karst also suggests that aliens, even lawful, permanent resident aliens, may be properly regarded as outsiders to the nation's "political community" by virtue of the primary allegiance they maintain to their home states. As a consequence, he maintains, they may legitimately be denied political rights, including the right to vote.[144] The principle of equal citizenship, in this context, permits and perhaps even requires the exclusion of outsiders from the political community— the same community in which the commitment to universal equal citizenship is deemed fundamental.

The condition of undocumented immigrants, especially, illustrates the dynamic. As we saw in chapter 3, the equal citizenship principle is usually understood to demand the extension of core constitutional rights to the undocumented. The Supreme Court expressed the point plainly: "Even one whose presence in this country is unlawful, involuntary, or transitory is entitled to [basic] constitutional protection."[145] Yet many proponents of equal citizenship also tolerate the exclusion of these immigrants—particularly the culpable adults—from other core benefits of membership,[146] and most seem to regard as acceptable, and perhaps even necessary, their subjection to deportation on grounds of unlawful entry or presence.[147] Furthermore, the threat or actuality of deportation works to undercut these immigrants' equal citizenship not merely directly but also indirectly by way of the "everpresent threat of deportation,"[148] since they are often unwilling to invoke the rights they are formally entitled to for fear of coming to the attention of the immigration authorities.[149] The result, once again, is that although equal citizenship requires rights for everyone, it also tolerates, and perhaps even demands, the legal exclusion of certain territorially present non-nationals for some purposes, with the effect that the inclusive force of the principle of equal citizenship is both directly and indirectly compromised.

The ambiguous status of aliens under an equal citizenship regime makes clear that the marriage of personhood with equal citizenship proposed by Karst and others is bound to be a partially unstable union. However compatible the idea of equal citizenship is with rights for persons *qua* persons in most cases, the idea of citizenship also presupposes a bounded national community, one characterized by exclusionary commitments, both political and territorial, that will inevitably clash with a pure personhood rights approach.

Constitutionally Divided Citizenship

For all of these reasons, the claims by Karst, Bobbitt, Ely, and the others to the effect that aliens can be the subjects of citizenship and that the revitalization of the idea of constitutional citizenship need not, in principle, result in a total diminution of rights for aliens each seem quite plausible. Yet there is an intrinsic limit to the citizenship that aliens can enjoy. Theirs is something of a second-class citizenship—though this is not second-class citizenship in its classic form, pursuant to which those afforded the formal status of citizenship are denied many of the substantive rights of citizenship. Instead, the individuals involved here enjoy many substantive citizenship rights even in the absence of formal citizenship status; and yet the scope of the rights they enjoy is simultaneously constrained by virtue of citizenship's other substantive commitments, including a commitment to national exclusivity and closure.

It is in this respect that constitutional citizenship is a divided condition. It is divided conceptually—as between status and rights—and it is divided normatively, through its embodiment of both universalist and nationalist commitments. These divisions complicate the efforts by scholars to revive constitutional citizenship as the basis for individual rights jurisprudence. At the very least, it requires those promoting the citizenship turn in constitutional law to recognize citizenship's multiple dimensions and to engage directly with them in their work. As an important part of this process, we should hope to see increasing intellectual incursions in both directions across the professional divide that now separates scholars of rights citizenship and status citizenship. We should also hope for more direct acknowledgment among equal citizenship advocates of the usually unrecognized premises of normative nationalism embedded in their project.

I do not mean to suggest that increased engagement across citizenship's various fracture lines will lead, in the end, to a more coherent and unitary theory of constitutional citizenship. On the contrary, I suspect that it will simply put us in a better position to understand constitutional citizenship's ultimate lack of unity and coherence. In his sweeping book *Civic Ideals*, political scientist Rogers Smith describes what he calls "the huge iceberg of anomalies and contradictions that lurk below the surface of American citizenship laws."[150] Smith's description, it seems to me, aptly characterizes not merely our citizenship laws in general[151] but also the concept of constitutional citizenship itself. This is our condition, and constitutional theorists need to come directly to terms with it.

CHAPTER 5

Borders, Domestic Work, and the Ambiguities of Citizenship

CITIZENSHIP TALK, as we have seen, trades in both universalism and particularism. From an internal perspective, the citizenship ideal is warm and inclusive, extending, in theory, to embrace "everyone." But this embrace is, in fact, circumscribed; the ideal of citizenship, from a boundary-conscious perspective, is exclusive, demarcating not merely a class of national community members but also, in the process, a class of community outsiders. And since citizenship's boundaries are not fully coextensive with territorial borders but extend into the national society's interior, these two understandings of citizenship—the universal and the exclusive—sometimes run up against each other on the national inside. It is that moment of interaction that interests me here.

In this chapter, I examine the relationship between the discourses of universal and bounded citizenship as they are implicated in the context of a particular scholarly debate, one that concerns the relationship between and among women, citizenship, and work. For many feminists, the struggle to achieve fulfilling, decently remunerated work lies at the heart of any political effort to achieve "citizenship" for women. In much of this literature, citizenship-through-work is portrayed, romantically, as the highest fulfillment of emancipatory aspiration. Yet the idea of citizenship in this context is double-edged. As much feminist scholarship has made clear, it is impossible to think usefully about women and work without addressing the social organization of domestic and reproductive labor. Domestic labor has become increasingly commodified as women have entered the formal labor force in even greater numbers. And because that commodification has taken increasingly transnational form—because it is increasingly performed by transnational migrant women—attention to such labor necessarily brings citizenship in the exclusive, bounded sense into the conversation.

Acknowledging the relevance of status citizenship in the context of the women/work nexus in turn presents us with new conceptual challenges. We see that what many theorists characterize as the achievement of emancipatory citizenship for some women through participation in paid work often depends on the labor of citizenshipless others. The chapter goes on to ask how we ought to think about the configuration of "citizenships" in this situation. What does it mean that, whatever equal citizenship (or democratic citizenship or economic citizenship) some women in wealthy countries may achieve through public- or market-sphere work, it is often facilitated, in structural terms, by the employment of people from poorer countries who themselves lack status citizenship in the country in which they labor?

It is rhetorically tempting to suggest that women in the developed countries acquire their citizenship *at the expense of* the citizenship of their domestic workers. But this characterization does not capture the nature of the relationship between equal citizenship and status citizenship as they are usually conceived. Citizenship is not a single currency that is transferred from some women to others in zero-sum fashion. The concept, instead, is constituted by very distinct discourses associated with different practices and institutions, and each has a surprising degree of autonomy from the others. Neither bounded citizenship nor equal/democratic citizenship fully presupposes or entails the other. They are, in important respects, nonconvergent.

That is not to say that they are unrelated. Citizenship is always understood to denote membership of some kind—membership in a political community or a common society. And certainly, both equal/democratic citizenship and status citizenship are understood as modes of organizing membership. But how, precisely, are these membership concepts connected?

According to some observers, the two forms of citizenship function as complementary parts of a larger whole, with bounded citizenship providing the necessary bordered framework for the pursuit of equal/democratic citizenship within. This hard- on-the-outside, soft-on-the-inside conception of citizenship represents a widely accepted, commonsense view as we have seen. Yet, I argues here that it fails to capture important contemporary understandings and practices of citizenship, mainly because it presumes a degree of separation and separability between the community' s edges and its interior that simply does not exist.

The chapter concludes with some reflections on the desirability, given these confusions, of employing *citizenship* as the central normative idea in progressive political and social thought, including the scholarship on women and work. Arguably, the kinds of conceptual divisions and normative conflicts that characterize citizenship as we conventionally understand it reflect and contribute to an unfortunate overuse and imprecision in the term, which could be redressed by abandoning the normative discourse of citizenship altogether. I feel some sympathy with this critique, but in the end, it is comprehension, rather than correction, that is required. Our ideas about citizenship reflect many of the core political and moral dilemmas we currently face, and in turn shape the way we think about these dilemmas. In this respect, the idea of citizenship and the practices and institutions and experiences that the term is used to represent are ultimately inseparable.

Citizenship and Domestic Work

In the past several years, social and legal theorists have shown a renewed interest in redistributive concerns. This recent turn to redistribution, though variously formulated, is commonly expressed in the language of citizenship. Many scholars deploy the idea of "economic citizenship," and sometimes "social citizenship," to convey a critique of the material exclusion of the disadvantaged and to evoke a commitment to redress that exclusion through law and policy. Some argue that the achievement of "equal citizenship" requires close attention to matters of economic justice; others maintain that the practice of "democratic citizenship" requires a citizenry that enjoys basic material security. Whatever the specific language or emphasis, however, the idea of citizenship is increasingly linked to the enjoyment of economic rights in the political community.[1]

Among the central concerns of the new economic citizenship literature is the subject of work. Many scholars have urged a shift in conceptual focus from welfare to work in the arena of social citizenship, and among these, many maintain that ensuring "decent work for everyone" is an indispensable condition of equal citizenship today.[2] Some, like William Forbath and Kenneth Karst, have made the argument in constitutional terms, contending that the U.S. Constitution can and should be understood to require "a right to decent work . . . and an acceptable income for all."[3] Forbath, for instance, argues that addressing the crisis of work requires us to recover American constitutional and political traditions that embrace a firm commitment to an inclusive economic citizenship.[4] Others have made more general political and moral arguments on behalf of policy designed to ensure decent work. Judith Shklar was among the first to write about the essential role played by the "right to earn" as a foundation of American citizenship;[5] a decade later, Vicki Schultz argued that ensuring "everyone full and equal participation in decently-paid, life-sustaining, participatory forms of work" must serve as the "platform on which equal citizenship [is] built."[6] Here and elsewhere, the right to decent work is characterized as essential as a matter of social justice.

By now, the linkage between redistributive concerns—work in particular—and citizenship is commonplace. Yet the conjoining of citizenship and economy would not always have seemed either natural or coherent.

In its early understandings, citizenship was treated as remote from—even directly opposed to—specifically economic concerns. Aristotelian theory approached citizenship as a mode of distinctly *political* engagement,[7] while in early liberal thought, citizenship came to mean entitlement to legal protection from others' interference in one's private life (including one's economic life). It certainly did not entail any affirmative right to public guarantee of economic goods or benefits.[8] Marxist thought likewise counterposed citizenship to economy by maintaining that the formal equality of citizenship status masks relations of drastic inequality prevailing in "material life,"[9] including—and perhaps especially—the domain of work.

Since the mid-twentieth century, however, application of the concept of citizenship to the economic sphere has been increasingly common. The social theorist T. H. Marshall treated the right to work as an element of "civil citizenship"; and he further developed the concept of "social citizenship," which included the right to basic material well-being through government provision. Many social theorists have since embraced and elaborated this notion.[10] By now, the concept of citizenship is less often confined to the political or civil domains, and many scholars have come to deploy the idea as part of a larger project on behalf of economic justice.[11]

While many scholars have contributed to the process of forging this link between citizenship and work, feminist scholarship has played an especially central role. Feminist scholars have long argued that women need to be fully integrated into the labor market in order to achieve equal citizenship. Notable recent articulations of this view include the work of Alice Kessler-Harris, who has maintained in her book, *In Pursuit of Equity,* that "access to economic equality" through work is "a necessary condition of citizenship" for women.[12] Vicki Schultz has likewise argued in an influential article that paid labor constitutes the necessary foundation of equal citizenship for women.[13] This literature echoes the work of earlier feminist political theorists such as Carole Pateman, who wrote several years ago that "paid employment has become the key to citizenship, and the recognition of an individual as a citizen of equal worth to other citizens is lacking when a worker is unemployed."[14]

All of this scholarship stresses meaningful integration into the world of work as the route to economic citizenship. As Kessler-Harris defines the term, economic citizenship entails "the achievement of an independent and relatively autonomous status that marks self-respect and provides access to the full play of power and influence that defines participation in a democratic society." Access to economic citizenship, she continues, "begins with self-support, generally through the ability to work at the occupation of one's choice, [but] it does not end there. Rather, it requires customary and legal acknowledgment of personhood, with all that implies of expectations, training, access to and distribution of resources, and opportunity in the marketplace."[15]

This is the paradigm vision of women's work and citizenship, and it is widely accepted. In some of its aspects, however, the integrationist vision has generated controversy among feminist theorists themselves. Among other things, some feminist scholars have posed a powerful, and inescapable, question to its proponents: How, structurally, is women's participation in this world of work made possible? When women as well as men participate fully in the paid labor market, who is it that undertakes the preconditional work of social reproduction in the domestic arena ? How does the work of dependency or care—of childrearing, food preparation, housecleaning and myriad other physical, emotional, and organizational maintenance tasks—get accomplished?

Work in the traditionally conceived public domain is enabled, according to this critique, by essential but often invisible care work at home.[16] And it is women who perform the overwhelming share of this work, whether or not they work in the paid labor force. It is for this reason that many scholars have urged that ensuring for women the chance to participate in decent, paid work outside the home is an inadequate foundation for equal citizenship. Some sort of public recognition of, and provision for, care work is also necessary. Indeed, one commentator has written, "care work must become a recognized component of citizenship, for both women and men."[17]

This idea has been expressed in various ways. Scholars such as Martha Fineman have suggested that public responsibility for dependency through social subsidy "marks a right of citizenship no less important and worthy of government protection than civil and political rights."[18] Here, the government support for care is regarded as an entitlement, like food, shelter, or medical attention, on the grounds that it is necessary for full human functioning and dignity.[19] Others have suggested that care should be treated as a public value for more instrumental reasons. The "republican idea . . . of citizenship . . . could support care as a moral and public value," Linda McClain has written, "and as a precondition to civic and democratic life." [20] In this latter argument, the family is conceived as a "school for citizenship," as well as the site of bodily reproduction. [21] Others still have contended that care work must be socially remunerated in some fashion; the idea here is that failure to formally recognize the value of domestic work is itself a denial of citizenship.[22]

Diverse though it is, all of this literature contributes to a critique of the tendency in some feminist scholarship to downplay the domestically based preconditions for the pursuit of citizenship by way of "public sphere" employment. Whether urging us to conceive of the activities of the domestic arena as an essential backdrop to public sphere citizenship or as itself constituting an arena of citizenship (in which case the practices of citizenship are conceived of as taking place within the domain of the family or household), this scholarship insists on highlighting the linkages between women's citizenship and the demands of social reproduction.

Few feminists would disagree with the contention that the domestic sphere needs to become more visible in social and political theory and more valued in practice. Certainly, theoretical and political differences abound here, principal among them those concerning the normative and economic value feminists should accord to the practices and identities associated with "domesticity," in Joan Williams's term.[23] But all of the critics insist on maintaining a focus on the demands of social reproduction in any discussion of citizenship and work.

These debates about women, work, and citizenship have, of course, unfolded in a specific historical context. This is a moment when, as a matter of fact, increasing numbers of women, including mothers, do now engage in remunerated work outside their own homes (at least relative to a generation ago). To give just one relevant statistic, according to recent Bureau of Labor Statistics data, 72% of mothers with minor children in the United States work for pay outside their homes. Partly because domestic work *en famille* is not financially compensated, and partly as a consequence of a broad range of economic and social developments over the past half century that have brought women in large numbers into the paid labor market,[24] ever-growing numbers of families are two-job families, and increasing numbers of households are headed by single mothers who work in the labor market.

This development has not meant that women now in the paid labor market are no longer extensively engaged in the practice of socially reproductive labor at home. Women continue to do a disproportionate share of the domestic work in their own homes, even when they work for wages.[25] The concept of the "second shift" is a broadly familiar shorthand for this phenomenon. And it is a phenomenon that affects women's lives not merely at home but also, in blowback fashion, on the job. Many scholars have shown that women's greater domestic commitments have had discernible impacts on their career status in the labor market.[26]

One clear concomitant of all of these trends, however, is that a good deal of the care work that was previously performed by wives and mothers is now performed by non-family members pursuant to commercial exchange or contract. The commercialization of domestic work, in turn, has involved drawing upon, and further developing, a labor market whose great majority of providers are other women. Correspondingly, increasing numbers of women who work outside their own homes perform aspects of the commercialized care work on a for-pay basis. In this way, women's work in the paid labor market now relies significantly on the commodification of domestic care work, and care work has itself become a significant commodified sector of the labor market for women.

A good deal of this newly delegated care work, we know, is performed outside the home in the broader service economy. The surge of employment in restaurants, take-out food operations, laundries and dry-cleaning services, day care facilities, nursing homes, cleaning services, elder home-care services, and tutoring operations, to mention just a few sectors, reflects the transfer of a great deal of care work once performed by women at home to the market. But in addition, and of particular interest to me here, an important share of the care work traditionally performed by wives and mothers is being performed in the home by other women, pursuant to contract, in the form of what the U.S. Census Bureau calls "private household service."[27]

Delegation of care work by some women to others within the household is certainly not a new development. As a rich and extensive body of historical literature on the subject makes clear, there is a long history of both coerced and market-based female domestic labor in the United States and other developed countries. Yet while paid domestic labor was "once the most common female occupation in the United States," in the post-World War II period it declined enormously in economic significance. As noted by Ruth Milkman, Ellen Reese, and Benita Roth, "by the early 1970s, some sociologists were writing obituaries for [the occupation]."[28] Nevertheless, the institution of paid domestic work has been making a substantial comeback in this country and others. Many employed women, especially those of the professional and managerial classes, now "purchase on the market much of the labor of social reproduction traditionally relegated to them as wives and mothers."[29]

In response to these developments, studies of contemporary domestic work relationships have proliferated across the disciplines. There is by now an extensive literature in feminist thought about domestic wage labor. Much of the literature makes clear that this broadening of the delegation of care work to third-party women does not bring society closer to eliminating work and family conflict. Indeed, the reliance upon low-wage workers to perform domestic tasks actually reinforces gendered divisions of labor: it makes it possible to free one class of women from the performance of some of this work while at the same time ensuring that the work remains *women's* work.[30]

This literature makes clear, moreover, that the debate over citizenship and work is deeply imbricated in relations of class. The scholarship highlights the stratifications that are produced or reinforced among groups of women when domestic tasks "are shifted from unpaid female family members to the shoulders of low wage female . . . workers"[31] (whose own families are then themselves disadvantaged, Mary Romero argues, by virtue of enjoying "lower amounts of unpaid reproductive labor").[32] The literature emphasizes, moreover, that this household work is often performed under substandard conditions and is poorly remunerated, making it hardly a model of the kind of "decent work" that citizenship theorists have aspired to.[33]

Beyond class segmentation, futhermore, the story of care and work and citizenship is, of course, a story about race. In the United States, the vast share of domestic labor has historically been performed by women of color. Racial stratification has been a critical part of the history of domestic work, as Evelyn Nakano Glenn, Dorothy Roberts, and others have shown, with white women commonly "delegat[ing] the more onerous tasks onto women of color."[34] The trend persists today: the great majority of women doing paid domestic care work in this country are Hispanic, Asian, and black.[35]

But in addition to the class and race features of domestic labor's commodification, there is another dimension that is of particular interest to me here. A rising number of the women who perform this commodified household labor are (and have for some time been) immigrants.[36] By this I mean they are persons who have crossed national borders, often specifically for the purpose of work, and who now reside and labor outside their countries of origin. Many of these immigrants are themselves people of color. But the fact of their immigrant identities points to another dynamic in the organization of paid domestic labor: what has developed is a political economy of care that is transnational in scope. The changing place of women in the domestic economy draws upon a globalized market in domestic labor,[37] one that is subject to distinct barriers but is nonetheless thriving and expanding.[38]

It is this last dimension of the political economy of care work that brings us directly to a range of questions about the nature of the relationship between women's work and citizenship. As we have seen, many feminists have argued that achievement of citizenship for women requires access to decent-quality, socially valued work. In such claims, the idea of citizenship functions as a powerful normative ideal. There are differences among feminists about what citizenship consists in substantively (with some emphasizing rights, others democratic participation), and differences as well regarding their conceptions of citizenship's domain of action (whether public sphere, workplace, domestic arena, or elsewhere). But however precisely it is conceived, citizenship is represented as the very highest political and social aspiration. And at the core of this aspiration lies a commitment to an anti-exclusionary ethic. Those who invoke the idea are responding to long (though differential) histories of exclusion of women from rights and recognition. They are seeking to make real the prevailing "ideal of universal citizenship," in Iris Young's phrase,[39] by reconceiving the character of that citizenship, and by ensuring that the apparent gender neutrality of the citizenship idea is no longer used to mask structures of gender subordination.

Of course, the very scope of the "universal" has been a principal issue of debate among feminists theorists, including feminist theorists of work. Because the idea of the universal has been deployed to exclude as well as include,[40] it seems prudent to ask: universal citizenship for precisely whom? Most theorists understand themselves as working on behalf of a citizenship for "everyone,"[41] including, and especially, "all women."[42] At the broadest normative level, universalism represents a shared and deeply felt commitment among the advocates of women's citizenship.

Yet the fact that domestic work—which, one way or another, lies at the heart of the women and citizenship story—possesses an increasingly transnational character complicates the use of the idea of citizenship to express such aspirations. Acknowledgment of the global dimension of this work brings to the table another citizenship discourse, one that is not about universalism at all but about boundaries and exclusivity. Citizenship, in this understanding, is premised on the existence of national borders, and often presupposes an affirmative commitment to them. Most citizenship aspirants in feminist theory, as elsewhere, pay little attention to this "other" citizenship discourse. But given the realities of globalized labor, it cannot be avoided. And once it is addressed, the perennial question, citizenship for whom? is rendered substantially more complicated.

CITIZENSHIP, NONCITIZENSHIP, AND THE TRANSNATIONALIZATION OF DOMESTIC LABOR

The transnationalization of labor, including domestic labor, is commonly invoked as a key measure of increasing economic globalization. But the prevalence of transnational labor migration by no means signals the demise of the contemporary nation-state system. Rather, the trend has unfolded squarely in the context of a system of bordered nation-states. It is true that in recent years, investments and production and goods have enjoyed increasing (though still partial) freedom from the constraints of borders, but national borders remain relatively rigid when it comes to the movement of persons, including workers. Many people migrate cross-nationally, but most states place restrictions on the numbers of admittees and impose conditions on their stay.

These restrictions are grounded in, and are a function of, a set of institutions we conventionally call "citizenship." This is not the citizenship embraced by feminist theorists, which is concerned with achieving egalitarian and democratic relations among the recognized members of a political community. *This* citizenship is concerned with the community's threshold—with the boundaries of that community in the first instance. This citizenship is a status which assigns persons to membership in specific political communities—ordinarily, nation-states. Different states have different policies regarding admission to citizenship. But while citizenship is always assigned automatically to some people based on birth in the territory or parentage (or both), citizenship is almost never automatically granted to those who affirmatively seek it.[43] It is, instead, subject to some rationing by the state. Rationing of this kind is accepted as a matter of international law; states are deemed fully sovereign with respect to decisions about whom to admit to membership.

Possession of citizenship status in a particular state, in turn, has consequences. Among other things, those who are status citizens may travel unconditionally into the country of citizenship, whereas noncitizens' opportunity for ingress is limited and conditional. (Indeed, it is precisely because of their lack of national citizenship status that many prospective immigrants—including many who would seek work in the domestic care sector—are prevented from entering the country of employment, or are required to wait for years to enter, or feel compelled to enter surreptitiously.)

At the international level, then, citizenship conventionally stands not for normative universalism but for an (at least relative) ethic of closure. But we have seen repeatedly that status citizenship does not entail closure *only* at the national border. States of immigration rarely treat an individual's physical entry into state territory as a sufficient condition for full national membership within. Instead, foreigners who do enter another state ordinarily reside there for at least some period of time in a condition short of full citizenship status. In legal terms, such people reside and work in the state of immigration as aliens, or *noncitizens* by legal definition.

Among the immigrant women who labor in the domestic labor arena in the United States and elsewhere, analysts estimate that there are considerable numbers who lack formal citizenship status.[44] Some of these noncitizen women are here as lawful permanent residents and, as such, are theoretically en route to citizenship (though citizenship is not guaranteed by the state, nor will it necessarily be chosen by the immigrants themselves). Yet as noncitizens, or aliens, they are denied certain basic political and social rights, including the right to vote and certain rights of social provision. And they are always potentially subject to the immigration enforcement authority of the state.

A great many other domestic workers are not merely noncitizens but are present on a formally unauthorized basis, as undocumented immigrants or "illegal aliens." (In the United States, this category of immigrant domestic worker was recently brought to public awareness in the wake of the Zoe Baird nomination episode and ensuing "Nannygate" controversies,[45] though the media focused far more on the plight of the employers than on the employees themselves.[46]) Under the terms of current national immigration laws, most such women face the prospect of permanent alienage, with no realistic path to status citizenship. They are denied many basic rights beyond those denied to lawful permanent residents; in the United States, for example, they are ineligible for virtually all forms of government-sponsored benefits, educational loans, and, in many states, driver's licenses. They are additionally at ongoing risk of apprehension and deportation by virtue of their unauthorized status, and so are often reluctant to enforce those rights that they do have for fear of coming to the attention of the immigration authorities.[47]

A final group of domestic workers enter this country legally on temporary work visas; of these, many are sponsored and hired by diplomats and international organization officials. These noncitizen workers suffer distinct vulnerabilities because (in most cases) their right to stay in this country is contingent upon their remaining with the sponsoring employer.[48]

Attention to the increasingly transnationalized character of the domestic labor market thus necessarily introduces the subject of status citizenship into the conversation about women and work. In fact, a growing number of scholars of domestic labor have recently highlighted the issue, with their work vividly describing how a lack of formal citizenship status serves, for these women, as an additional "axis of inequality" and exploitation on the job.[49] These women are vulnerable to deportation; they are often afraid to invoke the rights they have for fear of being reported to the immigration authorities, and they lack state-sponsored income alternatives to the job.

THE INTROVERSION OF CITIZENSHIP DISCOURSE

While the dynamics of bounded citizenship are thus essential to the political economy of domestic work, most theorists of citizenship, including the feminist work scholars, pay little attention to citizenship in its bounded, area, form. Despite all the differences that divide scholars in this area citizenship as formal national status is usually ignored and invisible (with the exception of the literature on migrant domestic workers, to which I have referred and to which I will return below).

When I say that the national status aspect of citizenship is usually invisible in this literature, I do not mean merely that these scholars pay little or no attention to the presence and condition of noncitizen immigrants and their role in the accomplishment of domestic labor in many countries, although this is true. I mean, more broadly, that their political and social vision tends to be unreflectively insular and nationalist. The feminist work scholars are concerned with the state of relations that prevails among presupposed members of the national society. These scholars rarely acknowledge that this society is a society that is situated in a wider world and that it is a bounded territorial community that limits access to membership. In most of this work, the national society is simply treated as the total universe of analytical focus and normative concern.

The invisibility of the world beyond the nation is sometimes palpable (paradoxically) in the text. Vicki Schultz, for instance, has written:

> I believe that it is imperative to create a world in which all women and men can pursue their chosen callings and all working people can live with justice, equality and dignity. . . . [I support] a utopian vision in which women and men from all walks of life can stand alongside each other as equals, pursuing our chosen projects and forging connected lives. In the process we come to view each other as equal citizens and human beings, each entitled to equal respect and a claim on society's resources because of our shared commitments and contributions. . . . We must remake our laws and culture to create a world in which everyone has the right to participate in the public world of work. . . . Paid work has the potential to become the universal platform for equal citizenship. (pp. 4, 6)

Schultz here treats "world" and "society" as fully substitutable concepts. The society with which she is concerned is a national society, though this is presumed rather than stated. The "everyone" she invokes is a national "everyone," and the universality she champions is clearly a nationally framed universality. In this vision, we, apparently, *are* the world, and as a consequence, the world beyond the national society is simply effaced.[50]

This is not to say that Schultz would not endorse a vision of equality, justice, and dignity through work for people beyond the nation. But the matter is never directly addressed. If it were to be addressed, it would raise some sticky policy and normative questions about how universal achievement of decent work in this country can be achieved under conditions of economic globalization. There is, in particular, the subject of international labor competition—the so-called race to the bottom. Is a nationally framed work-based economic citizenship even achievable in the absence of various protectionist measures such as trade tariffs, investment restrictions, and plant-closing laws? Supporting such measures has been endorsed by many labor unions and other workers' rights organizations that are specifically dedicated to achieving decent work for Americans. Obviously, though, the imposition of protectionist measures would implicate the well-being and interests of people beyond our nation. To what extent, if any, are these interests of relevance to us and our own citizenship?

Schultz gestures briefly toward the subject of economic globalization when she notes that "as corporations seek more flexible forms of production and labor around the globe, more and more people face greater insecurity and reduced opportunities to shape their lives around a coherent narrative involving steady, life-sustaining work." But there is no follow-up. The nation-centered analytic that Schultz and others employ erases all that is outside the national frame and therefore avoids all issues, practical and normative, that arise about cross-national distribution, trade, and production—questions that are necessarily implicated in any claims about achieving justice through paid work within the national community.

Deployment of this analytic also allows Schultz, and others, to avoid addressing the fact that the national community *within which* universal citizenship is championed is a community that is constituted by boundaries that keep nonmembers out. Such disregard means that all the challenging questions that some theorists (usually, the immigration scholars) ask about migration and work and justice remain unaddressed. Under what circumstances is it legitimate for a wealthy national society to restrict access to territory and membership? To what extent is the achievement of economic justice—or economic citizenship—within the national society contingent upon such restriction? What obligations do we owe to people whose opportunities for decent work in their own societies have been thwarted, in part, by a system of international political economy that has served to benefit our own nationals? Do such obligations, if any, include the obligation to provide access to our own national labor market? My point is that when scholars approach the national community as the world entire, its boundaries are going to be difficult to see, and critical questions will remain unaddressed.

Crucially, it is not merely the boundaries at the community's territorial edges that will be rendered invisible. As we have seen, the status of alienage—noncitizenship in the status sense—represents the legal operation of national boundaries *within* the national territory. Those internal boundaries do not register in most of the women-and-citizenship literature either. Even granting that the "everyone" with whom these analysts is concerned is a nationally framed "everyone," one still needs to know precisely how far this formulation extends. Is the goal of economic citizenship (or equal citizenship, or democratic citizenship) meant to extend to all *citizens*? To all "Americans"? To all residents? To all territorially present workers? For a group of scholars whose project is guided by a stated commitment to universalism, disregard of the internal boundaries of citizenship may be a more serious failing than inattention to the territorial threshold.

DIVIDED CITIZENSHIPS

Once we acknowledge that both universalist and bounded conceptions of citizenship are in play in the domestic labor arena, we need to think about their relationship. Viewed broadly, we are faced with an apparent paradox: women's pursuit of citizenship—equal citizenship or economic citizenship or democratic citizenship—by way of work in the developed world is facilitated, in part, by the employment of women from mostly third-world countries who themselves are in a condition of citizenshiplessness as a matter of status. The citizenship of one group of women seems to be constructed in reliance on the labor of citizenshipless others. How are we to understand this picture? How ought we to think about the configuration of citizenships in this situation?

It is rhetorically tempting to suggest that first-world women acquire whatever citizenship that labor in the market or public sphere affords them *at the expense of* the citizenship of their domestic workers. On this account, what is at stake is some sort of system of citizenship exploitation, whereby the achievement and enjoyment of citizenship by first-world women is reaped via the expropriation of the citizenship of immigrant others.[51] Some commentators have suggested as much: the case of migrant domestic workers illustrates, one author has written, "how the rights of citizenship in one state can be gained precisely because these are denied" to noncitizen immigrant women.[52]

Despite its rhetorical attractions, however, this formulation does not quite capture what is going on. It can't be the citizenship itself that is the object of transfer or expropriation. I am very sympathetic with critiques of the transnational organization of reproductive labor developed by various feminist commentators who forcefully argue that these arrangements reflect systemic inequality and privilege as between classes of women internationally.[53] There arguably *is* an expropriation—of labor, care, and maybe even of love (as Arlie Hochschild suggests)[54]—from south to north in the context of a market exchange, and it is an expropriation that often redounds to the greater benefit of the employer than the employee. It is an exchange that is contingent on economic inequality—international and domestic—and histories of gender and racial subordination, as well as on the operation of national immigration controls.

But it would be misleading to describe the situation as a transfer of *citizenship* from one group to another, to say that first-world women's citizenship comes at the expense of the citizenship of their household workers. It would be misleading because it would entail a conflation of the citizenships at stake; it would entail treating them as if they were a single, fungible kind of good and characterizing the problem as if it were entirely a matter of unequal distribution and control of that good. The trouble with doing so, however, is that there is no single quantity called citizenship that is at stake in this situation. The kind of aspirational equal citizenship or economic citizenship that women may hope to achieve through participation in the paid labor market is just not the same social good as the status citizenship that many immigrant domestic workers are lacking. The idea of citizenship in each case is constituted by very distinct discourses, associated with often nonconvergent sets of institutions and practices and normative commitments. Their distinctiveness makes them nontransferrable in this way.

The distinctions between these citizenships becomes clearer when we look at the configuration of *noncitizenships* at play in the domestic work situation itself. I'll start with the employers. Most of the women in the more developed countries who hire domestic workers to support their return to decent jobs in the paid labor force already have status citizenship: the problem is that they experience (or some experience) marginalization and subordination in various respects notwithstanding that status. There is a term we use to describe this condition: we call it "second-class citizenship." The term second-class citizen, as we saw in chapter 4, generally refers to people who are status citizens but who nevertheless lack citizenship in a more meaningful substantive sense. It is this kind of noncitizenship—the noncitizenship of nominal citizens—that Alice Kessler-Harris, Carol Pateman, Vicki Schultz, and other work feminists are concerned with redressing.

The noncitizenship that transnational domestic workers suffer, by contrast, is compound in nature. On the one hand, many lack formal status citizenship in the United States, which is itself disadvantaging. Additionally, however, many domestic workers also suffer from some of the same kinds of economic noncitizenship (or second-class citizenship) that their employers do on account of gender, as well as on the additional grounds of class and nationality and, sometimes, race. In fact, from virtually any perspective, these women suffer far *more* economic citizenshiplessness (as a rule) than their employers do. To the extent that we want to characterize the struggle for economic well-being and economic dignity as a struggle for citizenship, it is clear that these domestic workers are seeking, through their housecleaning and childcare and other care work in private households, to likewise achieve a degree of economic citizenship for themselves and their families.

Of course, to say that noncitizen domestic workers are seeking economic citizenship presents us with a version of our now-familiar conceptual puzzle: can we sensibly speak of the pursuit of economic citizenship, or equal citizenship, by *aliens*? One might want to argue that, to the extent these immigrants wish to enjoy citizenship in the substantive sense (economic citizenship, equal citizenship, democratic citizenship, and so forth), they presumably need to *be* national citizens first. After all, citizenship is for citizens—isn't it? What is required, in this view, is first to ensure their access to status citizenship, and the rest can, presumably, follow from there.

The fact is, however, that these immigrants' lack of economic citizenship will not be redressed merely by their acquisition of status citizenship. Obviously, if these women *were* somehow able to acquire status citizenship, it would improve their situations: as I have said, the possibility of deportation and the lack of access to certain social benefits, as well as denial of the vote (all conditions associated with alienage), directly and indirectly serve to disadvantage noncitizens in the workplace and elsewhere. But possession of citizenship status alone does not guarantee achievement of economic citizenship (or equal citizenship or democratic citizenship), as the condition of the people we call second-class citizens makes very clear.

Furthermore, and conversely, possession of citizenship status is not always a prerequisite for the enjoyment of substantive citizenship. In the United States, as in most other liberal democratic states, a great many of the rights commonly associated with equal citizenship and economic citizenship are not confined to status citizens at all but are available to territorially present persons. As discussed in chapters 3 and 4, all aliens in the United States, including the undocumented, formally enjoy most fundamental rights, including due process rights in criminal proceedings, expressive and associational rights, basic economic liberties such as contract and property rights, and even the right to attend public school. Citizenship, it turns out, is *not* actually "the right to have rights," despite the conventional wisdom.[55] In many situations, only personhood is required.

It is also true that someone need not be a status citizen in order to engage in various political activities and practices we conventionally associate with democratic citizenship.[56] Noncitizen immigrants are often deeply involved in civil society organizations: many are active in unions, neighborhood associations, and schools. Increasingly, they are organizing on their own behalf on issues like access to driver's licenses, in-state tuition for undocumented immigrants, and amnesty.[57]

Indeed, we might go so far as to say that in liberal democratic states like the United States, the animating ideals of equal citizenship and democratic citizenship and economic citizenship stand for a commitment to the rights and participation not of *citizens* but of *persons*. Kessler-Harris's definition of economic citizenship captures this understanding: economic citizenship "requires customary and legal acknowledgment of *personhood*, with all that that implies." Others have likewise maintained that the equal citizenship principle stands for ensuring the rights of persons: recall chapter 4's discussion of the constitutional principle of equal citizenship, as interpreted by Kenneth Karst and others.[58] On reflection, this is not surprising at all, given that the ethical foundation of this understanding of citizenship is universalism (though, once again, it is an introverted universalism—a universalism framed within the boundaries of the national society).

The point is that status citizenship is neither a necessary nor a sufficient condition for the enjoyment of rights citizenship and the practice of republican citizenship. Instead, we find that citizens lack citizenship in some respects, while noncitizens often enjoy it in others. To speak of the noncitizenship of citizens and the citizenship of noncitizens (or the citizenship of aliens) may sound provocative and paradoxical on its face. But the fact that these formulations can be intelligible in descriptive terms underlines the basic non-coincidence of the citizenships at stake here and, it seems to me, makes unconvincing the idea of citizenship expropriation.

Complementary and Competing Citizenships

Yet even if it is true that the status citizenship and equal/economic citizenship at stake in these debates are analytically severable, we are still left with the question of how to think about the nature of the relationship that does exist between them. It can hardly be an accident, some will argue, that a single word is conventionally used to describe both bounded and universal belonging. Even allowing for citizenship's internal dividedness, shouldn't we view the concept of citizenship as representing a single overarching idea denoting (some version of) community membership? According to this argument, citizenship may have various dimensions and aspects, but they *all add up* to a single, broader phenomenon.

The most compelling version of this account relies on a separate spheres argument of the kind discussed in chapter 3. On this approach, we would say that universal and bounded citizenship have different domains of action. Universal citizenship is the prevailing ethic (however imperfectly achieved) within the political community, while bounded citizenship operates at the community's threshold. In Walzerian fashion, citizenship's boundaries are enabling boundaries: exclusivity at the edges, and the constitution of community that this exclusivity makes possible, allows universality to flourish within.[59] This is hard-on-the-outside, soft-on-the-inside model of citizenship, which, as we have seen, is the prevailing and commonsense normative account (assuming citizenship's competing meanings register at all).

Clearly, viewing citizenship as having a hard outer shell and a soft interior raises some important practical and normative questions: questions about whether boundaries really are necessary for the pursuit of liberal democracy, and questions about their legitimacy. But those questions aside, there is a problem with the account's descriptive premise. By positing that threshold and interior are, in fact, jurisdictionally separate and separable, the hard-outside, soft-inside model misrepresents the actual structure of contemporary citizenship relations in the United States and other liberal democratic states. Bounded citizenship norms and practices are *not* entirely confined to the territorial threshold but operate also inside the community's territorial perimeters, through the state's laws on immigration and alienage. [60] They work to keep national outsiders from entering a political community, but they also regulate the status of foreigners once they are present, until such time as they are accorded status citizenship. Given that millions of people cross national boundaries and enter other states every year (both lawfully and unlawfully), and given that these states rarely grant automatic and immediate citizenship status to those entrants (and indeed, given that those present unlawfully are usually ineligible for status citizenship altogether), there is a large population of people within the receiving state's territory who are, at least for some period of time, governed by the introjected norms and practices of bounded citizenship.

Universal and bounded citizenship norms, in short, are not always jurisdictionally separate but often occupy the same terrain.[61] And it is in relation to the class of people we call aliens that both sets of norms are relevant and both are at stake. The law has developed a set of elaborate rules for accommodating both regimes, as we saw in chapter 3. But sometimes there is conflict, in principle and in practice, about which set of norms will govern in a given case.[62] Should aliens be treated as national outsiders and governed by the norms of the bounded citizenship regime, or should they be treated as subjects of liberal equality and as part of the nationally framed, universal "we"? Which regime trumps which under various circumstances, and how are we to decide? Disputes about the condition of status noncitizens are chronically shaped by these questions.

The Language of "Citizenship"

Given the various citizenship-related confusions at play in the domestic work arena, what are we to conclude? One possibility is to take the position that the kinds of conceptual divisions and normative conflicts that characterize our understandings of citizenship here (as elsewhere) reflect, more than anything else, an unfortunate linguistic turn of events. In this view, the idea of citizenship has become a terribly overworked concept in social and political and legal thought over the past few years, one that it is now invoked to represent so many diverse practices and institutions and experiences that it has ceased to be analytically meaningful. It is the overly casual and even promiscuous use of the term, together with a habit of unconsciousness about its multiple meanings and their implications, that is responsible for all of the confusion.

Add to this the concern that the profusion of aspirational citizenship talk in political and legal theory, including feminist theory, is not only confusing but potentially dangerous rhetorically in that it may work to undermine the claims and interests of status noncitizens. Given the tendency to conflate and entangle the various meanings of citizenship, articulation of a commitment to social justice in the language of citizenship almost inevitably communicates an exclusionary message toward status noncitizens, whether or not this is intended.

Perhaps, in this view, we should abandon the concept of citizenship altogether. We might substitute various other terms: instead of talking about citizenship in the status sense, we could talk about nationality or formal state membership.[63] And in place of talking about citizenship in the aspirational sense, we could talk about equality, democracy, and belonging. Doing this would permit us to avoid some of the apparently contradictory (and certainly awkward) analytical formulations—"the citizenship of noncitizens," "the noncitizenship of citizens"—we are otherwise stuck with. Giving up the language of citizenship would also avoid the rhetorical concerns I have raised about the inward-looking citizenship discourse: instead of using an aspirational political term that seems to presuppose a particular, predefined set of national subjects, it would leave the question of subjects more open for discussion and debate.

Sympathetic as I am with this critique,[64] I am also aware that playing the role of word police is usually a vain undertaking; language cannot be so easily disciplined.[65] And citizenship will not be given up easily, in any event: people are clearly attached to the idea. This is a concept that has a long and distinguished history, and it is infused with enormous political and moral resonance.

It is also true that our ideas about citizenship have not been static; as with other key political concepts, understandings change, though gradually. Indeed, citizenship's long association with egalitarian and democratic ideals in some of its understandings has made it a powerful term of progressive political rhetoric. It has been this feature of citizenship that has led to many ongoing efforts to reshape and extend the term to new subjects and new domains. There are always those who want to hold the line in one way or another, and who will continue to insist on citizenship's inherently limited meaning and bounded character. But these protests simply illustrate that the question of how citizenship is defined and who gets to claim it is always contested.[66]

It may be that what is most important about citizenship is precisely the fact that it is so divided. The divisions I have outlined reflect concrete political and social dilemmas. These are the dilemmas experienced by a political society that is formally committed to liberal egalitarian norms but in which the abiding premise of insularity does not actually obtain. They are the dilemmas of a society that is committed to a degree of territorial closure but whose borders are actually relatively porous, so that many foreigners cross them from the outside and come to join those who were there before them. In such a society, our understandings of citizenship and its boundaries will inevitably be divided. To the extent we continue to use the language of citizenship to express our deepest political and moral aspirations, it is essential that we bring those divisions to consciousness.

CHAPTER 6

Separate Spheres Citizenship and Its Conundrums

How should we think about the status of noncitizens in liberal democratic societies? For many political and legal theorists, as I have shown, the conceptual and normative dilemmas associated with status noncitizenship are more or less invisible. Yet increasing numbers of scholars and advocates have begun to focus directly on matters of citizenship status and the implications of its absence. Especially in the past decade, the category of alienage has garnered substantial attention within the burgeoning cross-disciplinary field of immigration studies.

Much of this literature is historical or empirical in character. But there is also a growing stream of scholarship in legal and political theory that addresses the normative question of how noncitizens ought to be treated in immigrant-receiving societies. Not surprisingly, scholars' responses to this question vary widely. But their inquiries and conclusions tend to have a common structure, one that reflects their thinking about the relationship between the regulatory domains of the political community's border and its interior. The organizing questions in this literature are jurisdictional ones: To what extent may the political community's authority to regulate admissions at the threshold legitimately extend to shape and constrain the lives of noncitizens already present and residing within that community? Alternatively, to what extent must a person who is residing in the territory be insulated from the regulatory reach of the border and be subject exclusively to the (generally more protective) norms governing territorially present persons?

In response to these questions, parties to the scholarly debate tend to line up in one of two broad camps. On one side are those who believe that the political community's vital interests in border regulation continue to play a legitimate and even essential role in defining the condition of immigrants who are now physically present within the territory. Rather than a binary, in-out decision, membership for new immigrants is understood as a continuum, or as a series of concentric circles, with citizenship the ultimate prize at the core.[1] Along the way, the individual's treatment is properly structured by the receiving society's border-driven, membership-related interests, until such time as the individual graduates to full membership in the innermost circle.[2]

On the other side are those who believe that it is generally illegitimate to structure immigrants' status within the national territory according to the community's border-regulative interests or imperatives.[3] Once the alien is present and participating in the national society, she ought to be subject, for the most part, to the rules and norms governing community residents, regardless of immigration status. Whether the motivating concern for this norm is protecting the rights of the immigrants themselves or ensuring against the development or perpetuation of caste relationships within a society ostensibly committed to norms of equal and democratic citizenship, the view, in essence, is that border norms ought to be confined to the border.

The distinction between these camps is, in effect, the distinction between the sphere separation and sphere convergence models, to use the Walzerian terms as I described them in chapter 3. In the case of the separation approach, the sphere of membership regulation must remain more or less confined to the border. In the case of convergence, the norms of the border properly penetrate the distributive spheres internal to the national society.

I do not wish to overstate the dimorphism between positions here. Good scholarship is qualified and complex, and the positions I have described are, in practice, only relative. Convergence partisans usually allow that resident noncitizens are entitled to some degree of insulation from the imperatives of the border, while separation proponents are rarely as strict about their separation commitments as one might predict from their rhetoric; some convergence is usually tolerated.[4] For this reason, it is perhaps more accurate to say that scholars addressing the status of noncitizens in liberal democratic societies tend to fall somewhere on a spectrum between the poles of separation and convergence, with the majority clustering toward either end.

Yet for my purposes in this concluding chapter, it is important to recognize how limited and partial the disagreement between these two poles of the alienage debate actually is. The two sides, in fact, share a great deal; most significantly, both maintain the crucial conviction that membership regulation *is* appropriate "within its own sphere." Both sides accept that a liberal democratic national society is properly a bounded society; the disagreement centers instead on those boundaries' proper jurisdiction. For the convergence advocates, boundaries act legitimately on the inside as well as at the border, whereas for the separationists, those boundaries must be confined (more or less) to the territorial frontier.

The argument among the normative alienage theorists, therefore, usually does not concern the question whether the national society is legitimately "hard on the outside," because just about everyone thinks it must be, at least to some degree.[5] The question is, rather, whether the hardness of the outer shell has any legitimate role to play on the inside in relation to territorially present immigrants, or whether that shell must necessarily be confined to the territorial perimeter, thereby insulating from incursion an otherwise "soft" interior.[6]

This book's earlier chapters were largely concerned with the fact and the consequences of sphere incursion. In various ways I contended that the enforcement of exclusionary citizenship norms against territorially present aliens both directly and indirectly undermines the inclusionary and egalitarian citizenship values to which liberal democratic national societies are at least formally committed. I argued, in other words, on behalf of sphere separation.

In this last chapter I shift emphasis and problematize the separationists' hard-on-the-outside, soft-on-the-inside conception of citizenship itself. I show, first, how widespread and unquestioned the model of hard-outside, soft-inside citizenship—or separate spheres citizenship—is in much legal and political theory. I then reflect on the model's deep attractiveness to many theorists, and suggest that the idea represents an understandable effort to resolve the chronic tensions between norms of universalism and particularism—between liberal equality and national exclusivity—that plague liberal theory. The desired resolution comes by way of a strategy of splitting, with the conflicting norms assigned to distinct regulatory domains. But I maintain that actual resolution remains elusive, because separation between these jurisdictional domains cannot be achieved. Under real-world conditions, border and interior are inevitably imbricated, most directly and graphically in the person of the alien. The impossibility of splitting citizenship means that citizenship's contrasting normative impulses are bound to remain directly in contention *within* liberal democratic communities. The dilemma that alienage represents cannot be willed away.

Hard Outside, Soft Inside

A normatively divided conception of citizenship is presupposed in the work of almost any theorist who is committed to ensuring and extending norms of democratic equality within a political community while simultaneously accepting, or taking as given, the community's boundedness at the threshold. Usually the normative divide is only implicit. Yet it is sometimes affirmatively articulated, for example, in the influential stream of social and political theory commonly described as "liberal nationalist" in orientation. Liberal nationalists differ widely among themselves about what the national *inside* should look like.[7] But they share a basic conception of the overall structure of our normative commitments, one in which there is a proper and necessary division between territorial inside, where some version of inclusionary, universalist commitments prevails, and the territorial threshold, which is properly and necessarily bounded.[8]

Although often unacknowledged, this hard outside, soft inside conception of citizenship represents liberal democracy's commonsense moral template of community belonging. And it is a vision that, upon reflection, has substantial normative appeal. It is attractive because it seems to promise to resolve the long-standing tension between the "conflicting conceptions of responsibility," in political theorist Samuel Scheffler's terms, that lie at the heart of contemporary liberal political thought. Tensions between universalist and particularist commitments—between "the underlying values of loyalty and moral equality"—plague liberalism, far more chronically than most of us usually acknowledge.[9] Yet the conception's mechanism for accommodating these contrasting norms is not intimate engagement so much as it is firm compartition. The idea is to split these commitments jurisdictionally so that they do not come into direct conflict but instead are relevant in, and applicable to, different domains. Normative responsibility is conceived in Janus-like terms, with universalist commitments directed inward and an exclusionary stance facing outward at the border. The result is a model of bounded solidarity in which compatriot insiders "take priority"[10] over non-national others and in which the territorial border encircling compatriots is policed against penetration by those others.[11]

Citizenship conceived as bounded solidarity, or bounded caring,[12] would thus seem to provide a neat solution to a messy problem. The unpalatable (because illiberally exclusionary) impulses endemic to liberalism are partially disavowed (though not entirely discarded) through their ejection from the inside of the liberal community to its edges.

The question whether such a resolution is normatively justifiable is, of course, a terribly important one. I am sympathetic to those ethical cosmopolitan theorists who have raised fundamental questions about its legitimacy.[13] But a more immediate problem with envisioning citizenship as bounded caring, in my view, is that it depends on a set of empirical premises that are largely implausible. In a hypothesized (Rawlsian) world in which populations are fixed and no one moves in or out, and in which boundaries are established and set for all time, the normative splitting that bounded solidarity entails is formally possible (although again, it is not necessarily just). But this is not the actual world: boundaries and populations are not fixed; people do move across borders; communities dispute, and sometimes war over, the location of boundaries. The strategy of dividing normative commitments between inside and outside, therefore, always depends on the resolution of prior questions about where and how the lines between inside and outside are drawn.[14]

We know, as a matter of fact, that states usually claim the right to make their own admissions decisions, in Walzer's terms—to decide who will be permitted to enter and who will remain outside. And they do so pursuant to the logic of bounded caring: decisions about whether or not to admit outsiders are undertaken with the interests of the current insiders in mind.[15] This may or may not mean imposing restrictions on access to entry and membership, although it usually does.[16]

But assuming some restrictions are imposed on the entry of outsiders, the binary picture of bounded solidarity I described above needs revision. Characterizing the world as divided into the domains of inside and outside is simply inadequate. We have to introduce another domain into the equation—that of the border between them. The border is a site that divides insiders and outsiders, and where decisions about who may or may not become insiders are made. It is, moreover, a sphere with its own normative logic, one that itself is structured neither entirely by inside nor outside but which lies at the interface between them.

Splitting and the Border

"The border" is a term that designates the community's threshold—a site where states maintain physical and administrative boundaries toward the outside world. It is the regulatory locus of the admission of foreigners, and, correspondingly, of their exclusion. It is, more broadly, the regulatory domain of citizenship in the status sense; it is the site where citizenship as status originates and in which it is governed.

Generally speaking, the norms governing border policy are ethically particularist; they are designed to meet the interests of already existing members. This is not to say that border policies are always exclusionary in substance; indeed, such policies are sometimes relatively welcoming. Furthermore, border policies in liberal democratic states are sometimes influenced by universalist commitments. In the U.S. context, for example, elimination of express racial preferences in the admissions system in the 1960s might be said to represent the transposition to the border of universalist norms ordinarily applicable in the interior.[17] The guarantee to non-citizens of certain due process protections in immigration proceedings likewise reflects a degree of universalization in the border process. Nevertheless, the predominant norms operating at national borders, as we have seen, are exclusivity and closure.

What is often uncertain, however, is how far, in space and in time, "the border" legitimately extends. We know that the border's jurisdiction is not strictly confined to the territorial threshold, nor is it strictly limited in its application to the national outsider's moment of entry. The very fact that immigrants are not automatically accorded citizenship status upon entry—that they subsist for (at least) some period in a status we call alienage—makes this clear; the norms of the border structure their status even within the liberal democratic society.

But in what respects and to what extent can that structuring legitimately occur? Once having entered the country, we know that aliens are also subject to the more (formally) universalistic norms governing the treatment of territorially present persons. Here is where the relationship between universalism and particularism—between the hard and soft norms I have been describing—becomes acutely contested. Since both sets of norms are applicable, how are they to be accommodated? In case of conflict, which controls?

One prevailing response to this question, as we have seen, is to regard the border norms as properly trumping norms of territorial personhood in the treatment of aliens, at least for some period of time. In this view, membership is conceived on the model of a continuum,[18] with the restrictive norms associated with the border initially decisive in regulatory effect, but increasingly less relevant and displaced by "soft" interior norms to the extent that the immigrant properly progresses toward full membership.

An alternative view, however, regards this convergence model as antithetical to liberal democratic values. The most theoretically explicit version of this critique is set out by Walzer in his analysis of the status of metics. We are familiar with the account: membership norms, which are legitimately particularist and restrictive, must be limited jurisdictionally to the political community's perimeter. Inside the community, more inclusive and universalistic norms apply. Justice requires that each sort of norm remain confined to its own domain.

Walzer, however, is hardly alone. A great many liberal intellectuals who have considered the issue of immigrant status have endorsed the same kind of strict separation approach. A notable recent example is Owen Fiss, who wrote the lead essay in a symposium issue of the *Boston Review* on the constitutional status of noncitizens in the United States in which he lambasted the imposition upon them of social and economic "disabilities." In the article, Fiss takes as given the current restrictions on immigrant admissions.[19] "My point," he writes, "is not to subvert the admission process or otherwise open the borders." Instead, his focus is the treatment of those immigrants who already reside within the political community. Fiss wants to "insist that laws regarding admission cannot be enforced or implemented in ways that would transform immigrants into pariahs."[20]

By invoking the idea of pariah, Fiss is expressing what he maintains is the American constitutional commitment to antisubordination or anticaste values. While restrictions are properly enforced at the border, we must maintain egalitarian values within. Fiss's rationale for his position is thus not humanitarianism nor a general concern with "the other"; his focus, rather, is on "us" and the state of our own political and constitutional culture. "We ought not to subjugate immigrants," he writes, "not because we owe them anything, but to preserve our society as a community of equals."[21]

Notably, Fiss does not defend an absolutist separation position. He distinguishes between social and political disabilities, treating only the latter as acceptably imposed on aliens—at least so long as the path to naturalization is relatively open.[22] But the basic separation commitment remains and is articulated by him quite plainly: "Admission laws can be enforced by fences at the borders, deportation proceedings, or criminal sanctions, not, I maintain, by imposing social disabilities."[23] While legitimate in themselves, in short, admissions laws must be exercised within their own sphere.

In his recent book, *Semblances of Sovereignty*, Alex Aleinikoff similarly embraces a hard outside/soft inside approach to citizenship. He is more critical than Fiss of the substantive forms that border exclusion can and do take—"membership decisions may display virulent intolerance based on race, political opinion or lifestyle," he recognizes[24]—but he accepts as given that admissions policies—"the classification of aliens and the establishment of procedures for their entry and removal"—are necessary and legitimate. What Aleinikoff objects to is a normative theory pursuant to which the enjoyment of rights and recognition of membership are made contingent on the possession of citizenship status. Such a theory, he argues, misrepresents the American constitutional tradition, which is concerned with protecting " 'persons'—a category that includes aliens and citizens as subsets."[25]

Consequently, Aleinikoff seeks to decouple our conceptions of citizenship and membership.[26] Viewing citizenship as membership may be an appropriate conception of belonging at the community's edges, but it is contrary to constitutional norms when enacted within the community's interior. Notice, however, that although Aleinikoff describes himself as wanting to "decenter citizenship," his intention is not to displace citizenship altogether but to substitute a different and more inclusive citizenship vision. He posits a conception of citizenship based on equal membership and belonging, but it is one that entails, as he puts it, "identification with and commitment to a national state and its future."[27] This is a vision that, by definition, depends on enforcement of national territorial borders.

There are many other liberal theorists who make separation arguments more or less explicitly. Both Rogers Smith and Kenneth Karst, for example, have trenchantly criticized internal subordination of noncitizens in their work. Yet both presuppose, and sometimes affirm, the action of exclusionary borders.[28]

Again, what distinguishes this group of theorists from the continuum or concentric circles proponents is their insistence on separation of the normative domains of border and interior. Pursuant to the principle of bounded solidarity, the line between inside and outside is acceptably, even necessarily, drawn, and in some circumstances outsiders may legitimately be prevented from joining the national community. But once someone is territorially in, she has to be fully *in*, and the "soft" norms of equal or democratic citizenship must govern.

INCOMPLETE SEPARATION

Or such is the theory. For as we have seen, the theory of strict separation is usually less stringent than its rhetoric would seem to require. Walzer, remember, allows for membership consequences to be visited, both directly and indirectly, upon aliens residing within the territorial community.[29] Similarly, Fiss, Aleinikoff, and Karst each accept the imposition of certain disabilities on noncitizens. The recognition of membership or equal citizenship for aliens is insisted upon only to a point: political exclusions are uniformly accepted, and the government's right to deport resident noncitizens in some circumstances is defended or taken as given. The separation of border norms from universalistic interior norms that they propound, in the end, is partial and incomplete.

What are we to make of the incompleteness of the separation project? Perhaps we should treat it simply as a matter of transition at the margins. This is not a perfect world; as Walzer himself has recognized, there will always be troubling cases at the boundaries between spheres.[30] The separation approach is not meant to be mechanistically air-tight; it is simply a general normative framework to guide democratic practice.

We might also say that any regime of full separation is impracticable, especially in the immigration context. A true and exacting regime of separate spheres would require the extension of full citizenship status to an immigrant the moment she sets foot in the country. A modified version would perhaps exempt short-term visitors but would require immediate extension of citizenship status to anyone coming to work or settle. Regardless of whether such a regime would be desirable, it seems unlikely to be accepted as a practical matter.

Yet of course, to the extent full membership upon entry is not required, advocates of universal citizenship norms find themselves sanctioning, or acceding to, conditions of less than full equality within the community. It is precisely the desire to contain this anomaly—to limit the effects of the operation of border norms in the interior—that has prompted many liberal theorists of immigration to insist that immigrants' acquisition of citizenship through naturalization—what Walzer calls "second admissions"—must be routinely swift and simple.

Certainly, a requirement for fast-track naturalization would go some distance toward ameliorating the effects of internal border enforcement; the sooner these people become status citizens, the sooner exclusionary border norms are no longer relevant to them. Still, a liberalized naturalization policy does not eliminate the difficulty entirely. So long as they remain noncitizens, immigrants are understood to be rightfully precluded from (at least some) important forms of political participation, including the franchise, and as properly subject to removal from the country in some circumstances. Arguably, a regulatory regime that permits denial of both access to political voice and security against banishment to large numbers of its residents, even temporarily, is problematic under "soft," liberal universalist principles.

More fundamentally troubling is the prospect that these exclusions will not be temporary at all. Most countries of immigration, including the United States, have large populations of undocumented immigrants living and working within who have no prospect of ever regularizing their immigration status, and therefore no prospect of applying for naturalization, at least under current requirements. Although many liberals support versions of legalization or amnesty for certain existing undocumented immigrants (the beneficiaries of which eventually would be eligible to apply for naturalization), most continue to defend national border control norms. Given this commitment, legalization must necessarily be understood as an exception to the norm, a deviation from the usual prerogative of closure. For if undocumented immigrants were legalized routinely and ongoingly—if amnesties were issued annually, or if all territorial entrants were immediately and automatically recognized as lawful permanent residents—what would be left of the rule? Even assuming the occasional legalization program, in other words, some set of undocumented immigrants face the prospect of permanent alienage.[31]

There is, in addition, the case of so-called guest workers, who enter receiving countries to work pursuant to state-sponsored short-term migrant labor programs. These programs nearly always expressly preclude any opportunity for the participating migrant to pursue a path to citizenship; indeed, this was the hallmark of the European guest worker programs that Walzer denounced in his critique of metic status. And guest worker programs are not a thing of the past: one such program recently proposed in the United States would specifically deny participants the opportunity to regularize their status by way of program participation, and would therefore foreclose acquisition of citizenship through such participation as well.[32]

It is partly in response to the prospect of indefinite alienage and the normative and practical difficulties this poses for liberal democratic societies that legal scholar Ruth Rubio-Marin has proposed that liberal states ought, under some conditions, to guarantee to immigrants "a path to automatic membership."[33] In her book *Immigration as a Democratic Challenge,* Rubio-Marin argues that so long as the case can adequately be made that certain rights of membership may legitimately be limited to national citizens,[34] justice requires "having the whole of the state's ordinary resident population . . . included within the body of nationals and thus within the sphere of civic equality." Under this model, citizenship would be assigned, unconditionally, to long-term immigrants, including most settled undocumented immigrants, after some period of residence[35] (although requirements would remain more stringent for the undocumented).

Rubio-Marin's hope is to ameliorate the "legitimacy gap" that alienage produces for a liberal democratic society by, in effect, legislating the class of aliens away. If implemented, this strategy would, in fact, produce a radical shrinkage in the size of the class of noncitizens and move us closer to the ideal in-or-out binary promoted by the separation theorists. Yet while this proposal makes an important contribution to the debate at the level of policy,[36] it does not entirely resolve the problem. By the proposal's terms, not every immigrant will be eligible for automatic membership, nor is automatic membership immediately available to any immigrant upon territorial entry. Under this model, in other words, alienage remains with us. The model continues to presuppose a hard outer shell encircling the liberal democratic community into which migrants travel and accepts as given that that "hardness" will not be confined exclusively to the territorial border but will accompany the alien into the interior, at least for some period and to some degree.

If it is impracticable to imagine a regime in which all entrants can be immediate and automatic citizens—a citizenship regime, in other words, without aliens—there remains another well-trodden route to redress the legitimacy gap: assuming we *are* going to have aliens, we can make the condition of alienage, or status noncitizenship, essentially inconsequential.[37] Instead of seeking citizenship status *for* aliens, in other words, we can insist upon recognition of equal rights for status noncitizens—or, differently stated, we can insist upon recognition of the equal citizenship *of* aliens.[38] This, in effect, is the strategy pursued by Walzer, Karst, and many of the other separationists I have discussed, and it is an approach with which I strongly identify.[39] Nonetheless, the idea of alien citizenship can be, in the end, only a partial citizenship. Given both the national political

imaginaries of liberal democratic communities and the prevailing acceptance of hard (or hardish) borders around those communities, citizenship
status is going to continue to matter to some extent.

All of which means that we are left, irreducibly, with alienage: with the
person of the alien, and with the social and political condition that alienage represents. Assuming, in other words, that we are going to maintain
a normative citizenship model of bounded solidarity in a world of cross-
national population movements, the category of alienage is inevitable.
And the inevitability of alienage, in turn, belies the possibility of full separation of normative spheres, and more generally casts in skeptical light
what we might call the "ideology of separate spheres" in liberal citizenship theory.[40] Liberal democracy's allegedly soft interior cannot be entirely insulated from its exclusionary edges; rather, through alienage, that
exclusion routinely penetrates the interior as well.

Comparing Noncitizenships

That citizenship as practiced within the bounds of liberal democratic
communities cannot be characterized as entirely universalistic will
hardly be news to most social critics. Indeed, most scholarship on citizenship published in recent years is devoted to illustrating precisely that
point. Although citizenship within the liberal nation-state ostensibly
stands for universalist values, in reality it falls far short, often catastroph-
ically so. The history of citizenship, as many have shown, is the history
of subordination and exclusion as much as it is the history of progressive
incorporation and belonging. Whether this exclusion derives from illib-
eral regressive strands endemic to many national cultures or is inherent
in liberal democracy itself,[41] modern citizenship regimes have tolerated,
and quite often concealed, some of the worst forms of social exclusion
and injustice. As a concurrent critique, many analysts have charged that
the very ideal of universal citizenship is nonemancipatory at the core. Iris
Young and others have forcefully argued that citizenship's universality
is typically conceived not merely as referring to "everyone," but more
specifically to "everyone the same."[42] Universal citizenship, as conventionally understood, demands social conformity; it is hostile to plural
modes of identity and experience, and functions, in this respect, as a
coercive and repressive norm.

Hence, while the ideal of universal citizenship remains the official governing norm within liberal democratic states, it has a great deal to answer
for. And many liberal and progressive scholars, as I have said, devote
themselves to pressing for answers. The result has been the elaboration
of a powerful and diverse body of critical literature across the disciplines

that takes as its task the exposure of the various disjunctures between political ideal and social reality that characterize citizenship in liberal democratic societies.[43]

Most of these scholars, we now know, are *not* thinking about alienage. They are thinking about exclusions and subordinations associated with race and gender and ethnicity and sexual identity and disability and poverty. That is not to say that their insights are irrelevant to the condition of alienage. Indeed, from the point of view of the immigration scholar, close attention to the experience of other marginalized and subordinated groups is essential for several reasons. First, it situates the exclusions of alienage in a broader frame. It reminds us that aliens are not the only group to have been excluded from the franchise (indeed, in many states in the United States, aliens had the right to vote at one time when many nominal citizens did not), nor to be denied access to public benefits. Neither are aliens the first and only group within liberal democratic societies to be denied the status of citizenship, or to suffer social stigma or violence on account of their status.

Attending to the experience of other subordinated groups, futhermore, helps to shed light on some of the dilemmas that immigrants rights advocates face at the level of political strategy and representation. When we protest alienage discrimination, for example, are we claiming that discrimination against noncitizens is unjust because they are distinctly vulnerable and need to be recognized as such, or because they are sufficiently like citizens that distinctions drawn on this basis are irrational and therefore illegitimate?[44] The difficult trade-offs between claims of sameness and difference in arguments over equal protection for noncitizens are familiar to social justice advocates in the areas of race and gender and elsewhere, many of whom find themselves facing analogous choices.

Finally, paying heed to other structures of subordination helps us to recall that the exclusion and subordination that aliens experience do not occur in a vacuum. Alienage interacts with other forms of subordinated status in all kinds of ways that powerfully affect social outcomes. A paradigm example of this "intersectionality" is California's Proposition 187—the 1994 ballot initiative that would, if enforced, have denied undocumented immigrants access to education, health care, and other services, and would have required service providers to report to immigration authorities those suspected of unlawful status. Proposition 187 has come to be understood not merely as a product of antiforeigner or nativist sentiment, though it surely was that, but also as a result of anxieties about the increasing presence and power of Mexicans and Central Americans in California.[45] Similarly, antiterrorist responses in the U.S. post 9–11 cannot be described merely as a recapitulation of the kind of antiforeign sentiment emerging in earlier moments of national crisis;[46] the responses have taken a specific racialized form, targeting persons perceived to be of Muslim faith or Middle Eastern descent.[47] What an intersectional analysis make clear is that there is, in fact, no essential alien. Alienage is inevitably tied up with race and gender, as well as with sexual orientation and national origin and religion and disability, in ways that can heighten disadvantage or can minimize or ameliorate it.[48] This is why it is important that scholars of status citizenship engage with the work of critical scholars concerned with various other forms of status inequality—many of whom, as we have seen, characterize their projects in the language of equal or democratic citizenship.[49]

I have, on the other hand, been mainly concerned in this book with a lack of intellectual engagement in the converse direction. I have sought to press inward-looking scholars of equal and democratic citizenship to take greater cognizance of the social structures of bounded citizenship, and of alienage in particular. Status citizenship has mostly been off the radar screen in this scholarship, including the self-identified critical scholarship. Recently the subject seems to be receiving somewhat more acknowledgment.[50] If this trend persists, it is a good thing, not least because it will produce a more complete and accurate understanding of the social world with which these theorists are concerned. Subordination of status noncitizens needs to be made visible and, to the extent it is acknowledged, needs to be regarded as something more than a mere proxy for other forms of oppression.

Rethinking National Privilege

But once we place alienage on the agenda and begin to consider its distinctive character, what exactly will we see? As I said in chapter 1, it is not enough simply to add alienage to the already lengthy list of injustices that concern us. We have to think about the difference that alienage makes in our thinking about everything else. We need to understand what it is that, to recast Bonnie Honig's question about foreignness,[51] alienage does for us—does, specifically, at the level of our theoretical work on subordination.

In my view, what alienage does for us, or should do for us, is force us into engagement with our often unacknowledged normative nationalist commitments. By "normative nationalism" I mean that prevailing set of baseline premises according to which the territorial nation-state is the rightful, if not the total, world of our normative concern. It is the conviction—again, usually unacknowledged—that "compatriots take priority," that the interests of our conationals or coresidents are rightfully privileged over those of national or territorial outsiders.[52] It is the predominant experience of collective self-preference in the contemporary world.[53]

What is most striking about normative nationalism is its taken-for-grantedness. In most popular discourse, and in much academic discourse as well, it is the air we breath; it is our common sense. Upon reflection, this apparent obviousness is not surprising. As John Dunn has asked, "if we ourselves are not for us, who else is likely to be?"[54] Of course, there are alternative traditions in modern political thought, both cosmopolitan and internationalist, pursuant to which primary ethical solidarities are defined not by national ties but by other kinds of bonds—whether of humanity in general or grounded in common experiences or convictions or structural locations.[55] But these tend to be marginal views in mainstream discourse. Overall, it is fair to say that normative nationalism represents our "common idiom of contemporary feeling."[56] It is certainly the prevailing ethic in the inward-looking citizenship literature.[57]

Yet normative nationalism can itself take various forms. We have seen that for many inward-looking citizenship theorists, the solidarities associated with normative nationalism are understood in territorial rather than status terms. Those proponents of equal and democratic citizenship that I have termed the separationists would reject the claim that compatriots take priority, if compatriot is understood to mean cocitizen in the status sense. Their normative nationalism extends, at least for many purposes to include all persons residing in (sometimes, present in) the national territory. On reformulation of the norm, it might be more accurate to say that under a separationist reading of normative nationalism, conational residents take priority.

Notice, however, that even if national coresidents, and not merely compatriots, take priority—even if coresidents as well as compatriots are understood to be ethically privileged for us over territorial outsiders—the fact of *being* a coresident or a compatriot itself represents a privilege. This is the privilege of already being national. It is the privilege of already being within, and in some respect part of, the community presumed to be the locus of solidarity and privilege, whether as a matter of formal status *or* as a matter of territorial presence.

Yet, of course, the privilege of already being national and of remaining national presupposes its own set of exclusions. This privilege most often arises at the moment of initial access to national citizenship. We live in a world in which the citizenship status of the vast majority of people is assigned automatically at birth. When the institution of birthright citizenship is considered from an inward-looking national perspective, the discussion usually centers on the relative merits of *jus soli* and *jus sangunis* citizenship assignment: should citizenship be automatically extended to those born in the national territory or to those born of already-national parents? The trend internationally is a movement toward territorial birthright citizenship, and there are good reasons for this:[58] a territorial citizenship rule protects against hereditary caste within liberal states and, the experience of many states shows, is an essential mechanism of democratic inclusion.[59]

Once we step outside the inward-looking normative framework, however, and look at allocation of citizenship from a global perspective, we see that territorial birthright citizenship rules are, as much as rules allocating citizenship by blood or descent, fundamentally exclusionary. As the legal theorist Ayelet Shachar has recently observed, *all* birthright citizenship rules[60] make citizenship "an inherited entitlement," one that "secures the ability of its holders to enjoy a share in specific rights, protections and wealth-creating assets held in common by those who count as members, while excluding all others . . . by the state's membership rules."[61] For those born outside a particular national territory, the chances of acquiring citizenship in that state at a later point via naturalization are usually very slim. In this respect, a system of territorially-based hereditary citizenship, whether administered together with, or as an alternative to, the institution of citizenship-by-descent, ensures that the normative preference we extended to conational residents is (mostly) hoarded for members by birth. In a world of vast disparities in wealth and resources, this is a practice that, Shachar compellingly argues, serves to "sustain global inequality."[62]

But again, the privilege of already being national is not always a function of privileged access to citizenship status. It may also derive from privileged access to national residence via the immigration process. Many of the separationists would count themselves among those who support liberalized national immigration policies. They endorse greater opportunities for admission to residence for conationals' family members, for refugees, and (sometimes) for providers of labor. Most also oppose enforcement of various removal provisions against lawful permanent residents, including those based on ideology, political association, and minor criminal activity.[63] Still, even if these policy positions reflect an attitude of relative openness to outsiders seeking to join or remain within the ranks of the nation's coresidents, they only go so far. The fact that there *are* borders to territory and residence is not itself challenged by the separationists, and can not easily be. For even though they understand social exclusion of national coresidents within the nation to be unjust, the fact of national territorial borders also appears essential to them, as a necessary precondition for the preservation of the community within which the ends of equal citizenship are pursued.[64]

Of course, taking territorial borders as given means taking as given that some people who would wish to gain access to residence in the national state in question (often a very great number of people at the global level) will not have the chance to do so. And by not having that chance, these people end up excluded in a double sense. They are excluded from the various economic, social, political, and personal benefits that may come with coresidence, and in addition, they are excluded from membership in the community of normative priority—in the community of people toward whom (according to the logic of normative nationalism) we understand ourselves to bear special responsibility.[65]

The privilege of already being national, then, may be a function of privileged access to citizenship status or privileged access to national residence via immigration. But there is one more layer of possible national privilege. For the separationists, the priority accorded to conationals extends not only to citizens and to lawful residents but also, to an important extent, to people who are territorially *here*, even if they are here in a status short of citizenship or lawful resident status. The fact of their national hereness, we might say, represents its own privilege.[66]

The privilege of presence can be seen most clearly in relation to undocumented immigrants: those territorially present noncitizens who lack formal government authorization for that presence. We have already seen that the separationists regard the undocumented as rightfully and necessarily included within the domain of national priority for some purposes, and that they defend the extension of many fundamental rights and protections to them on this basis.[67] Yet because, in conjunction with their vision of a soft interior, separationists embrace a hard-on-the-outside vision of national community, they also endorse the existence of a regime of national territorial border control. They may (and often do) criticize particular border control policies and practices, but they support such control in principle.

To the extent that national borders are policed, of course, there is a world of aspiring entrants who are prevented from crossing into the territory and achieving the presence that would place them (for at least some purposes) within the domain of national priority. Although millions of people manage to achieve territorial presence despite these border controls, far greater numbers do not (and a tragic number also die or suffer harm trying to evade them).[68] In comparison to the territorially present undocumented (who may either have directly evaded border controls upon entry or violated the terms of their initial admissions once in), those on the outside enjoy none of the priority that extends to the territorially here.

The fact that they do not raises important questions about the justifiability of a political ethics that depends on the contingency of location. What sense does it make, we might ask, to draw a line of normative consequence at the Rio Grande when success at crossing into or remaining within the national territory is quite often a fortuitous affair? What is the sense when most undocumented immigrants who are currently here have family members and friends who were not so lucky as they, and when many of the undocumented travel back and forth across the border with relative frequency in any event?[69] Membership in the class of people who happen to be territorially present at any given time is both adventitious and mutable. But that being the case, it becomes clear how arbitrary it is to claim as nationally privileged only those individuals who happen to have crossed the geographic frontier.[70]

The usual rejoinder is that hereness is a measure (even if imperfect) of the ties to the community a person maintains; and the existence of ties itself justifies a degree of normative priority. This is the antiformalist membership-as-social-fact approach, and it is a critically important response to exclusion when we are proceeding from an inward-looking perspective.[71] It allows us to say that a person's participation in, and contribution to, a common social world with already recognized members ought to provide the basis for community recognition.

But things look different when we approach the issue from a global vantage. We might ask, if actual community ties represent an important foundation of ethical responsibility, why not include those who lived and worked here at one time but who are not currently present? Why not include the large numbers of people around the world who are intimately linked to the nation—familially, culturally, economically, politically—without being territorially present?[72] Indeed, why not include those who were less lucky at the border or who are aspiring to come for the first time, all of whom may possess the same desire to rejoin family, to work, to contribute, to build the nation, as many who are already here?

Some commentators have suggested that the apparent arbitrariness involved casts doubt on the legitimacy of extending important protections to undocumented immigrants in the first instance. For after all, why should the contingency of their hereness be turned to such advantage? The inverse argument, however, is just as easily made: why stop at the water's edge? Indeed, if it is the moral arbitrariness of territorial location that one is concerned about, why not take aim at the entire system of territorial birthright citizenship, and at the commitment to border restrictions altogether?

Wherever one stands on the moral significance of borders, there is no escaping the empirical reality that prompts the discussion: territorial presence now serves as a constitutive element of the privilege of already being national as a matter of fact. Given the prevailing commitment to territorial borders, not just anyone can achieve this presence: it is hard to come by. Once achieved, though, it is consequential; it produces real advantage—a fact that is driven home when we compare our legal system's treatment of any undocumented immigrant with her otherwise similarly situated compatriot who happens to be located on the other side of the line.

Yet while significant privileges attend territorial presence, this presence is not always itself an indefeasible privilege. Only status citizens can count on it unqualifiedly. For status noncitizens—for aliens—the privilege of presence is conditional. In the case of lawfully present aliens, a variety of factors may trigger the process of territorial removal. In the case of the undocumented, it is, additionally, the very fact of their *hereness* that renders them deportable.

I have emphasized throughout this book that this potential subjection to deportation structures the lives of aliens in ways that are disadvantaging. This is a convergence effect that separationists should, in theory, oppose. And they do, but only to an extent. Because, in the end, their normative commitment to national borders prevents them from fully repudiating the disadvantages inherent in alienage.

It is precisely here that the separationists' commitment to equal citizenship for aliens runs up against their normative nationalism. The condition of alienage, though sometimes lamented, is presupposed by the boundaries that are understood to make equal citizenship possible. The contradiction is most vivid in relation to the undocumented. While the social exclusion these individuals suffer is recognized as objectionable, the territorial exclusion that creates their status also seems essential, at least some of the time, as a precondition for achieving social justice within the community—and indeed, as a constitutive condition of the political community's existence altogether. Yet of course, it is precisely enforcement of these borders that produces the immigrants' social exclusion here in the first place.

It is in this sense that undocumented aliens are "impossible subjects," to borrow Mae Ngai's evocative phrase.[73] It is their territorial hereness that brings them within the circle of national normative concern, but it is also their territorial hereness that is objected to, that subjects them to potential territorial removal and renders them vulnerable to subordination in the process.

CITIZENSHIP AGAINST ITSELF

I understand the impulse to try to dissolve the ambivalence we suffer over citizenship's "who" questions through a strategy of splitting. Splitting holds out the promise of achieving a purely inclusionary inside—a promise that egalitarian liberals find deeply compelling. The splitting strategy is also attractive in practical political terms: it provides a rhetorical basis for insisting that the (internal) universality that citizenship aspires to stand for be effectuated in practice. Defenders of immigrants' rights within liberal democratic societies make use of this rhetorical strategy all the time. We deploy the community's articulated ideals to challenge its exclusionary practices;[74] we insist that it make good on its promise to include "everyone."

But in the end, elimination of the unpalatable (from a liberal perspective) exclusionary commitments through ejection to the community's geographic edges is simply not possible: exclusionary national boundaries are with us on the territorial inside as well. The category of alienage embodies the unachievability of pure separation. Aliens are liminal characters, subjects of contrasting and sometimes competing citizenship worlds. The worlds are ultimately inseverable at the point of alienage because it is alienage's very condition to be at their interface. Alienage, we might say, pits citizenship against itself.

The quest for unmitigated inclusion within the community can therefore serve as a regulative ideal, but in actuality, such inclusion is a fantasy. Our condition, on the inside, is one of ambivalence and ethical conflict.[75] However ostensibly committed we are to norms of universality, we liberal national subjects are chronically divided over the proper location of boundaries—boundaries of responsibility and boundaries of belonging. It is precisely these divisions that are at stake in our debates over the institutions and practices and experiences we have come to call citizenship.

Notes

1. Iris Marion Young, "Polity and Group Difference: A Critique of the Ideal of Universal Citizenship," 99 *Ethics* no. 2 (1989).

Of course, "universal citizenship" is itself a bitterly contested concept. Many critics from Marx onward have observed that citizenship's universal ideal is usually conceived in formal, rather than substantive, terms and have pointed out that the extension of formal recognition of citizenship under the law by no means undoes the myriad forms of substantive inequality and social exclusion suffered by various groups in liberal democratic societies. Critics have also made clear that, as understood and practiced, the ideal of universal citizenship often serves to reproduce subordination; it has been intolerant of difference, and has served as a formal cover for relations of domination and coercion. Indeed, one of the central projects of recent critical and egalitarian thought has been to unmask the false promises of liberal universalist conceptions of citizenship in one way or another. Yet despite its very real failures in fulfillment and (perhaps) conception, there is little question that universal citizenship remains a prevailing regulative ideal in our political and legal thought. "The inclusion and participation of everyone" (Young, "Polity and Group Difference") is by now a normatively incontestable value in liberal democratic societies. I address these points in chapters 2, 4, and 5.

2. Linda Bosniak, "The Citizenship of Aliens," 56 *Social Text* at 29–35 (1998).

3. John Rawls, *Political Liberalism* (Columbia Univ. Press, 1993).

4. John Rawls, *A Theory of Justice* 8 (Harvard Univ. Press, 1971).

5. *See, e.g.*, Charles R. Beitz, *Political Theory and International Relations* 129–136 (Princeton Univ. Press, 1999) (1979); Samuel Scheffler, *Boundaries and Allegiances: Problems of Justice and Responsibility in Liberal Thought* 32–47 (Oxford Univ. Press, 2001). For critiques of the Rawlsian premise as it applies to the immigration context, see, e.g., Joseph Carens, "Aliens and Citizens: The Case for Open Borders," 49 *Rev. Pol.* 251 (1987); Seyla Benhabib, "Citizens, Residents and Aliens in a Changing World: Political Membership in the Global Era," 66 *Soc. Res.* 709 (1999).

Other social theorists, though not responding specifically to Rawls, make a similar point about the liabilities of unexamined nation-centeredness in scholarly thought. Craig Calhoun states the problem succinctly:

> Nationalist thinking also pervades social science, which is one reason why developing an adequate critical stance toward it is difficult. Our very ideas about what "a society" is are shaped by understandings developed under the influence of nationalism and European state-making. Not least of all, we

> make national identities seem natural, or at least primordial, by building
> them into our very sense of history.

Calhoun, *Critical Social Theory* (Blackwell, 1995), at 233.

6. In this insular intellectual tradition, the only relationships extending beyond the community's edges that are addressed, if they are at all, are those among the political communities themselves. Rawls, *The Law of Peoples* (Harvard Univ. Press, 1999).

7. The idea of "globalization within" has been articulated and explored by various analysts in recent years, central among them Saskia Sassen, who has criticized the prevailing "national/global duality" in standard approaches to globalization and who has insisted that globalization "is not simply a matter of a space economy extending beyond a national realm." "Important components of globalization," she writes, "are embedded in particular locations within national territories." Saskia Sassen, "Whose City Is It? Globalization and the Formation of New Claims," in *Cities and Citizenship* (James Holston, ed., Duke Univ. Press, 1999), at 177, 186. The idea of globalization within underlines the fact that national states are in various respects penetrated by global processes and must inevitably contend with the practical and imaginative effects of that penetration.

8. International Organization for Migration, "Facts and Figures on Migration," http://www.iom.int/DOCUMENTS/PUBLICATION/EN/MPI_series_No_2_eng .pdf.

9. See "1-in-5 U.S. Residents Either Foreign-Born or First Generation, Census Bureau Reports," Census Bureau News, Press Release, U.S. Dept. of Commerce, Washington, D.C., Feb. 7, 2002.

10. Certainly, a good deal of this literature attends to the challenges of diversity, multiculturalism, and racism—issues that are obviously tied up with the incorporation of immigrants. Furthermore, some of this scholarship (particularly from the United States, but also from Australia and Canada) is informed in various ways by a background narrative about the countries' histories as "nations of immigrants." For a discussion of the self-identity of "nations of immigrants," see *Nations of Immigrants: Australia, the United States and International Migration* (Gary P. Freeman and James Jupp, eds., Oxford Univ. Press, 1992).

11. Michael Walzer, *Spheres of Justice: A Defense of Pluralism and Equality* (Basic Books, 1983), at 30. *See also* W. Rogers Brubaker, *Citizenship and Nationhood in France and Germany* 22 (Harvard Univ. Press, 1992).

12. Walzer, however, does not describe them in the language of citizenship. He employs the idea of membership to talk about initial belonging, and the idea of citizenship to talk about the condition of belonging among those already deemed community members.

13. Here my argument departs from Walzer's ideal "separate spheres" model. See chapters 3 and 6 for extensive discussion.

14. National boundaries are also enforced outside the borders of the territorial state, as in the case of a state's granting or denial of visas abroad, or more controversially through the interdiction of prospective asylum seekers on the high seas.

15. See Etienne Balibar, *We the People of Europe? Reflections on Transnational Citizenship* (James Swenson, trans., Princeton Univ. Press, 2004) for an important recent theoretical treatment of the interiorization of borders.

16. The examination of alienage and citizenship law I undertake here is set largely in the context of the United States, which is the case I know best. However, in its broad outlines, I believe the analysis is also relevant to the organization of citizenship and alienage in other liberal democratic states with robust individual rights traditions. For treatments of the status of aliens in other liberal democratic states compatible with my own, see, e.g., Yasemin Nohoglu Soysal, *Limits of Citizenship: Migrants and Postnational Membership in Europe* (Cornell Univ. Press, 1994); Ruth Rubio-Marin, *Immigration as a Democratic Challenge: Citizenship and Inclusion in Germany and the United States* 6 (Cambridge Univ. Press, 2000); Jacqueline Bhabha, " 'Get Back to Where You Once Belonged': Identity, Citizenship and Exclusion in Europe," 20 *Hum. Rts. Q.* 592 (1998). The discussion likewise bears on the ambiguous status of aliens under international law. The perennial tension in international law between state sovereignty and human rights in the treatment of aliens has many parallels with the border/interior divide in the national context. *See* Linda Bosniak, "Human Rights, State Sovereignty and the Protection of Undocumented Migrants Under the International Migrant Workers Convention," 25 *Int'l Migration Rev.* 737–770 (Winter 1991) (updated in Linda Bosniak, "Undocumented Immigrants Under the Migrant Workers Convention," in *Irregular Migration and Human Rights: Theoretical, European and International Perspectives* 311–41 (Barbara Bogusz et al., eds., Koninklijke Brill NV, 2004).

17. Iris Marion Young, "Status Inequality and Social Groups," in *Issues in Legal Scholarship: The Origins and Fate of Antisubordination Theory*, Article 9 (2002), *available at* www.bepress.com/ils/iss2/art9.

18. *Id.* at 6.

19. In this respect, noncitizens constitute a class-in-themselves but not often a class-for-themselves, in Marxian terms.

20. In each of these cases, noncitizens (and others) have worked to advance the condition of noncitizens *as* a class. See generally, Steven Greenhouse, "Riding Across America for Immigrant Workers," *New York Times*, Sept. 17, 2003, at A20; Robert F. Worth, "Push Is On to Give Legal Immigrants a Vote in the City," *New York Times*, April 8, 2004, at 1. *See also* Jennifer Gordon, *Suburban Sweatshops: The Fight for Immigrant Rights* (Belknap Press, 2005).

At the international level, increasing attention has been brought to bear on the human rights of noncitizens as a class. Efforts to support entry into force of the International Convention for the Protection of Migrant Workers and Members of Their Families served to elicit and channel a great deal of international activism. The convention obtained the necessary signatures and entered into force in 2003. For an overview of recent international efforts to protect the rights of noncitzens, see "The Global Campaign for Ratification of the Convention on Rights of Migrants," *available at* http://www.migrantsrights.org/.

21. For example, while alienage per se is not a "visible marker" of distinction in a multiethnic society (Jacqueline Bhabha, "The Mere 'Fortuity' of Birth? Are Children Citizens?" 15 *Differences: A Journal of Feminist Cultural Studies* 91, 94

(2004), alienage is unquestionably attributed to "foreign-looking" persons with great frequency.

22. Groups currently supporting an "expansive" view on rights for noncitizens and immigrant admissions include "ethnic groups, human rights and religious groups; [and the] AFL-CIO." Daniel J. Tichenor, *Dividing Lines: The Politics of Immigration Control in America* 276 (Princeton Univ. Press, 2002). For a critical view of the left's abandonment of its mid-twentieth century posture of immigration protectionism, see David Abraham, *Citizenship Solidarity and Rights Individualism: On the Decline of National Citizenship in the U.S., Germany and Israel* 12 (Center for Comparative Immigration Studies, Univ. of California, San Diego, Working Paper No. 53, May 2002) ("[T]hose legal forces and actors whom one would expect to represent the redistributional interests of the lower classes have been centrally responsible for the disappearance and exclusion of class and solidarity from the discourse of immigration policy and law and their replacement by concern with nondiscrimination and recognition."). See also Vernon Briggs, *Immigration and American Unionism* (Cornell Univ. Press, 2001); Editorial, *New York Teacher*, July 14, 2005, *available at* http://www.uft.org/news/teacher/labor/ 1_14_04__second/. ("[T]he reigning multicultural orthodoxy . . . equates even the slightest skepticism about open borders with kicking the underdog. Righting immigrant wrongs has been adopted by the political and cultural left. . . .").

23. E.g., Iris Young's important earlier work exemplified the nationally insular approach to citizenship that I criticize here. See especially Young, "Polity and Group Difference." In a 2003 article, however, Young attends (albeit briefly) to the categories of immigration and citizenship in an essay about the structure of subordination in liberal democratic societies. See Young, "Status Inequality and Social Groups."

24. The phenomenology of language and concept undertaken here is motivated by the conviction that, as William Connolly has written, "[t]he language of politics is not a neutral medium that conveys ideas independently formed; it is an institutionalized structure of meanings that channels political thought and action in certain directions. . . . [T]he discourse of politics helps to set the terms within which that politics proceeds." William E. Connolly, *The Terms of Political Discourse* 10 (Princeton Univ. Press, 1993).

25. Raymond Williams, *Keywords* (1983).

26. Quentin Skinner, "Language and Political Change," in *Political Innovation and Conceptual Change* 10 (Terrence Ball et al., eds., Cambridge Univ. Press, 1989). A word's appraisive meaning is its evaluative meaning; it refers to "the range of attitudes the term can standardly be used to express."

27. To see this process of legitimation at work is to see that "the social and political world is conceptually and communicatively constituted." Terence Ball, James Farr, Russel L. Hanson, "Editors' Introduction," in *Political Theory and Conceptual Change* 1 (Terence Ball et al., eds., Cambridge Univ. Press, 1989). The language we use reflects political and social norms and conflict over norms, but it does more than this. As Raymond Williams has written, "important social and historical processes occur within language in a variety of ways." Williams, *Keywords* at 22. Debates over powerful political concepts such as citizenship reflect competing efforts to reshape the social and political landscape as well as to repre-

sent it. *See also* Ball, Farr, and Hanson, "Editors' Introduction," in *Political Innovation and Conceptual Change* 3 ("To explore and criticize contradictions or incoherences in one's moral language is to begin to remake and rearrange one's moral or political world.").

28. This objection has been heard especially often in response to efforts to talk about citizenship beyond the nation-state—about transnational or global or cosmopolitan forms of citizenship. Invocations of citizenship in these latter terms are viewed by opponents as involving a fundamental category error. See chapter 2; *see also* Linda Bosniak, "Citizenship Denationalized," 7 *Ind. J. Global Legal Stud.* 447 (2000).

29. *E.g.*, Williams, *Keywords*; Skinner, "Language and Political Change," in *Political Innovation and Conceptual Change*; Ball, Farr and Hanson, "Editors' Introduction," in *Political Innovation and Conceptual Change*.

30. Ball et al., "Editors' Introduction," *Political Innovation and Conceptual Change* at 2.

31. Williams, *Keywords* at 17, 24. Williams criticizes "what can best be called a sacral attitude to words, and corresponding complaints of vulgar contemporary misunderstandings." *Id.* at 20. Certainly, "the original meanings of words are always interesting. But what is often most interesting is the subsequent variation. . . . The vitality of a language includes every kind of extension, variation and transfer, and this is as true of change in our own time (however much we may regret some particular examples) as of changes in the past, which can now be given a sacral veneer." *Id.* at 21.

32. For two exceptionally useful works on these themes, see Craig Calhoun, *Critical Social Theory* (Blackwell, 1995) (identity) and Samuel Scheffler, *Boundaries and Allegiances* (Oxford Univ. Press, 2001) (responsibility).

CHAPTER 2
DEFINING CITIZENSHIP: SUBSTANCE, LOCATION, AND SUBJECTS

1. Judith Shklar, *American Citizenship: The Quest for Inclusion* 1 (Harvard Univ. Press, 1991).

2. J.G.A. Pocock, "The Ideal of Citizenship since Classical Times," in *The Citizenship Debates* (Gershon Shafir, ed., Univ. of Minn. Press 1998); Michael Walzer, "Citizenship," in *Political Innovation and Conceptual Change* (Terence Ball, James Farr, and Russell L. Hanson, eds., Cambridge Univ. Press, 1989).

3. T. H. Marshall, *Citizenship and Social Class* (Cambridge Univ. Press, 1949). Marshallian citizenship theory has generated substantial interest among social theorists in recent years, with most commentators focusing on Marshall's concept of social citizenship. For a sampling (both sympathetic and critical), see Margaret R. Somers, "Rights, Relationality, and Membership: Rethinking the Making and Meaning of Citizenship," 19 *Law & Social Inquiry* 63 (1994); Nancy Fraser and Linda Gordon, "Civil Citizenship against Social Citizenship?," in *The Condition of Citizenship* (Bart van Steenbergen, ed., Sage, 1994); Lawrence M. Mead, "Citizenship and Social Policy: T. H. Marshall and Poverty," 14 *Social Philosophy and Policy* 197 (1997).

4. *See generally* Kenneth Karst, *Belonging to America: Equal Citizenship and the Constitution* (Yale Univ. Press, 1989); Shklar, 1991; Rogers M. Smith, *Civic Ideals: Conflicting Visions of Citizenship in U.S. History* (Yale Univ. Press, 1998).

5. Richard Flathman, "Citizenship and Authority: A Chastened View of Citizenship," in *Theorizing Citizenship* (Ronald Beiner, ed., State University of New York Press, 1995).

6. Joseph Carens describes this dimension as "psychological citizenship." Joseph H. Carens, "Dimensions of Citizenship and National Identity in Canada," 28 *Phil. F.* 111–12 (1996–1997) (distinguishing among the legal, psychological, and political dimensions of citizenship).

7. Martha Nussbaum, "Patriotism and Cosmopolitanism," in *For Love of Country* (Joshua Cohen, ed., Beacon Press, 1996).

8. Charles Taylor, *Multiculturalism and 'The Politics of Recognition'* (Princeton Univ. Press, 1992).

9. *E.g.*, Joseph Carens, "Aliens and Citizens: The Case for Open Borders," 49 *Rev. of Pol.* 251 (1987); *see also* Pamela Johnston Conover, "Citizen Identities and Conceptions of the Self" 3 *J. Pol. Phil.* 133, 134 (1995) (citizenship "encompasses a variety of elements, some legal, some psychological and some behavioral").

10. Conover, "Citizen Identities and Conceptions of the Self," at 134.

11. *E.g.*, Will Kymlicka and Wayne Norman, "Return of the Citizen: A Survey of Recent Work on Citizenship Theory," 104 *Ethics* 352 (1994).

12. Pocock, "The Ideal of Citizenship Since Classical Times."

13. Marx, "On the Jewish Question," in *Karl Marx: Early Writings* (Vintage, 1975). T. H. Marshall was likewise concerned with the contradiction in capitalist societies between civil and political equality, on the one hand, and economic inequality, on the other. As summarized by Margaret Somers:

> It is the relationship between the rights endowed by citizenship status premised on equality on one side and the fundamental inequalities inherent in the social class system on the other that most interests Marshall. The two sides represent, in his words, "warring principles"—those of status equality and right against contract inequality and markets. Developing a theory to account for the origins and consequences of these warring tensions in modern society forms the heart of his work.

See Margaret Somers, "Rights, Relationality and Membership," at 67. However, instead of viewing citizenship as a cover for economic inequalty, Marshall treated this contradiction as internal to citizenship itself.

14. This was an axiom of the legal realists and later of scholars identified with the critical legal studies movement. *See generally* Robert Gordon, "Critical Legal Histories," 36 *Stan. L. Rev.* (1984).

15. Iris Marion Young, "Polity and Group Difference: A Critique of the Ideal of Universal Citizenship," 99 *Ethics* 250 (1989).

16. *Id.*

17. E.g., Susan Moller Okin, "Women, Equality and Citizenship," in 99 *Queens Q.* 33 (Spring 1992); Carol Pateman, *Participation and Democratic Theory* (Cambridge Univ. Press, 1970). As Cass Sunstein has written, "[c]itizenship,

understood in republican fashion, does not occur solely through official organs." Cass Sunstein, "Beyond the Republican Revival," 97 *Yale L.J.* 1539 (1988).

18. The exact parameters of the sphere of civil society are subject to dispute. Most liberal theorists treat civil society as comprising those aspects of social life not encompassed in the state, and on this approach, the market is part of civil society. Other theorists distinguish civil society from both the state and the economy, in what one analyst has called a "three-part model" deriving from Gramsci. *See* Jean Cohen, "Interpreting the Notion of Civil Society," in *Toward a Global Civil Society* 35, 36 (Michael Walzer, ed., Berghahn Books, 1995).

19. *See, e.g.,* Benjamin Barber, "Clansmen, Consumers and Citizen: Three Takes on Civil Society," in *Civil Society, Democracy and Civic Renewal* (Robert K. Fullinwider, ed., Rowman & Littlefield, 1999); Robert Putnam, *Bowling Alone: The Collapse and Revival of American Community* (Simon & Schuster, 2000).

20. Richard Dagger, *Civic Virtues: Rights, Citizenship, and Republican Liberalism* 99 (Oxford Univ. Press, 1997).

21. William Forbath, "Class, Caste and Equal Citizenship," 98 *Mich. L. Rev.* 1 (1999); Shklar, *American Citizenship.*

22. Bruce Ackerman and Anne Alstott, *The Stakeholder Society* (Yale Univ. Press, 1999).

23. This literature draws on and elaborates T. H. Marshall's account of social citizenship. See, e.g., Nancy Fraser and Linda Gordon, "Civil Citizenship against Social Citizenship? On the Ideology of Contract-Versus-Charity," in *The Condition of Citizenship* (Bart van Steenbergen, ed., Sage, 1994).

24. Susan Moller Okin, "Women, Equality and Citizenship," supra note 16 at 56–69.

25. William Flores and Rina Benmayor, eds., *Latino Cultural Citizenship: Claiming Identity, Space and Rights* 57 (Beacon Press, 1997); Young, "Polity and Group Difference" 14.

26. Will Kymlicka, *Multicultural Citizenship: A Liberal Theory of Minority Rights* (Oxford Univ. Press, 1995).

27. *See especially* Ayelet Schachar, *Multicultural Jurisdictions: Cultural Differences and Women's Rights* (Cambridge Univ. Press, 2001).

28. *E.g.,* David Miller, *Citizenship and National Identity* (Polity Press, 2000).

29. Increasingly, however, analysts are making the assumption explicit. *See, e.g.,* David Jacobson, *Rights across Borders: Immigration and the Decline of Citizenship* 7 (Johns Hopkins Univ. Press, 1996) ("[C]itizenship and the nation-state are intricately linked to one another. Indeed, it is fair to say that citizenship is the linchpin of the nation-state."); Miller, *Citizenship and National Identity* at 81 ("[T]he practice of citizenship must, for as far ahead as we can reasonably envisage, be confined within the boundaries of national political communities.")

30. *See generally,* Richard Falk, "The Making of Global Citizenship," in *The Condition of Citizenship* (Bart van Steenbergen, ed., Sage, 1994); Yasemin Nohoglu Soysal, *Limits of Citizenship: Migrants and Postnational Membership in Europe* (Cornell Univ. Press, 1994); Andrew Linklater, "Cosmopolitan Citizenship," in *Cosmopolitan Citizenship* (Kimberly Hutchings and Roland Dannreuther, eds., St. Martin's Press, 1999). For an extensive discussion of this literature, see Linda Bosniak, "Citizenship Denationalized," 7 *Ind. J. Global Legal Stud.* 447 (2000).

31. Hannah Arendt, *Men in Dark Times* 81 (Harcourt, Brace & World, 1968).

32. Gertrude Himmelfarb, "The Illusions of Cosmopolitanism," in *For Love of Country* 1194 (Joshua Cohen, ed., Beacon Press, 1996). See also sources cited in note 28.

33. Bosniak, "Citizenship Denationalized."

34. It is true that people throughout much of the world enjoy formal legal memberships in subnational entities, including provinces, states, and municipalities. But these memberships are often subordinated to the demands of national citizenship as a matter of domestic law, and are almost always regarded as subsidiary in the international arena.

35. Linda Bosniak, "Multiple Nationality and the Postnational Transformation of Citizenship," in *Rights and Duties of Dual Nationals: Evolution and Prospects* (David A. Martin and Kay Hailbronner, eds., Kluwer Law International, 2002).

36. "Every citizen shall have the right to move and reside freely within the territory of Member States." European Union Treaty, art. 18 (1).

37. For a general discussion, see Hans Ulfich Jessurun d'Olivera, "Union Citizenship: Pie in the Sky?" in *A Citizen's Europe: In Search of a New World Order* (Allan Rosas and Esko Antola, eds., Sage, 1995).

38. The Treaty on European Union specifically defines EU citizens as those persons "holding the nationality of a Member State" (EU Treaty, art. 17), and it is national law that determines who will be citizens of the individual EU states. Hundreds of thousands of people live in Europe without national citizenship, which means that they lack EU citizenship as well. *See generally* Jacqueline Bhabha, "Belonging in Europe: Citizenship and Postnational Rights," 159 *UNESCO* 11 (1999). Furthermore, the entity in which this new citizenship is based is still controlled in important ways by the individual states that compose it; as one commentator put it, "the real *locus* of political power in the Community remains, as it has since the Community's foundations, with the governments of the Member States." Stephen Hall, *Nationality, Migration Rights and Citizenship of the Union* 11 (Martinus Nijhoff, 1995).

39. *See, e.g.,* Louis Henkin, *The Age of Rights* 23 (Columbia Univ. Press, 1990) (comparing the European human rights system, which "can claim dramatic successes," with the United Nations system, where "[t]he establishment of even a 'toothless' office such as a UN High Commissioner for Human Rights has been strenuously (and to date successfully) resisted.")

Rainer Baubock maintains that a "claim for citizenship rights always implies an appeal directed toward political institutions which could enforce the right." He suggests, therefore, that viewing human rights as transnational citizenship will ultimately entail a conception of a transnational polity equipped to enforce them and to ground political membership more broadly." Rainer Baubock, *Transnational Citizenship* 247–48 (Edward Elgar Publishing, 1994).

40. *See, e.g.,* Baubock, *Transnational Citizenship*; Soysal, *Limits of Citizenship*.

41. Michael Peter Smith, "Can You Imagine? Transnational Migration and the Globalization of Grassroots Politics," 39 *Soc. Text* 15 (1994).

42. This process has been described as "deterritorialized nation-state formation." Linda Basch, Nina Glick Schiller, and Cristina Szanton-Blanc, *Nations Un-*

bound: Transnational Projects, Postcolonial Predicaments and Deterritorialized Nation-States (Gordon and Breach, 2004).

43. Margaret E. Keck and Kathryn Sikkink, *Activists beyond Borders: Advocacy Networks in International Politics* (Cornell Univ. Press, 1998).

44. Falk, "The Making of Global Citizenship" at 39 (describes transnational activism as "global citizenship"); *see also* Warren Magnusson, *The Search for Political Space* 9–10 (Univ. of Toronto Press, 1996) (transnational social movements "involve people in active citizenship and thus lay claim to a political space that may or may not conform to the spaces allowed by the existing system of government").

45. On the common "citizenship" of members of the transnational capitalist class, *see* Aihwa Ong, *Flexible Citizenship: The Cultural Logics of Transnationality* (Duke Univ. Press, 1999); Falk, "The Making of Global Citizenship" at 43–44 (describing "deterritorialized and elite global culture").

46. Alejandro Portes, "Global Villagers: The Rise of Transnational Communities," in *American Prospect* 77 (Mar.–Apr. 1996).

47. *See* Linda Bosniak, "Multiple Nationality and the Postnational Transformation of Citizenship," 42 *Va. J. Int'l L.* 979 (2002) (on transnational citizenship).

48. David Jacobson, *Rights across Borders: Immigration and the Decline of Citizenship* (Johns Hopkins Univ. Press, 1996).

49. Miller, *Citizenship and National Identity,* at 96.

50. Bosniak, "Citizenship Denationalized" at 508.

51. Linklater, "Cosmopolitan Citizenship" at 36; Nussbaum, "Patriotism and Cosmopolitanism"; Thomas Pogge, "Cosmopolitanism and Sovereignty," 103 *Ethics* 48, 49 (Oct. 1992) ("The central idea of moral cosmopolitanism is that every human being has a global stature as ultimate unit of moral concern").

Critics of cosmopolitanism regard the posture of moral detachment presumed in this vision as implausible. Individuals are never truly detached, in the critics' view; they are unavoidably "situated selves," whose moral commitments are necessarily constituted by and within the communities where they live. David Miller, *On Nationality* (Oxford Univ. Press, 1995); Michael Sandel, *Liberalism and the Limits of Justice* (2d ed., Cambridge Univ. Press, 1998) (1984). Nor are people, by nature, actually capable of identifying with humanity at large, because the category is too big and too abstract to serve as the object of political love and identification. *E.g.,* Nathan Glazer, "Limits of Loyalty," in *For Love of Country* 63 (Beacon Press, 1996) (arguing that cosmopolitans "are often unrealistic about how far the bonds of obligation and loyalty can stretch.")

I am sympathetic to the methodological "situated self" critique, but it is important to note that it does not lead necessarily to ethical nationalism. It is perfectly possible to maintain that our commitments and identifications are constituted by and within various sub- and transnational communities, as well as national ones.

In response to the critics' argument that the world is "too big" as an object of identification and solidarity, Bruce Robbins has noted, correctly I think, that "[i]f cosmopolitanism were really too big, then the nation would be too big as well." Bruce Robbins, "Introduction, Part I: Actually Existing Cosmopolitanism," in *Cosmopolitics: Thinking and Feeling beyond the Nation* (Pheng Chea and Bruce Robbins, eds., Univ. of Minn. Press, 1998).

52. Falk, "The Making of Global Citizenship."

53. David Miller, *On Nationality* (Oxford Univ. Press, 1995). According to Miller, "the welfare state—and indeed, programmes to protect minority rights— have always been *national* projects, justified on the basis that members of a community must protect one another and guarantee one another equal respect." *Id.*, at 187.

54. Charles Taylor, "Cross-Purposes: The Liberal-Communitarian Debate," in *Liberalism and the Moral Life* (Nancy L. Rosenblum, ed., Harvard Univ. Press, 1989).

55. Jocelyne Couture and Kai Nielsen (with Michael Seymour), "Afterword," in *Rethinking Nationalism* 593 (Jocelyne Couture et al., eds., Univ. of Calgary Press, 1998).

56. Henry Shue, *Basic Rights: Substance, Affluence and American Foreign Policy* 132 (Princeton Univ. Press, 1980) (criticizing what he terms the "priority thesis").

57. *See, e.g.*, Linklater, "Cosmopolitan Citizenship"; Nussbaum, "Patriotism and Cosmopolitanism"; Falk, "The Making of Global Citizenship"; Carens, "Aliens and Citizens."

58. David Held, "The Transformation of Political Community: Rethinking Democracy in the Context of Globalization," in *Democracy's Edges* 103 (Ian Shapiro and Casiano Hacker-Cordon, eds., Cambridge Univ. Press, 1999).

59. *See generally id.*; Linklater, "Cosmopolitan Citizenship"; Falk, "The Making of Global Citizenship."

60. *See, e.g.*, Nancy Cott, "Marriage and Women's Citizenship in the United States, 1830–1934," in *American Historical Review* (Dec. 1998).

61. Marshall, *Citizenship and Social Class*, at 84 (my emphasis).

62. Walzer, "Citizenship."

63. Karst, *Belonging to America*, at 3.

64. Iris Marion Young, "Polity and Group Difference: A Critique of the Ideal of Universal Citizenship," at 250–251.

65. *See, e.g.*, Smith, *Civic Ideals*; Cott, "Marriage and Women's Citizenship in the United States"; Leti Volpp, " 'Obnoxious to Their Very Nature': Asian Americans and Constitutional Citizenship," 5 *Citizenship Studies* (2) 57 (2001).

66. *E.g.*, Fraser and Gordon, "Civil Citizenship against Social Citizenship?"

67. *See, e.g.*, Taylor, "Cross-Purposes"; Karst, *Belonging to America*.

68. *E.g.*, Barber, "Clansmen, Consumers and Citizen."

69. *See, e.g.*, Leti Volpp, "The Citizen and the Terrorist," 49 *UCLA L. Rev.* 1575, [ ] (2001–2003) ("Many of those racially profiled in the sense of being the targets of hate violence or being thrown off airplanes are formally citizens of the United States, through birth or naturalization. But they are not considered citizens as a matter of identity, in that they in no way represent the nation").

70. *E.g.*, Bart van Steenbergen, "Towards a Global Ecological Citizen," in *The Condition of Citizenship* (Sage, 1994).

71. J. P. McFadden, "Toward the New Future," 25 *The Human Life Review* (Jan. 1999).

72. For a review of the state of contemporary international law of nationality, *see* Peter Spiro, "Mandated Membership, Diluted Identity: Citizenship, Globalization and International Law," in *People Out of Place: Globalization, Human*

Rights and the Citizenship Gap (Alison Brysk and Gershon Shafir, eds., Taylor and Frances, 2004).

73. Peter Schuck and Rogers Smith, *Citizenship without Consent: Illegal Aliens in the American Polity* (Yale Univ. Press 1985).

74. *See generally Rights and Duties of Dual Nationals: Evolution and Prospects* (David A. Martin and Kay Hailbronner, eds., Kluwer Law International, 2003); Peter Spiro, "Dual Nationality and the Meaning of Citizenship," 46 *Emory L.J.* 1435 (1997); Linda Bosniak, "Multiple Nationality and the Postnational Transformation of Citizenship," 42 *Va. J. Int'l L.* 979 (2002).

75. Rogers Brubaker, *Citizenship and Nationhood in France and Germany* (Harvard Univ. Press, 1992).

76. Spiro, "Dual Nationality and the Meaning of Citizenship."

77. Alexander M. Bickel, *The Morality of Consent* 36 (Yale U. Press, 1975).

78. *See generally* Peter Schuck, "The Devaluation of Citizenship," in *Citizens, Strangers, and In-Betweens: Essays on Immigration and Citizenship* (Westview, 1998); Noah Pickus, *True Faith and Allegiance: Immigration and American Civic Nationalism* (Princeton Univ. Press, 2005).

79. *See generally* Michael Walzer, *Spheres of Justice: A Defense of Pluralism and Equality* (Basic Books, 1983).

80. Bruce Ackerman, *Social Justice in the Liberal State* (Yale Univ. Press, 1980).

81. Carens, "Aliens and Citizens."

82. See Brubaker, *Citizenship and Nationhood in France and Germany.*

83. Soysal, *Limits of Citizenship*; Schuck, "The Devaluation of Citizenship."

84. Linda Bosniak, "Membership, Equality and the Difference That Alienage Makes," 69 *N.Y.U. L. Rev.* 1047 (1994).

85. Brubaker, *Citizenship and Nationhood in France and Germany* at 31.

86. For characterizations of political and economic organizing among noncitizen immigrants as examples of citizenship practice (or of "the work of citizenship," in Jennifer Gordon's phrase), see, e.g., Jennifer Gordon, *Suburban Sweatshops: The Fight for Immigrant Rights* (Belknap, 2005), at 275, 278; Paul Johnson, "Transnational Citizenries: Reflections from the Field in California," 7 (2) *Journal of Citizenship Studies* 199 (July 2003).

CHAPTER 3
THE DIFFERENCE THAT ALIENAGE MAKES

1. On citizenship's consequentiality, see William Rogers Brubaker, "Introduction," in *Immigration and the Politics of Citizens in Europe and North America* 4 (William Rogers Brubaker, ed., University Press of America, 1989) (citizenship of a nation-state is understood, ideally, to be "socially consequential. . . . [It] should be objectively valuable and subjectively valued.").

2. *Graham v. Richardson*, 403 U.S. 365, 372 (1971) ("[C]lassifications based on alienage, like those based on nationality or race, are inherently suspect and subject to close judicial scrutiny.") (footnotes omitted).

3. *City of Cleburne v. Cleburne Living Ctr., Inc.*, 473 U.S. 432, 453 n. 6 (1985) (Stevens, J., concurring).

4. *Johnson v. Eisentrager*, 339 U.S. 763, 770 (1950).

5. *Cabell v. Chavez-Salido*, 454 U.S. 432, 439–40 (1982).

6. Michael Walzer, *Spheres of Justice: A Defense of Pluralism and Equality* (Basic Books, 1983).

7. Michael Walzer, "The Distribution of Membership," in *Boundaries: National Autonomy and Its Limits* 1–36 (Peter Brown and Henry Shue, eds., Rowman & Littlefield, 1981).

8. Walzer, *Spheres of Justice*, at 39.

9. *Id.* at 29, 31.

10. *Id.* at 32.

11. *Id.* at 32.

12. *Id.* at 29, 40, 61–62; Walzer, "The Distribution of Membership" at 21.

Notably, the political community's right of closure is not entirely unconstrained in Walzer's formulation. Walzer posits a variety of moral limits on state action at the political community's border, grounded in both "internal and . . . external principles." He asserts, for example, that a political community's admissions policies are constrained by its "shared understandings" of moral action; thus, he argues that the racial quotas codified by United States immigration law in the 1920s were morally wrong because Americans had already created a "pluralist society," and "the moral realities of that society ought to have guided the legislators of the 1920's." *Id.* at 34, 40.

He further argues that a national community may have particular commitments to specific groups of people, namely, to "national or ethnic 'relatives' " located outside state borders (as in the case of Israel or in Germany before reunification), which it is morally enjoined to act upon. This constraint he terms the "nationality principle"; it establishes affirmative obligations to grant admission to those with whom we share some "national affinity." *Id.* at 42. United States immigration law, he points out, acts on this principle by favoring the admission of the relatives of members; and most states honor obligations of this nature in practice, if not in law. *Id.* at 41. (On the other hand, Walzer argues, although shared national affinity may under some circumstances constrain a state in denying admission, a lack of shared national affinity cannot provide a legitimate basis for the expulsion of aliens already within its borders. This is because a state is more than a family; it is also a territorial space within which people construct their lives:

> The state owes something to its inhabitants simply, without reference to their collective or national identity. And the first place to which the inhabitants are entitled is surely the place where they and their families have lived and made a life. The attachments and expectations they have formed argue against a forced transfer to another country.

Id. at 43.

Finally, Walzer, contends, the right of closure is to some degree constrained by the "external" principle of mutual aid, of "Good Samaritanism," in the face of needy foreigners. Walzer cites Rawls for a recent articulation of the Good Samaritan principle. *Id.* at 33, *citing* John Rawls, *A Theory of Justice* (Belknap Press of Harvard Univ. Press, 1971). For example, where a country has "superfluous" territory (a concept he leaves undefined), and others nearby are driven by famine to seek entry, mutual aid might require the wealthy country to allow for the admission of the starving—that is, it might be required to redistribute membership. On the other hand, claims of necessity have to be weighed against the right of the host community to maintain its "ways of life" (see Walzer, "Distribution of Membership"), which might well include the desire for ethnic homogeneity. A redistribution of membership could clearly interfere with such commitments. Therefore, argues Walzer, it might also be legitimate under the principle of mutual aid for the wealthy country to relinquish land or wealth, thereby meeting their obligation while also maintaining the cultural identity it wishes to preserve.

On the other hand, Walzer maintains, there are some necessitous strangers whose needs cannot be met by the relinquishing of territory or even the export of wealth. These are *refugees*, whose need, as it happens, "is for membership itself" (Walzer, *Spheres of Justice* at 48). As to this group of needy persons, the principle of mutual aid may require admission to the extent "we have helped turn [them] into refugees." *Id.* at 49.

Walzer's fundamental message, though, is not about the moral limitations on a country's admissions decisions but about the enormous discretion that such decisions entail. The heart of his argument is that admissions decisions are the legitimate and essential prerogative of the current members of any particular national community.

13. *See, e.g.,* Joseph H. Carens, "States and Refugees: A Normative Analysis," in *Refugee Policy: Canada and the United States* 22 (Howard Adelman, ed., Center for Migration Studies of New York, 1991) (Walzer "rejects the idea that all states should be morally required to have open borders with one another. . . . States may choose to be open in this way . . . but they may also legitimately choose to be closed, at least for the most part").

Many cite Walzer approvingly in support of this proposition. *See, e.g.,* Peter H. Schuck and Rogers M. Smith, *Citizenship without Consent: Illegal Aliens in the American Polity* 36 (Yale Univ. Press, 1985) ("[A]s Michael Walzer has argued, permitting a democratic community the power to shape its own destiny by granting or refusing its consent to new members is essential if the community is to be able to protect its interests, maintain harmony, and achieve a unifying sense of shared values."); Peter H. Schuck, "Membership in the Liberal Polity: The Devaluation of American Citizenship," 3 *Geo. Immigr. L.J.* 1, 15 (1989) ("Michael Walzer has hinted at an underlying emotional dynamic of [national] communities in his assertion that 'neighborhoods can be open only if countries are at least potentially closed' ") (citation omitted); Sanford Levinson, "Constituting Communities Through Words That Bind: Reflections on Loyalty Oaths," 84 *Mich. L. Rev.* 1440, 1446 (1986) ("According to Walzer, a 'sovereign state' must be permitted to 'take shape and claim the authority to make its own admissions policy, to control and sometimes restrain the flow of immigrants.' ") (page citations omitted).

Others contest the nationalist communitarian vision that lies at the heart of Walzer's formulation and argue that his theory is insufficiently attentive to individual rights. *See, e.g.,* Joseph H. Carens, "Aliens and Citizens: The Case for Open Borders," 49 *Rev. Pol.* 251, 264–270 (1987) (arguing that Walzer insufficiently acknowledges liberal traditions in our own culture which provide the ground for a critique of the exclusive nationalist theory he expounds); Judith Lichtenstein,

"National Boundaries and Moral Boundaries: A Cosmopolitan View," in *Boundaries* at 79, 95–96 (critiquing Walzer on grounds that "some 'distributive choices' are to be determined by considerations to which facts about membership are irrelevant." Lichtenstein also critiques Walzer's view of "nations as essentially closed systems").

Others still critique his approach on utilitarian grounds. *See, e.g.*, Peter and Renata Singer, "The Ethics of Refugee Policy," in *Open Borders? Closed Societies? The Ethical and Political Issues* 121–22 (Mark Gibney, ed., Greenwood Press, 1988). (Walzer defends "the current orthodoxy [which] is based on a view of right in which the primary right is the right of the community to determine its own membership. . . . In contrast to the rights-based arguments discussed so far, we hold that immigration policy in general, and refugee intake in particular, should be based on the interests of all those affected, either directly or indirectly, whether as an immediate result of the policy or in the long run.)

14. Although he does not make the point explicit, it seems clear that Walzer should not be read as arguing that each and every alien who comes within the territorial bounds of a national community is entitled to membership in that community. Walzer's concern is with the status of those aliens who have been admitted to permanent residence, or who have been admitted temporarily to provide labor to the community. He appears, therefore, not to be concerned with the status of relatively short-term visitors (such as tourists and students) who do not come to provide labor. However, he never expressly indicates which classes of aliens would and would not fall within the scope of his injunction that aliens who work and reside in the community are entitled to community membership.

Because Walzer's concern is with aliens admitted to residence, the applicability of his theory to the status of undocumented aliens remains uncertain. Undocumented immigrants are people who reside and usually labor here, sometimes for many years, but who have not been formally admitted to residence.

15. Walzer, "The Distribution of Membership," at 23; Walzer, *Spheres of Justice* at 62. This lack of recognition constitutes a form of tyranny because it violates what Walzer regards as the fundamental precept of justice in democratic societies: "different goods to different companies of men and women for different reasons and in accordance with different procedures." *Spheres of Justice* at 26. See discussion of this principle, which Walzer terms "complex equality," in the text.

16. Walzer, *Spheres of Justice*, at 54–55.

17. *Id.*

18. *Id.* at 58.

19. *Id.* at 60–61.

20. *Id.* at 62.

21. However, the prospect of an expanded guest worker program is back on the policy agenda in the United States. President Bush announced his support for a new temporary worker program in 2004 (*see* "President Bush Proposes New Temporary Worker Program," The White House, *available at* http://www.whitehouse.gov/news/releases/2004/01/20040107–3.html) and as of 2005, Congress is considering various proposed guest worker programs. The question whether any new program will provide participants with a "path to citizenship" or will insist

on temporariness is one of the central issues in contention in these debates. See discussion in chapter 1.

22. Still, at least a few scholars have not been deterred: one has invoked Walzer in support of extending lawful permanent resident aliens the right to vote in local elections, *see* Jamin Raskin, "Legal Aliens, Local Citizens: The Historical, Constitutional and Theoretical Meanings of Alien Suffrage," 141 *U. Pa. L. Rev.* 1391, 1448, n. 300 (1992); and some have enlisted him in support of lenient naturalization requirements, *see, e.g.,* Aleinikoff, "Citizens, Aliens, Membership and the Constitution," 7 *Const. Comm.* 9, 29, n.77 (1990) (citing Walzer for the proposition that "the communitarian perspective may favor easy terms of naturalization"). A few courts have cited Walzer as well: *U.S. v. Marta Concepcion, aka Marta Martinez, et al.,* 795 F.Supp. 1262, 1274 (E.D.N.Y. 1992) (Weinstein, J.) (" 'political justice is a bar to permanent alienage' ") (quoting Walzer, *Spheres of Justice* at 61). Others still have cited his metic analysis on behalf of affording undocumented aliens recognition as full national community members; *see, e.g.,* David Schwartz, "The Amorality of Consent," 74 *Cal. L. Rev.* 2143, 2163 (1986) (*reviewing* Peter H. Schuck and Rogers Smith, *Citizenship without Consent: Illegal Aliens in the American Polity* (Yale Univ. Press, 1985) (arguing that Walzer's theory implicitly supports full membership for undocumented aliens)).

23. Walzer, *Spheres of Justice* at 63 (emphasis added).

24. *See generally* Michael Walzer, *Interpretation and Social Criticism* (Harvard Univ. Press, 1987).

25. Walzer, *Spheres of Justice* at xiv.

26. *Id.* at 19.

27. *Id.* at 3. The notion of social good excludes privately valued goods, such as beautiful sunsets. *Id.* at 7.

28. Walzer posits the existence of the following distributive spheres: membership, security and welfare, the market, labor/work, "office" (by which he means political power), leisure, education, kinship and love, and "divine grace" (religion). However, he also acknowledges that "[n]o account of the meaning of a social good, or of the boundaries of the sphere within which it legitimately operates, will be uncontroversial." Walzer, *Spheres of Justice,* at 21. Elsewhere he writes, "[W]e never know where to the put the fences [between spheres]; they have no natural location. The goods they distinguish are artifacts; as they were made, so they can be remade. Boundaries then, are vulnerable to shifts in social meaning, and we have no choice but to live with the continual probes and incursions through which these shifts are worked out." *Id.* at 319.

29. *Id.* at 10.

30. "I call a good dominant if the individuals who have it, because they have it, can command a wide range of other goods. . . . [A]ll good things come to those who have the one best thing. Possess that one, and the others come in train. Or, to change the metaphor, a dominant good is converted into another good, into many others, in accordance with what often appears to be a natural process but is in fact magical, a kind of social alchemy." *Id.* at 10–11.

31. *Id.* at 26. Goods have "shared meanings" which are internal, and specific to those goods and those goods only. *Id.* at 9. "When meanings are distinct," Walzer argues, "distributions must be autonomous." *Id.* at 10.

It is worth noting that Walzer devotes very little effort to grounding the autonomy principle in "common understandings." He states merely that the appeal of complex equality is to "our ordinary understanding, and at the same time, against our common acquiescence in illegitimate conversion patterns." The arguments for complex equality "depend for their force on some shared understanding of knowledge, influence and power." *Id.* at 19. The principle thus often appears to have a kind of foundational, transcontextual status in Walzer's analysis.

32. *Id.* at 19.

33. *Id.* at 315.

34. *Id.* at 19. Walzer elsewhere describes tyranny as "a continual grabbing of things that don't come naturally, an unrelenting struggle to rule outside one's own company." *Id.* at 315.

35. *Id.* at 312.

36. *Id.* at 17.

37. *Id.* at 10.

38. *Id.* at 317.

39. *Id.* at 320.

40. *Id.* at 10.

41. Walzer suggests as much in the following statement: "No citizen's standing in one sphere or with regard to one social good can be undercut by his standing in some other sphere with regard to some other good" (*Id.* at 19). He also more explicitly adopts this approach in the chapter entitled "Hard Work," where he argues that poverty is a negative good that ought not to have effects in other spheres. *Id.* at 165–183.

42. *Id.* at 58.

43. Robert Fullinwider characterizes this position as the "full membership" principle, which he attributes to Walzer. *See* Robert K. Fullinwider, "Citizenship and Welfare," in *Democracy and the Welfare State* 261, 268 (Amy Gutmann, ed., Princeton Univ. Press, 1988).

44. Walzer, *Spheres of Justice* at 59.

45. It is not entirely clear whether Walzer's allowance of status differentials during the transition to citizenship represents a departure from his basic commitment to sphere separation. At first glance, it would appear to. In Walzer's account of the path to naturalization or "second admissions," the social good of membership is not merely distributed via the community's decision at the initial threshold about whether to admit the stranger; it is distributed as well through a process of incorporation of the alien into the political community, a process that culminates in naturalization. This approach presumes that there are two gradations of membership that properly structure rights and relationships within the community. Although the transition period from one to the other is supposed to be brief, its effects are hardly insignificant. Walzer considers the sphere of politics "probably the most important sphere" in a national community (Walzer, *Spheres of Justice* at 321), and during the transition, Walzer treats the political disenfranchisement of the alien as legitimate.

46. Walzer, *Spheres of Justice* at 19.

47. *Id.* at 29 (emphasis added).

48. Walzer, *Spheres of Justice* at 26.

49. I should emphasize that Walzer himself does not treat this transition period to citizenship as a relaxation of his separability requirement. He does not even make an affirmative argument justifying the extension of membership principles into the interior. Instead, he simply assumes the penetration and makes a case for limiting it. He emphasizes its limitations in time and in effect, and he also stresses the "entirely constrained" nature of second (as distinct from first) admissions decisions. *Id.* at 62. Walzer's major concern is clearly prophylactic: he takes great pains to underline that political justice allows for only the most ephemeral and limited commingling of spheres. Still, the fact that a person's lack of power in the membership sphere may legitimately translate into disenfranchisement in the sphere of politics, even temporarily, points to an ambiguity in Walzer's own view of the proper scope, or jurisdiction, of membership principles.

I suspect Walzer himself would probably deny that his treatment of "second admissions" represents a departure from his commitment to sphere separability. In characterizing complex equality, Walzer posits, as a general matter, that "[w]hat happens in one distributive sphere affects what happens in the others; we can look, at most, for relative autonomy." *Id.* at 10. Thus, transition to citizenship might well be characterized as a case of relative, rather than absolute, autonomy. A limited overlapping of spheres, in this view, would simply be a matter of transition at the margins, and hardly an exception to the rule.

50. See text accompanying note 42.

51. In Europe, the question of the legitimacy of deporting an alien after he or she has completed a sentence for a criminal violation is characterized as a problem of "double jeopardy." For a general discussion, see Jacqueline Bhabba, "Belonging in Europe: Citizenship and Post-National Rights," *UNESCO* 159 (1999), 11–23.

52. In another work, Walzer explicitly states that law is a source of "social meaning." He writes:

> Every human society provides for its members—they provide for themselves through the medium of justification—standards of virtuous character, worthy performance, just social arrangements. The standards are social artifacts; they are embodied in many different forms: legal and religious texts, moral tales, epic poems, codes of behavior, ritual practices. In all their forms they are subject to interpretation.

Michael Walzer, *Interpretation and Social Criticism* at 47–48.

53. *Id.* at 21.

54. *Id.* at 318–19.

55. *See, e.g., Wong Wing v. United States,* 163 U.S. 228 (1896) (Fifth and Sixth Amendments); *Almeida-Sanchez v. United States,* 413 U.S. 266 (1977) (Fourth Amendment).

56. *Bridges v. Wixon,* 326 U.S. 135, 148 (1945); *Bridges v. California,* 314 U.S. 252 (1941).

57. *See Mathews v. Diaz,* 426 U.S. 67 (1976).

58. *Graham v. Richardson,* 403 U.S. 365 (1971).

59. *Cabell v. Chavez-Salido,* 454 U.S. 432 (1982) (parole officer); *Ambach v. Norwick,* 441 U.S. U.S. 68 (1979) (public school teacher).

60. *In re* Griffiths, 413 U.S. 717 (1973) (bar examination); *Bernal v. Fainter*, 467 U.S. 216 (1984) (notary public).

61. *See, e.g., Mathews v. Diaz*, 426 U.S at 84 ("it is the business of the political branches of the Federal Government, rather than . . . that of the States . . . to regulate the conditions of entry and residence of aliens"); *Graham v. Richardson*, 403 U.S. at 378 ("State laws that restrict the eligibility of aliens for welfare benefits merely because of their alienage conflict with these overriding national policies in an area constitutionally entrusted to the Federal Government.")

62. *See, e.g., Mathews*, 426 U.S. at 77–78 (stating that "[t]he fact that all persons, aliens and citizens alike are protected by the Due Process Clause does not lead to the further conclusion that all aliens are entitled to enjoy all the advantages of citizenship," and holding that Congress may distinguish between alien and citizen in the exercise of its plenary power over immigration).

63. *Compare Graham v. Richardson*, 403 U.S. 365, 371–72 (in a case involving state discrimination against lawful permanent resident aliens, the Court held that "classifications based on alienage, like those based on nationality or race are inherently suspect and subject to close judicial scrutiny") (footnotes omitted) *with Plyler v. Doe*, 457 U.S. 202, 219 n.19 (1982) ("We reject the claim that 'illegal aliens' are a 'suspect class.' ").

64. *Compare Graham* , 403 U.S. 365, *with Cabell v. Chavez-Salido*, 454 U.S. 432 (1982). For a discussion of the economic/political distinction in the state alienage discrimination cases, see text accompanying notes 119–140, *infra*.

65. *See Hampton v. Mow Sun Wong*, 426 U.S. 88, 105, 114 (1976).

66. The immigration power is also exercised extraterritorially; for instance, the United States staffs consulates abroad, which grant visas to potential visitors and permanent resident aliens. Moreover, the government has engaged in a form of extraterritorial border control through its interdiction policy toward Haitian and Chinese asylum seekers. For a discussion of extraterritorial border control as it was exercised against Haitian asylum seekers, see generally Hiroshi Motomura, "Haitian Asylum Seekers: Interdiction and Immigrants' Rights," 26 *Cornell Int'l L. J.* 695 (1993).

67. *See, e.g., Almeida-Sanchez v. United States*, 413 U.S. 266, 272 (1973) (pursuant to government's immigration authority, government may conduct routine searches of individuals or conveyances "not only at the border itself but at its functional equivalents as well" in the interior).

68. *See Fiallo v. Bell*, 430 U.S. 787, 792 (1977) (*quoting Oceanic Navigation Co. v. Stranahan*, 214 U.S. 320 (1909)); *Shaughnessy v. Mezei*, 345 U.S. 206, 210 (1953).

69. Among the many commentaries to this effect, see generally Peter Schuck, "The Transformation of Immigration Law," 84 *Col. L. Rev.* 1 (1984); Louis Henkin, "The Constitution and United States Sovereignty: A Century of *Chinese Exclusion* and Its Progeny," 100 *Harv. L. Rev.* 853, 862–63 (1987); Aleinikoff, "Citizenship, Aliens, Membership and the Constitution"; Steven Legomsky, *Immigration and the Judiciary* 177–222 (Oxford Univ. Press, 1987); Ibrahim Wani, "Truth, Strangers and Fiction: The Illegitimate Uses of Legal Fiction in Immigration Law," 11 *Cardozo Law Rev.* 51 (1989).

70. *See* Aleinikoff, "Citizens, Aliens, Membership and the Constitution" at 11; T. Alexander Aleinikoff, *Semblances of Sovereignty: The Constitution, the State and American Citizenship* (Cambridge: Harvard Univ., 2002), 11–38, 151–81.

71. *See, e.g., Chae Chan Ping v. United States* (The Chinese Exclusion Case), 130 U.S. 581 (1889); *Fong Yue Ting v. United States*, 149 U.S. 698 (1893). For a useful narrative account of this period, see Lucy Salyer, "Captives of Law: Judicial Enforcement of the Chinese Exclusion Laws, 1891–1905," 76 *J. Am. Hist.* 91 (1989).

72. *See, e.g., Harisiades v. Shaughnessy*, 342 U.S. 580 (1952) (holding constitutional statute providing for deportation of alien members of the Communist Party); *Boutilier v. INS*, 387 U.S. 118 (1967) (holding then-existing "psychopathic personality" ground of exclusion encompassed homosexuals). In 1990, many, though not all, of the "ideological exclusion" provisions in the Immigration and Nationality Act (INA) were repealed (see the discussion later in this chapter), as were the provisions providing for exclusion of homosexuals on grounds of "psychopathic personality." However, carriers of the AIDS virus remain excludable. *See* 8 U.S.C. § 212(a)(1)(A)(i).

For narrative accounts of the historical treatment of noncitizen radicals under the immigration laws, see, e.g., Cole, "Enemy Aliens"; William Preston, Jr., *Aliens and Dissenters: General Suppression of Radicals, 1903–1933* (Harvard Univ. Press, 1963); John Higham, *Strangers in the Land: Patterns of American Nativism, 1860–1925* (2d ed., Rutgers Univ. Press, 1988); For discussion of the history of American immigration policy toward homosexuals, see Jorge L. Carro, "From Constitutional Psychopathic Inferiority to AIDS: What Is in the Future for Homosexual Aliens?" 7 *Yale L. & Pol'y Rev.* 201 (1989).

73. Motomura, "Haitian Asylum Seekers."

74. *See, e.g., United States ex rel. Knauff, v. Shaughnessy*, 338 U.S. 537, 544 (1950); *Fernandez-Roque v. Smith*, 734 F.2d 576, 582 (11th Cir. 1984).

In 2001, the U.S. Supreme Court held that certain resident aliens who have been ordered deported but whose countries of origin will not accept them may not be detained indefinitely. *Zadvydas v. Davis,"* 121 S. Ct. 2491 (2001). For further discussion, see Linda Bosniak, "A Basic Territorial Distinction," 16 *Geo. Immigr. L.J.* 407 (2002); T. Alexander Aleinikoff, "Detaining Plenary Power: The Meaning and Impact of *Zadvydas v. Davis*," 16. *Geo. Immigr. L. J.* 365 (2002).

75. *See, e.g.,* Louis Henkin, "The Constitution and United States Sovereignty: A Century of *Chinese Exclusion* and Its Progeny," 100 *Harv. L. Rev.* 853 (1987); T. Alexander Aleinikoff, "Federal Regulation of Aliens and the Constitution," 83 *Am. J. Int'l L.* 862 (1989); Legomsky, *Immigration and the Judiciary* 117–222 (1987).

76. *See Fiallo v. Bell*, 430 U.S. 787, 793 n. 5 (1977) (acknowledging a "limited judicial responsibility under the Constitution" to review immigration policy); *Zadvydas v. Davis*, 121 S. Ct. at 2501 (the plenary power doctrine is subject to "important constitutional limitations.")

77. *See Yamataya v. Fisher* (Japanese Immigrant Case), 189 U.S. 86 (1903).

78. Unlike aliens subject to removal on deportation grounds, "inadmissible aliens"—aliens who were not formally admitted into the country (whether or not they are actually physically present)—cannot claim much in the way of due process protections. With exceptions for returning permanent resident aliens—see *Landon v. Plasencia*, 459 U.S. 21 (1982)—the law remains more or less what it was nearly fifty years ago: "Whatever the procedure authorized by Congress is, it is due process as far as an alien denied entry is concerned." *United States ex rel. Knauff, v. Shaughnessy*, 338 U.S. 537, 544 (1950).

79. For example, despite (arguably) some ambiguity in the immigration statute, the Supreme Court held that Congress intended that the government prove its charges of deportability against the alien by "clear, unequivocal and convincing evidence" rather than by a preponderance, as the government had urged. *Woodby v. INS*, 385 U.S. 276 (1966).

80. *See generally* Hirosh Motomura, "Immigration Law after a Century of Plenary Power: Phantom Constitutional Norms and Statutory Interpretation," 100 *Yale L.J.* 545 (1990); Hiroshi Motomura, "The Curious Evolution of Immigration Law: Procedural Surrogates for Substantive Constitutional Rights," 92 *Colum. L. Rev.* 1625 (1992).

81. *Wong Wing v. United States*, 163 U.S. 228, 239 (1886) (J. Field, concurring in part and dissenting in part). His characterization of the government's position is based on "what seemed to [him] to be harsh and illegal assertions, made by counsel of the Government, on the argument of this case." *Id.* Justice Field also writes that "[t]he contention that persons within the territorial jurisdiction of this republic might be beyond the protection of the law was heard with pain on the argument at the bar." *Id.* at 243.

82. *Brief for the United States* at 12, *Wong Wing*, 163 U.S. 228.

83. *Id.*

84. *Id.* at 19.

85. Commentators have long described the *Wong Wing* decision as "'one of the bulwarks of the Constitution.'" *See, e.g.*, Gerald M. Rosberg, "The Protection of Aliens from Discriminatory Treatment by the National Government," *Sup. Ct. Rev.* 329 (1977), *quoting* Henry Hart, "The Power of Congress to Limit the Jurisdiction of Federal Courts: An Exercise in Dialectic," 66 *Harv. L. Rev.* 1362, 1387 (1953).

86. *Id.* at 237. (This was, of course, the era of Chinese Exclusion.) The Court stated that if detention or temporary confinement were provided for "as part of the means necessary to give effect to the provision or expulsion of aliens," this would be valid. Likewise, "it would be plainly competent for Congress to declare the act of an alien in remaining unlawfully within the United States to be an offence, punishable by fine or imprisonment, if such offence were to be established by a judicial trial." *Id.* at 235.

87. *Id.* at 237.

88. The Court here invokes the case of *Yick Wo v. Hopkins*, 118 U.S. 356 (1886), in which the Court had held that aliens are persons protected under the Fourteenth Amendment.

89. The holding in *Wong Wing* followed the Court's decision three years earlier in *Fong Yue Ting v. United States*, 149 U.S. 698 (1893), in which the Court had

concluded that deportation per se was not punishment. Thus, while the Court holds in *Wong Wing* that imprisonment at hard labor is punishment that requires full criminal due process before imposition, the Court continues to presume that deportation itself is not a punishment, and therefore that procedures in pursuance thereof are not limited by the constraints of due process or the right to trial by jury. The presumption that deportation is not punishment remains a fundamental tenet of immigration law today, though it has been roundly criticized.

90. *Id*. at 241.

91. *Yick Wo v. Hopkins*, 118 U.S. 356 (1886).

92. It is common for immigration law scholars to characterize the rights that aliens enjoy outside the immigration sphere as deriving from "the *Yick Wo* tradition." For a discussion, see Linda Bosniak, "Membership, Equality and the Difference That Alienage Makes," 60 *N.Y.U. L. Rev.* 1049, 1059–65 (1994).

93. The state's articulated objective for the ordinance was "to prevent our people from being burned in their beds at night by careless and irresponsible people using dangerous fires in wooden shanties so inflammable that no underwriter would insure them." *See* Points and Authorities for Defendant and Respondent at 87, *Yick Wo*, 118 U.S. 356 (1886).

94. *Yick Wo*, 118 U.S. at 1070.

95. *Plyler*, 457 U.S. 202, 215 (1982).

96. Of course, *Yick Wo* and *Plyler* differ from *Wong Wing* in one fundamental respect. The government power at issue in the former cases was that of the states, whereas in *Wong Wing* the power at issue was federal. In the state cases, the articulated government purpose had nothing to do with immigration regulation per se, whereas in *Wong Wing*, the government was expressly concerned with regulating immigration—in that case, the immigration of Chinese nationals. But the significance of the federal/state distinction in this context is largely irrelevant. Today, courts and commentators usually invoke *Yick Wo* and *Wong Wing* in the same breath when addressing the constitutional status of aliens and virtually never distinguish between them based on their respective institutional histories. The cases are understood to have articulated the principle that the constitutional rights of territorially present persons, citizens and aliens alike, are guaranteed as against *any* governmental power.

97. *See, e.g., Martinez v. Fox Valley Bus Lines*, 17 F.Supp. 576 (N.D. Ill., 1936) ("[I]t is the general rule that aliens, other than enemy aliens . . . may maintain suits in the proper courts to vindicate their rights and redress their wrongs."); *Bolanos v. Kiley*, 509 F.2d 1023 (2d Cir. 1975) ("[T]he familiar combination of 42 U.S.C. § 1983 and 28 U.S.C. § 1343(3) affords [all aliens, including illegal aliens] access to the federal courts to assert a claim of violation of [their constitutional rights]."). Many of the cases specifically addressing the rights of aliens to sue in tort and contract are cases that deal expressly with undocumented aliens. *E.g., Mendoza v. Monmouth Recycling Corp.*, 288 N.J. Super. 240, 248 (App. Div. 1996) ("[A] well established body of law holds that illegal aliens have rights of access to the courts and are eligible to sue therein to enforce contracts and redress civil wrongs such as negligently inflicted personal injuries.").

98. *See, e.g., Espinoza v. Farah Mfg. Co.*, 414 U.S. 86 (1973) (aliens protected from illegal discrimination under Title VII); *E.E.O.C. v. Tortilleria La Mejor*, 758

F. Supp. 585, 589 (E.D. Cal. 1991) ("We agree that aliens are protected from discrimination under the [Civil Rights Act of 1964]."). *But see Bhandari v. First Nat'l Bank of Commerce*, 887 F. 2d 609 (5th Cir. 1989) (en banc), *cert. denied*, 494 U.S. 1061 (1990) (§ 1981 does not prohibit alienage discrimination by private actors).

99. 326 U.S. 135 (1945).

100. *See, e.g., Almeida-Sanchez v. United States*, 413 U.S. 266, 273 (1973) (although, in the exercise of its plenary power to enforce the immigration laws, the federal government has wide latitude to conduct administrative searches of individuals and conveyances at the national border or "its functional equivalents" without probable cause, beyond the border region, government must have probable cause); *Illinois Migrant Council v. Pilliod*, 540 F.2d 1062, 1069 n.5 (1976) ("Congress' power to exclude aliens cannot be interpreted so broadly as to limit the Fourth Amendment rights of those present in the United States,").

These cases had been presumed to apply to all aliens in the United States. However, the Supreme Court more recently called into question—albeit in *dicta*—whether undocumented aliens in the United States are protected under the Fourth Amendment. *See United States v. Verdugo-Urquidez*, 494 U.S. 259 (1990). The matter of undocumented immigrants' protection under the Fourth Amendment remains unresolved. For helpful discussion, see, e.g., Victor Romero, "The Domestic Fourth Amendment Rights of Undocumented Immigrants: On *Guttierez* and the Tort Law-Immigration Law Parallel," 35 *Harv. C.R.-C.L. L. Rev.* 57 (2000).

101. Upon holding in *Plyler* that undocumented aliens are "persons within the jurisdiction" of the state for Fourteenth Amendment purposes, Justice Brennan wrote that this "only begins the inquiry. The more difficult question is whether the Equal Protection Clause has been violated. . . ." 457 U.S. at 215.

102. *Graham v. Richardson*, 403 U.S. at 372.

103. *Id*. at 378. The Court pointed out that although Congress had provided, pursuant to its immigration power, that indigent aliens were excludable (or non-admissible), Congress had not made aliens deportable who had become indigent by virtue of causes arising after their entry, but instead had determined to treat aliens, while they are here, like all other "persons within the jurisdiction of the United States" as entitled to "the full and equal benefit of all laws and proceedings for the security of persons and property as is enjoyed by white citizens." *Id*. at 377.

104. 426 U.S. 67 (1976).

105. *Id*. at 80.

106. *Id*. at 83. Specifically, the Court concluded that "it is unquestionably reasonable for Congress to make an alien's eligibility depend on both the character and the duration of his residence." *Id*.

107. *Id*. at 80.

108. The *Mathews* decision, in short, is based on the following syllogism: Congress's power to regulate the admission and expulsion of aliens is plenary and not (except perhaps in the most extreme circumstances) subject to judicial review; it was an act of Congress which excluded a class of aliens from access to social security benefits; therefore, this congressional action is subject to only the most deferential judicial review.

109. Rosberg, "The Protection of Aliens from Discriminatory Treatment by the National Government" at 294. Although Rosberg suggests that the federal government may have a special interest in matters concerning immigration, he adds that this merely "explain[s] why the federal government [may be able to] demonstrate a compelling need for a particular classification even though a state could not. . . . [I]t does not in any obvious way explain why the burden of justification on the federal government should be different from the burden on a state." *Id.*

110. *Adarand Constructors Inc. v. Pena*, 515 U.S. 200 (1995).

111. The *Mathews* analysis is untenable in the view of some critics because immigration regulation and the denial of social benefits to aliens implicate very different policy concerns and cannot, therefore, reasonably be painted with a single brush. *See* T. Alexander Aleinikoff, "Federal Regulation of Aliens and the Constitution," 83 *Am. J. Int'l L.* 862, 869–70 (1989) ("It should be apparent that some statutes burdening aliens are based on considerations other than a policy judgment regarding the number and classes of aliens who may enter or remain in the United States."). This represents a classic argument on behalf of "separation," as I have described it.

112. Rosberg points out that "[a]part from its comment [in *Graham*] that 'aliens as a class are a prime example of a 'discrete and insular minority,' " the Court has offered no theoretical explanation for bringing aliens within the suspect classification doctrine." Rosberg, "The Protection of Aliens from Discriminatory Treatment by the National Government" at 299. Rosberg himself discusses various possible rationales for treating aliens as a suspect class: the stigma theory, the immutable characteristics theory, the political powerlessness theory, and others. However, he concludes that whatever rationales are used to support suspect class status in the context of state discrimination, those rationales must support it with respect to federal discrimination as well.

113. For a typical articulation of this distinction, see Jesse Choper, "Discrimination Against Aliens," in *The Supreme Court: Trends and Developments 1981–1982* (Jesse Choper et al., eds., National Practice Institute, 1983) at 17: "If the Equal Protection Clause applies to the federal government, why is there this exception for aliens? Well, there is a reason why the Equal Protection clause does not apply full force to the federal government when discrimination against aliens is involved. It is that Congress has specifically delegated power in Article I of the Constitution to regulate immigration and naturalization of aliens."

114. *Mathews v. Diaz*, 426 U.S. 67, 84–85 (1976).

115. *See In re Griffiths*, 413 U.S. 717, 729 (1973) (holding that Connecticut's wholesale ban of resident aliens from admission to the bar violates the equal protection clause); *Sugarman v. Dougall*, 413 U.S. 634, 646 (1973) (holding as violative of the equal protection guarantee a New York law that allowed only citizens to hold permanent positions in the competitive class of the state civil service.).

116. *See especially Toll v. Moreno*, 458 U.S. 1 (1982), where the Supreme Court bypassed equal protection analysis altogether when faced with a challenge to Maryland's denial of in-state tuition benefits to nonimmigrant aliens and struck down the state law on preemption grounds.

117. Michael J. Perry, "Equal Protection, Judicial Activism, and the Intellectual Agenda of Constitutional Theory: Reflections on, and Beyond, *Plyler v. Doe*," 44

U. Pitt. L. Rev. 329, 334–335 (1983). For a more critical view of preemption analysis in this context, see Harold Koh, "Equality with a Human Face: Justice Blackmun and the Equal Protection of Aliens," 8 *Hamline L. Rev.* 51, 96–98 (1985) (Preemption analysis "effectively subordinates fourteenth amendment equal protection doctrine governing discrimination against resident aliens to the vagaries of federal immigration policy.").

118. Whether Congress possesses the power to authorize states to discriminate against aliens by devolving the federal government's immigration authority to the states has not been resolved by the courts. The Supreme Court in *Graham* specifically stated that Congress does "not have the power to authorize the individual states to violate the Equal Protection Clause." However, in that case, the Court concluded that Congress had not, in fact, authorized the states to discriminate, so the matter was not squarely addressed. Furthermore, in recent years, Congress *has* specifically authorized states to discriminate against aliens, most notably in the 1996 Welfare Reform Act. For contrasting views on whether states should be permitted to discriminate against aliens on federal authorization, see Michael J. Wishnie, "Laboratories of Bigotry? Devolution of the Immigration Power, Equal Protection, and Federalism," 76 *N.Y.U. L. Rev.* 493 (2001), and Howard Chang, "Migration Regulation Goes Local: The Role of the States in U.S. Immigration Policy: Public Benefits and Federal Authorization for Alienage Discrimination by the States," 58 *N.Y.U. Ann. Surv. Am. L.* 357 (2002).

119. *See, e.g., Bernal v. Fainter,* 467 U.S. 216, 220 (1984) ("We have . . . developed a narrow exception to the rule that discrimination based on alienage triggers strict scrutiny. This exception has been labeled the 'political function' exception. . . .").

120. *Sugarman v. Dougall,* 413 U.S. 634, 643, 649 (1973) (recognizing "the State's broad power to define its political community" and stating that "alienage itself is a factor that reasonably could be employed in defining 'political community' ").

121. *Foley v. Connelie,* 435 U.S. 291, 295 (1978) (*quoting Sugarman,* 413 U.S. at 648).
The Court wrote:

> It would be inappropriate . . . to require every statutory exclusion of aliens to clear the high hurdle of 'strict scrutiny,' because to do so would 'obliterate all the distinctions between citizens and aliens, and thus depreciate the historic values of citizenship. . . .' Accordingly, we have recognized 'a State's historical power to exclude aliens from participation in its democratic political institutions,' as part of the sovereign's obligation 'to preserve the basic conception of a political community. . . .' The practical consequence of this theory is that . . . [t]he State need only justify its classification by a showing of some rational relationship between the interest sought to be protected and the limiting classification. . . . [I]t represents the choice, and right, of the people to be governed by their citizen peers.

Id. at 295–96 (citations omitted).
Here, New York State's law requiring prospective police officers to possess citizenship was held to meet the test: "The police function fulfills a most fundamental

obligation of government to its constituency. Police officers in the ranks do not formulate policy, per se, but they are clothed with authority to exercise an almost infinite variety of discretionary powers." *Id.* at 297–98.

122. 454 U.S. 432 (1982).

123. Other jobs designated as peace officer positions included "toll takers, cemetery setons, fish and game wardens, furniture and bedding inspectors, voluntary fire wardens, racetrack investigators, county coroners, State Supreme Court and Courts of Appeal bailiffs, messengers at the State Treasurer's office, and inspectors for the Board of Dental Examiners." *Cabell*, 454 U.S. at 450–51 (Blackmun, Jr., dissenting).

124. *Id.* at 447.

125. *Id.* at 438. The Court continued: "We recognize a State's interest in establishing its own form of government, and in limiting participation in that government to those who are within 'the basic conception of a political community.' " *Id.* at 438–39 (*quoting Sugarman v. Dougall*, 413 U.S. 634, 642 (1973) (citation omitted)).

126. *Id.* at 439–40.

127. *Id.* at 439.

128. As the *Cabell* Court described it, "*Graham* implied that there would be very few—if any—areas in which a State could legitimately distinguish between its citizens and lawfully resident aliens." *Id.* at 438.

129. *Id.* at 439.

130. *Sugarman v. Dougall*, 413 U.S. 634, 641 (1973) (citation omitted).

131. *Id.* at 648. Not everyone agrees that voting rights should be confined to citizens. The question of whether aliens should be allowed to vote has recently been of special interest to scholars. For three very useful discussions of the issue, see generally Gerald L. Neuman, "We Are the People: Alien Suffrage in German and American Perspective," 13 *Mich. J. Int'l L.* 259 (1992) (arguing, *inter alia*, that although in the United States, liberal individualist and nationalist-communitarian conceptions of popular sovereignty compete, the liberal vision is more fundamental and allows for extending the right to vote to noncitizens); Raskin, "Legal Aliens, Local Citizens" at 1395–96 (1993) (arguing that providing aliens with access to the franchise is neither forbidden by the Constitution nor compelled by it, and making a normative case for alien suffrage based in a "politics of presence," pursuant to which "all community inhabitants, not just those who are citizens of the superordinate nation-state, form the electorate"); Gerald M. Rosberg, "Aliens and Equal Protection: Why Not the Right to Vote?," 75 *Mich. L. Rev.* 1092 (1977) (arguing for a return to the tradition of alien suffrage in the United States).

132. *Foley v. Connelie*, 435 U.S. 291, 298 (1978) (upholding exclusion of aliens from jobs as police officers).

133. *Ambach v. Norwick*, 441 U.S. 68, 78 (1979) (upholding exclusion from jobs as schoolteachers)

134. *Cabell v. Chavez-Salido*, 454 U.S. 432, 445 (1982) (upholding exclusion from probation officer positions).

135. *Foley*, 435 U.S. at 297 ("The essence of our holdings to date is that although we extend to aliens the right to education and public welfare, along with

the ability to earn a livelihood and engage in licensed professions, the right to govern is reserved to citizens.").

136. *Id.* at 303 (Marshall, J., dissenting) (*quoting Sugarman v. Douglall*, 413 U.S. 634, 647 (1973)).

137. *Id.* at 304.

138. *Id.* at 310 (Stevens, J., dissenting).

139. Gerald Rosberg, "Discrimination against the 'Nonresident' Alien," 44 *U. Pitt. L. Rev.* 399, 400 (1983).

140. *Bernal v. Fainter*, 467 U.S. 216, 220 (1984). As Justice Marshall concluded for the majority, "a notary's duties, important as they are, hardly implicate responsibilities that go to the heart of representative government. Rather, these duties are essentially clerical and ministerial." *Id.* at 225. The Court therefore applied strict scrutiny and found the state statute wanting. *Id.* at 227.

141. Although Walzer has not directly addressed the status of undocumented immigrants in his writing, he has suggested in conversation that justice—and his membership theory—would require legalization of those undocumented aliens who reside and work here. Conversation with Michael Walzer in New York, N.Y. (Oct. 19, 1993).

142. *Wong Wing v. U.S.*, 163 U.S. 228, 238 (1896); *Plyler v. Doe*, 457 U.S. 202, 215 (1982).

143. The Supreme Court has since suggested in *dicta* that the question whether undocumented aliens enjoy the protections of the Fourth Amendment remains an open one. *See United States v. Verdugo-Urquidez*, 494 U.S. 259, 272 (1990). Writing for the majority, Justice Rehnquist questioned the Court's assumption in *INS v. Lopez-Mendoza*, 468 U.S. 1032, 1050–51 (1984) that the Fourth Amendment applies to undocumented aliens. Justice Rehnquist distinguished the provisions of the Fifth and Sixth Amendments, which speak "in the relatively universal term of 'person,' " from the provisions of the Fourth Amendment, which are guaranteed only to "the people" (*Verdugo-Urquidez*, 494 U.S. at 269), and suggested that undocumented aliens, while clearly constitutional *persons*, are not necessarily among *the people* of the United States. *Id.* On the other hand, Justice Rehnquist suggested that, as compared with nonresident aliens involuntarily present in the national territory (who, he concluded, could definitively not be counted among "the people," and could therefore not invoke the Fourth Amendment's exclusionary rule), the undocumented had at least entered "the United States voluntarily and presumably had accepted some societal obligations." *Id.* at 272–73. In this way, he suggested that the undocumented might be entitled to greater levels of constitutional protection than at least some nonresident aliens. (Note that the nonresident alien who was "involuntarily present" in the United States in this case had been forcibly transported here as a prisoner by law enforcement authorities.) *Id.* at 262. As of this writing, the issue has not been addressed by the Supreme Court again. Lower courts have been divided on the language's significance. *See U.S. v. Esparza-Menoza*, 265 F. Supp. 2d 1254 (D. Utah 2003) (*aff'd*, 386 F.3d 953 (10th Cir. 2004)) (Fourth Amendment does not apply to undocumented immigrants) and *Martinez Augero v. U.S.*,

2005 U.S. Dist. Lexis 2412 (2005) (undocumented immigrant may claim protections of the Fourth Amendment).

144. *See generally* Linda S. Bosniak, "Exclusion and Membership: The Dual Identity of the Undocumented Immigrant under U.S. Law," 1988 *Wis. L. Rev.* 955, 977–87 (1988) (discussing the limited, but still significant, civil and social rights enjoyed by undocumented noncitizens).

145. *Moreau v. Oppenheim*, 663 F.2d 1300, 1307–08 (5th Cir. 1981); *see also Montoya v. Gateway Ins. Co.*, 401 A.2d 1102, 1104 (1979) (*cert. denied*, 81 N.J. 402 (1979)) (holding that in contract dispute between undocumented alien and insurance company, alien may sue because the "public policy of discouraging illegal immigration will not be subverted by according [undocumented] aliens access to our courts"); *Mendoza v. Monmouth Recycling Corp.*, 288 N.J. Super. 240, 248 (App. Div. 1996) ("illegal aliens have rights of access to the courts") (*citing Montoya*, 401 A.2d at 1102).

146. *See, e.g., Sure-Tan, Inc. v. NLRB*, 467 U.S. 883, 890 (1984) (National Labor Relations Act); *In re Reyes*, 814 F.2d 168 170 (5th146. Cir. 1987) (Fair Labor Standards Act); *EEOC v. Tortilleria La Mejor*, 758 F. Supp. 585, 590 (E.D. Cal. 1991) (Title VII); *Rajeh v. Steel City Corp.*, 813 N.E.2d 697, 702 (Ohio App. 2004) (Lebanese alien was an employee within meaning of state workers' compensation act, despite his status as alien subject to deportation); *but see Granados v. Windson Dev. Corp.*, 257 Va. 103 (1999) (holding claimant who was illegal alien was not an "employee" under Workers' Compensation Act). Soon after *Granados* was decided, the Virginia legislature amended the definition of employee in the Virginia Workers' Compensation Act to include "[e]very person, *including aliens* and minors, in the service of another under any contract of hire . . . *whether lawfully or unlawfully* employed." *See* Va. Code Ann. § 65.2–101. See also *Mendoza*, 288 N.J. Super. 240 (illegal alien with work-related injury was eligible for workers' compensation benefits).

147. Although undocumented immigrants are deemed covered persons under most employment protective legislation, they have been held ineligible to obtain important remedies for violations of these acts. See, most significantly, *Hoffman Plastics Compounds, Inc. v. Nat'l Labor Relations Bd.*, 122 S. Ct. 1275 (2002) (notwithstanding a finding that alien was illegally fired for exercising his rights under the National Labor Relations Act to form a union, he was denied remedy of back pay on grounds that he could not show he was "available for work" due to lack of employment authorization). For recent discussion of *Hoffman* and associated cases, see Ruben Garcia, "Ghost Workers in an Interconnected World: Going beyond the Dichotomies of Domestic Immigration and Labor Laws," 36 *U. Mich. J.L. Reform* 737 (2003); Katherine Fiske and Michael Wishnie, "The Story of *Hoffman Plastic Compounds, Inc. V. NLRB*: The Rules of the Workplace of Undocumented Immigrants," in *Immigration Stories* (David A. Martin and Peter Schuck, eds., Foundation Press, 2005).

148. *Plyler v. Doe*, 457 U.S. 202, 215–16 (1982). The challenged statute withheld state funds from school districts for the education of children not "legally admitted" into the United States, and permitted local districts to deny public

school enrollment to these same children. *Id.* at 205. Pursuant to the statute, several Texas school districts imposed a tuition fee on those children who were not "legally admitted aliens." *Id.* at 205 n.1.

149. *Id.* at 246 (Burger, C.J., dissenting) (*quoting Mathews v. Diaz*, 426 U.S. 67, 80 (1976)).

150. *Id.* at 245.

151. *Id.* As to why the *Mathews* analysis should be relevant in a case involving a challenge to a *state* alienage classification, the dissent merely stated that although "the Constitution imposes lesser constraints on the Federal Government than on the states with regard to discrimination against *lawfully* admitted aliens . . . the same cannot be said when Congress has decreed that certain aliens should not be admitted to the United States at all." *Id.* at 246 n.7.

152. Id. at 250. Justice Brennan criticizes the dissent's analysis here as circular, writing, "[t]he state must do more than justify its classification with a concise expression of an intention to discriminate." *Id.* at 227 (citation omitted).

Note that there is an important ambiguity on the preemption issue in the *Plyler* majority opinion. While arguing that states enjoy no power to classify aliens, Justice Brennan nevertheless wrote that "we cannot conclude that the States are without any power to deter the influx of persons entering the United States against federal law, and whose numbers might have a discernable impact on traditional state concerns." *Plyler*, 457 U.S. at 228 n.23 (*citing DeCanas v. Bica*, 424 U.S. 351, 354–56 (1976)). The question consequently becomes: When is a state law that regulates the status of aliens in some way a "classification" of aliens, which is prohibited, and when is it an effort to protect against "a discernable impact on traditional state concerns," which is not? Of course, this is a version of the question that plagues the alienage jurisprudence more globally: When is an alienage questions an equality question and when is it an immigration question—and how are we to tell the difference?

153. *Plyler*, 457 U.S. at 223. Counsel for the aliens, not surprisingly, sought to have the Court apply the same strict scrutiny that it had applied in *Graham*, on the theory that the children's undocumented immigration status should have no bearing on their equality interests, particularly in light of their status as minors.

154. *Plyler*, 457 U.S. at 228, 230. There is some ambiguity in the opinion about exactly which level of scrutiny was being applied. The Court held that the Texas law "can hardly be considered rational unless it furthers some substantial goal of the state." *Id.* at 224. Most commentators describe the Court's approach as an example of "intermediate scrutiny," but some argue otherwise.

155. *Id.* at 228.

156. *Id.* ("[E]ven making the doubtful assumption that the net impact of illegal aliens on the economy of the State is negative, we think it clear that '[c]harging tuition to undocumented children constitutes a ludicrously ineffectual attempt to stem the tide of illegal immigration. . . .'") (*quoting Doe v. Plyler*, 458 F. Supp. 569, 585 (E.D. Tex. 1978)).

157. *Id.* at 272. That deprivation takes on "inestimable toll . . . on the social, economic, intellectual and psychological well-being of the individual" who suffers

it, and acts as an overwhelming obstacle to the improvement of her status. *Id.* at 222 (*citing Brown v. Bd. of Educ.*, 347 U.S. 483 (1954)).

158. *Plyler*, 457 U.S. at 221. Later, the Court wrote: "It is difficult to understand precisely what the State hopes to achieve by promoting the creation and perpetuation of a subclass of illiterates within our boundaries, surely adding to the problems and costs of unemployment, welfare and crime." *Id.* at 230.

159. *See, e.g.*, Perry, "Equal Protection, Judicial Activism, and the Intellectual Agenda of Constitutional Theory" at 329 ("The Court's decision in *Plyler* . . . was unmistakably and fundamentally activist in character, and . . . contributed to the analytical confusion of earlier cases.").

160. Kenneth Karst, "Paths to Belonging: The Constitution and Cultural Identity," 64 *N.C. L. Rev.* 303, 324 (1986) (citation omitted).

161. California's 1996 anti-immigrant initiative Proposition 187 represented a frontal challenge to *Plyler*. If enforced, the California ballot initiative would have (among other things) excluded undocumented aliens from the public schools. Its supporters consistently described the law as providing " 'a promising vehicle for the Court to reverse its position [in *Plyler*].' " Seth Mydans, "Move in California to Bar Service to Aliens," *N.Y. Times, May 22,* 1994, at A18 (quoting a Proposition 187 campaign official). For general discussion, see Linda Bosniak, "Opposing Prop. 187: Undocumented Immigrants and the National Imagination," 28 *Conn. L. Rev.* 555 (1996). Prop. 187 was eventually invalidated in federal court, but strong antipathy to *Plyler* persists among restrictionist organizations. *See, e.g.*, Mark Levin, "Citizenship Up for Grabs: The Supreme Court and Immigration," Center for Immigration Studies, Mar. 2005 (describing *Plyler v. Doe* as "perhaps the most egregious of the Court's immigration rulings").

162. Other scholars have made this point. *See, e.g.*, T. Alexander Aleinikoff, "Good Aliens, Bad Aliens and the Supreme Court," in IX *Defense of the Alien* 46, 48 (L. Tomasi, ed., 1986) ("*Plyler* [ ] is properly understood not as a 'pro-alien' case, but rather as a case about innocent children."); Schuck, "The Transformation of Immigration Law," at 55 ("[I]t was the 'innocent' children, not their 'guilty' parents, to whom Texas denied equal protection. . . . Had Texas adopted an analogous system of free public *adult* education or job training . . . the Court apparently would not have upheld an equal protection claim by the *parents*.").

163. *Plyler v. Doe*, 457 U.S. 202, 220 (1982) (*quoting Trimble v. Gordon*, 430 U.S. 762, 770 (1977)).

164. The majority's assumption that all undocumented alien adults possess this status as the result of their own "voluntary" action is problematic. To begin with, many undocumented aliens have fled their countries in fear of persecution but have nevertheless not presented themselves to the authorities in the United States to apply for political asylum because they believe, often rationally, that their chances of success are exceptionally low. During the 1980s, for example, political asylum applications filed by nationals of Guatemala and El Salvador were granted at the rate of approximately 2 percent and 3 percent, respectively (*see* Bill Frelick, "No Central Americans Need Apply," *L.A. Times, June 25,* 1991, at B7), and many aliens remained underground rather than risk deportation. At some

level, it is difficult to describe such individuals as having "voluntarily" assumed undocumented status.

Furthermore, the notion of voluntariness can itself be problematic, at least at the margins. For instance, has an undocumented alien who came to this country to ensure that she can support her family acted "voluntarily?" Has she been, in David Martin's terms, "drawn or driven?" *See* David A. Martin, "Reforming Asylum Adjudication: On Navigating the Coast of Bohemia," 138 *U. Pa. L. Rev.* 1247, 1275 (1990) (arguing that most asylum applicants in the United States are "*both* drawn and driven") (emphasis added).

165. While the Court declined to treat education as a "fundamental right" whose deprivation would require strict judicial scrutiny, Justice Brennan stated that education is not "merely some governmental 'benefit' indistinguishable from other forms of social welfare legislation." *Plyler*, 457 U.S. at 221. Throughout the opinion, the Court emphasized the " 'supreme importance' " of education in "maintaining our basic institutions." *Id.* (*quoting Meyer v. Nebraska*, 262 U.S. 390, 400 (1923)).

166. *Id.* at 219. These aliens "should be prepared to bear the consequences" of their illegal action, "including, but not limited to, deportation." *Id.* at 220.

167. *Id.* at 218–19 (footnotes omitted).

168. *Id.* at 219 n.18 (*quoting Doe v. Plyler*, 458 F.Supp. 569, 585 (E.D. Tex. 1978)).

169. Walzer, *Spheres of Justice* at 9.

170. 8 U.S.C.A. § 1324a (authorizing fines and imprisonment for employers who knowingly hire undocumented aliens and monetary penalties for those who fail to verify employees' authorization to work in this country). It is generally acknowledged that, for a variety of reasons, the U.S. employer sanctions regime has failed to curtail the entry and residence of undocumented immigrants in this country. Nearly two decades after their implementation, the numbers of undocumented immigrants here are at an all-time high (as of 2004, the population of undocumented immigrants was estimated to be at least 10 million; see, e.g., Urban Institute, "Undocumented Immigrants: Facts and Figures," January 2004, http://www.urban.org/urlprint.cfm?ID=8685). However, with sanctions on the books, advocates and courts can less easily seek to point to the government's patent lack of commitment to interior enforcement as a rationale for protecting the rights of the undocumented.

171. This is also true in the statutory context. Even more explicitly than in *Plyler*, the Court's holding in *Sure-Tan, Inc. v. NLRB*, that undocumented aliens are covered employees under the National Labor Relations Act (discussed in the text), was premised on the absence of employer sanctions provisions. The Court there wrote:

> This Court has observed that '[t]he central concern of the INA is with the terms and conditions of admission to the country and the subsequent treatment of aliens lawfully in the country. . . .' The INA evinces 'at best evidence of a peripheral concern with employment of illegal entrants. . . .' For whatever reason, Congress has not adopted provisions in the INA making it un-

lawful for an employer to hire an alien who is present or working in the United States without appropriate authorization. . . . Since the employment relationship between an employer and an undocumented alien is hence not illegal under the INA, there is no reason to conclude that application of the NLRA to employment practices affecting such aliens would necessarily conflict with the terms of the INA.

Sure-Tan, Inc., 467 U.S. at 892–93 (citations omitted).

Following the passage of employer sanctions, however, the Supreme Court held that although undocumented immigrant workers remain protected employees, they are not entitled to backpay as a remedy (pay they would have earned in the absence of the labor violation) because they cannot be deemed "available for work." *Hoffman Plastics Compounds, Inc. v. Nat'l Labor Relations Bd.*, 122 S. Ct. 1275, 1282 (2002). At present, the courts appear to distinguish between monetary remedies for work performed (available) and monetary remedies for work that would have been performed but for the violation (not available). For further discussion, see Fiske and Wishnie, "The Story of *Hoffman Plastic Compounds, Inc. v. NLRB*: The Rules of the Workplace of Undocumented Immigrants."

172. Walzer, *Spheres of Justice* at 58.

173. *Id.* at 57.

174. Here again, we see the ambiguity in Walzer's work about the propriety of deporting resident aliens. It would appear that Walzer is not arguing that governments should abandon their deportation power altogether; we know that he thoroughly endorses the right of a national society to regulate its own membership. Yet he is disturbed by the effects of the specter of deportability on the life of the noncitizen residing in the political community. The difficulty with his argument is that, at least to some degree, the specter of deportability *always* shapes the experience of noncitizens inside the political community because, in virtually all countries, noncitizens are subject to expulsion in at least some circumstances.

175. *See generally* 8 U.S.C.A. § 1251(a) (classes of deportable aliens). The Act also contains various provisions that ameliorate the effect of the deportation provisions by providing relief from removal.

176. *See* Aleinikoff, "Citizens, Aliens, Membership and the Constitution," " at 27 n.67 ("Actually, as long as the deportation power exists, there remains a huge difference between aliens and citizens. While expanding our concept of constitutional membership may impose limits on the power to deport, we would have to travel a lot of ground to get rid of the deportation power altogether. . . .").

177. *See* Mae Ngai, *Impossible Subjects: Illegal Aliens and the Making of Modern America* (Princeton Univ. Press, 2004). *See also* Bosniak, "Exclusion and Membership."

178. *See, e.g.*, Bosniak, "Exclusion and Membership" at 986 ("Undocumented aliens often fear exposing themselves to the exclusionary powers of the state and will often forego the exercise of . . . rights in order to avoid such an eventuality. Undocumented immigrants commonly decline to report private or official abuse and are frequently unwilling to pursue civil claims in court or to step forward to receive benefits to which they are entitled.").

179. Sometimes, the "everpresent threat of deportation" functions not just collaterally and indirectly but directly and formally. California's Proposition 187 contained provisions requiring educators, health care providers, and public entities providing social services to report the presence of any apparent or suspected undocumented immigrants they encountered. Under these provisions, the very act of seeking to enforce non-immigration-related rights would have directly subjected undocumented immigrants to immigration penalties.

Proposition 187 was struck down by a federal court on preemption grounds. *League of United Latin American Citizens v. Wilson*, 908 F. Supp. 755 (C. D. Cal. 1995). In 1999, after a change of governor and a federal court-directed mediation process, the state of California dropped its appeal of the decision. *See* Patrick McDonnell, "Davis Won't Appeal Prop. 187 Ruling, Ending Court Battles," *Los Angeles Times*, July 29, 1999, at A1.

180. On the other hand, they have often been subject to *indirect* challenge. In many of the cases challenging the INS's (now DHS's) enforcement procedures, for example, immigrants and their representatives were presumably motivated by a desire to protect noncitizens from the collateral effects of the government's power to regulate the borders. They sought, and achieved, certain limits on where and how the government can enforce the immigration laws. According to these decisions, aliens are not fair game for INS enforcement during every waking moment of their lives. *See, e.g., United States v. Brignoni-Ponce*, 422 U.S. 873, 886–87 (1975) ("The likelihood that any given person of Mexican ancestry is an alien is . . . a relevant factor, but standing alone it does not justify stopping all Mexican-Americans to ask if they are aliens."); *Orhorhaghe v. INS*, 38 F.3d 488, 497 (9th Cir. 1994) (holding "foreign-sounding name" insufficient basis for a seizure under the Fourth Amendment). Procedural constraints on government actions such as these have served to lessen the collateral impact that the "everpresent threat of deportation" has on the lives of undocumented aliens. In theory, they have helped to enforce the *separation* of the zone of territorial personhood from the imperatives of the border.

Note, however, that the Supreme Court has held that the Fourth Amendment's exclusionary rules does not apply to civil deportation hearings. This means that evidence seized in violation of the Fourth Amendment can still be used in deportation proceedings. *See INA v. Lopez-Mendoza*, 468 U.S. 1032 (1984). *See generally* Victor C. Romero, Note, "Whatever Happened to the Fourth Amendment?: Undocumented Immigrants' Rights after *INS v. Lopez-Mendoza* and *United States v. Verdugo-Urquidez*," 65 S.Cal. L. Rev. 999 (1992); *see also* Bosniak, "Exclusion and Membership" at 971–77.

181. *Sure-Tan Inc. v. NLRB*, 467 U.S. 883 (1984); *Hoffman Plastics v. NLRB*, 535 U.S. 137 (2002); *EEOC v. Tortilleria La Mejor*, 758 F.Supp. 585 (E.D. Cal. 1991).

182. *Sure-Tan Inc.*, 467 U.S. 883 Note, however, that the employer sanctions provisions of the immigration laws prohibit employers from employing or continuing to employ an individual that the employer knows to be unauthorized to work in the United States. *See generally* 8 U.S.C. § 1324(a). Often, the employer will claim to have contacted the immigration authorities pursuant to his or her duty to comply with employer sanctions and not as an effort to thwart protected labor

activity. Consequently, the initial question in these cases often concerns the factual issue of employer motivation.

183. Supporters of the current rules permitting immigration authorities to make use of otherwise tainted information about the immigration status of undocumented workers maintain that the government should not be penalized for the bad acts of employers; the borders still need enforcing. Yet the effects of permitting such use are perverse. A legal regime that deters undocumented immigrants from pressing for formally granted labor rights will often serve to enhance their attractiveness to employers and, hence, employer demand for their labor. This increased demand, in turn, likely exacerbates the rates of unauthorized migration.

Note also that the undocumented immigrant employee who suffers from illegal employment action is not entitled to the full panoply of remedies that other employees enjoy. Undocumented workers fired from their jobs in violation of law cannot be reinstated (*Sure-Tan*), nor can they receive "back pay"—the salary they would have received but for the legal violation (*Hoffman Plastics*). On the other hand, undocumented immigrants are still able to enforce their right to salary for work already performed. For general discussion of the interplay between immigration and labor law regimes and their impact on undocumented immigrants, see generally Garcia, "Ghost Workers in an Interconnected World"; Fiske and Wishnie, "The Story of *Hoffman Plastic Compounds, Inc. V. NLRB*"; Rebecca Smith and Amy Sugimori, "Undocumented Workers: Preserving Rights and Remedies after *Hoffman Plastic Compounds v. NLRB*", National Employment Law Project, Apr. 2003, *available at* www.nelp.org/iwp/rights/organize/nlghoff040303.cfm.l.

184. The immigration statute provides, among other things, that an alien who is convicted of a "crime involving moral turpitude" within five years of entry and sentenced to or imprisoned for a year or more is deportable, as is an alien who has committed multiple crimes at any point. *See generally* 8 U.S.C.A. § 1251(a)(2)(A)(i)&(ii). Likewise, an alien who commits an "aggravated felony" (a term that is defined exceptionally broadly by statute) is subject to deportation at any time. § 1251 (a)(2)(A)(iii). In this context, the rules of membership and the criminal law effectively occupy the same terrain. The result is a compounding of penalties for the noncitizen; a noncitizen who commits a crime is subject to the same criminal punishment that would be imposed on any convicted criminal *and also* to the immigration penalties the law prescribes. The same conduct, in other words, is subject to regulation and penalty both within the sphere of membership and the spheres governing territorial personhood. The convergence of spheres entailed in this context would seem to violate Walzer's autonomy principle, but Walzer does not address the issue. For a comment on the injustice of subjecting a person to deportation after, and in addition to, criminal punishment, see *Aguilera-Enriquez v. INS*, 516 F.2d 565, 573 (6th Cir. 1975) (cert. denied, 423 U.S. 1050 (1976)) (DeMascio, D.J., dissenting) ("In this case, the respondent, a resident alien for seven years, committed a criminal offense. Our laws require that he be punished and he was. Now, he must face additional punishment in the form of banishment.").

185. Prior to passage of the 1990 Immigration Act, the INA provided for deportation of aliens who, among other things, advocated or taught opposition to all organized government; who were members of or affiliated with the Communist

Party or any other "totalitarian" organization; who advocated the economic, international and governmental doctrines of world communism; and who wrote, published, or distributed materials that were subversive. *See generally* 8 U.S.C. § 1251(a)(6)(A)(H) (1988) (repealed 1990). These provisions were among those referred to as McCarran-Walter Act provisions, after the congressional sponsors who enacted them into law in 1952. The 1990 Immigration Act eliminated these deportation provisions (although totalitarian party membership remains a basis for the denial of *admission* for some aliens, *see* 8 U.S.C. § 1182(a)(3)(D)(I) (Supp. V 1993)). The 1990 Act did, however, include provisions making deportable aliens who have "engaged in . . . any terrorist activity." 8 U.S.C. § (a)(4)(B) (Supp. V 1993). The government's current interpretation of this latter provision allows it to deport individual aliens who have supported the lawful and legitimate activities of organizations that are themselves deemed to have engaged in terrorist activity. Cole, *Enemy Aliens* at 57–71.

186. *ADC*, 714 F. Supp. 1060 (C.D. Cal. 1989) (aff'd in part and rev'd in part on other grounds, vacated sub norm); *American-Arab Anti-Discrimination Committee v. Thornburgh*, 970 F.2d 501 (9th Cir. 1991). Specifically, the government charged the aliens with membership in or affiliation with the Popular Front for the Liberation of Palestine, an organization that, it alleged, advocated world communism and the unlawful destruction of property.

187. *See, e.g., Bridges v. Wixon*, 326 U.S. 135, 148 (1945) ("Freedom of speech and of press is accorded aliens residing in this country."); *see also U.S. v. Verdugo-Urquidez*, 494 U.S. 259, 271 (1990) (*citing Bridges*, 326 U.S. at 148) (noting that resident aliens enjoy First Amendment rights).

188. *Brandenburg v. Ohio*, 395 U.S. 444, 447 (1969).

189. *ADC*, 714 F. Supp. at 1077–78. The plaintiffs pointed out that in *Harisiades v. Shaughnessy*, 342 U.S. 580 (1952), the Supreme Court assumed that the same First Amendment standard generally applied to government regulation of expressive conduct also applied in the deportation context. *See ADC*, Plaintiffs' Memorandum; *see also ADC*, 714 F. Supp. at 1077–78. In *Harisiades*, the Court rejected the aliens' challenge to one of the ideological deportation provisions of the day on grounds that the provision did not run afoul of the then-prevailing First Amendment standard, thereby indicating that the deportation context was to be treated no differently from any other context for the First Amendment purposes. *Harisiades*, 342 U.S. at 592.

190. *See ADC*, Plaintiffs' Memorandum; *see also ADC*, 714 F. Supp. at 1081.

191. The plaintiffs argued that "but for the McCarran-Walter provisions . . . they would engage in the expressive activities that led the INS to charge them under the McCarran-Walter provisions in 1987." *Id.*

192. For a discussion of the rights noncitizens enjoy as territorial persons, see text accompanying notes 81–101.

193. *ADC*, 714 Supp. at 1074. *See also id.* at 1079 ("[T]he Government would have us conclude that while aliens have First Amendment rights generally, within the deportation forum these rights are 'irrelevant' and can be severely circumscribed.").

194. *Id.* at 1075.

195. The fact that the government's position here takes the form of a separation argument makes clear that the terms "separation" and "convergence" are relative terms, and that within the broader theory of complex equality, separation and convergence can cut both ways. (As Walzer writes, "[b]oundaries must, of course, be defended from both sides." *Spheres of Justice*, at 317.) Those who are concerned with defending the government's power to define the community's membership can and do argue that the membership domain requires greater insulation from penetration of the norms of equal personhood; they contend, in other words, that it requires greater "separation." In contrast, those who are concerned with individual rights can and do argue that a greater penetration of the norms of equal personhood into the membership domain is essential; they maintain, in other words, that a further "convergence" of spheres in this context is appropriate.

My concern in this chapter, however, is not with the status of noncitizens "inside" immigration law but instead with their status on the "outside" (to the extent, of course, that we can determine what lies inside and what out, which is precisely the question at issue). Therefore, in my use of the terms *separation* and *convergence* here, my point of reference is the general status of noncitizens in the various spheres of national life *other than* the membership sphere. When I speak of convergence, I refer to penetration of membership principles into those other spheres, and when I speak of *separation*, I refer to the insulation of those other spheres from the penetration of membership principles. This is how Walzer employs these concepts in his analysis of metic status; for him, separation means that the status of aliens within the society at large is insulated from the action of membership principles, whereas convergence means that membership principles have acted outside their proper domain to shape the lives of aliens in the civil, economic, and political domains of the national society. But once again, the government's argument in *ADC* shows that the terms "separation" and "convergence" are relative, and in particular, that separation arguments can be made on behalf of the government's immigration power as well as against it.

196. T. Alexander Aleinikoff et al., *Immigration: Process and Policy* (West, 3rd ed. 1995), *supra* at 515 ("The [ADC] decision . . . represents the first time in American history that a deportation statute has been invalidated on constitutional grounds"). Note, however, that the Supreme Court *has* struck down on constitutional grounds sub-parts of the Immigration and Nationality Act provision providing relief from deportation, and has invalidated particular applications of deportation-related provisions on constitutional grounds.

197. *ADC*, 714 F. Supp. at 1076. The court quoted, among other cases, *Fong Yue Ting v. United States*, 149 U.S. 698, 712, 713 (1893), an otherwise notorious plenary power case from the Chinese exclusion era, for the propositions that the "immigration power must be exercised 'consistent[ly] with the Constitution,' and [that] the judiciary must intervene where 'required by the paramount law of the Constitution.'" *Id.* at 1075 (citation omitted).

198. *See ADC*, 714 F. Supp. at 1078 (citing *Harisiades v. Shaughnessy*, 432 U.S. 580 (1952)). See *supra* note 356.

199. *Id.* Some commentators have raised questions about Judge Wilson's interpretation of *Harisiades*, arguing that alienage may well have been "a factor in the [*Harisiades*] analysis," because the Court "actually applied a standard that was more deferential to the government than [the prevailing first amendment standard] required." Katherine L. Pringle, "Silencing the Speech of Strangers: Constitutional Values and the First Amendment Rights of Resident Aliens," 81 *Geo. L.J.* 2073, 2088 (1993). *See also* Steven H. Legomsky, *Immigration Law and Policy* (Foundation Press, 3rd ed., 2002), at 84–85 (questioning whether the *Harisiades* Court had indeed applied then-prevailing First Amendment standards).

200. *ADC*, 714 F. Supp. at 1078 (quoting *Pacific Glass & Elec. v. Cal. Pub. Utilities Comm'n*, 475 U.S. 1, 8 (1986) (internal citation omitted)).

201. The analysis was subsequently reaffirmed by the court of appeals in this case: "The values underlying the First Amendment," the Ninth Circuit wrote, "require the full applicability of First Amendment rights to the deportation setting." *Am. Arab Anti-Discrimination Comm. et al. v. Reno*, 70 F. 3d 1045, 1064 (9th Cir. 1995).

202. *See, e.g., Galvan v. Press*, 347 U.S. 522, 531 (1954) (holding that the constitutional prohibition against ex post facto laws does not apply to deportation statutes).

203. *ADC*, 714 F. Supp. at 1081–82. In this analysis, Judge Wilson followed Justice Murphy, who in concurrence in *Bridges v. Wixon* wrote the following:

> Since resident aliens have constitutional rights, it follows that Congress may not ignore them in the exercise of its "plenary" power of deportation. . . . [T]he First Amendment and other portions of the Bill of Rights make no exception in favor of deportation laws or laws enacted pursuant to a "plenary" power of the Government. Hence, the very provisions of the Constitution negative the proposition that Congress, in the exercise of its "plenary" power, may override the rights of those who are numbered among the beneficiaries of the Bill of Rights.
>
> Any other conclusion would make our constitutional safeguards transitory and discriminatory in nature. Thus, the Government would be precluded from enjoining or imprisoning an alien for exercising his freedom of speech. But the Government at the same time would be free, from a constitutional standpoint, to deport him for exercising that very same freedom. The alien would be fully clothed with his constitutional rights when defending himself in a court of law, but he would be stripped of those rights when deportation officials encircle him. I cannot agree that the framers of the Constitution meant to make such an empty mockery of human freedom.

Bridges v. Wixon, 326 U.S. 135, 161–62 (1945) (Murphy, Jr., concurring).

204. *ADC*, 714 F. Supp. at 1081–82. For the most part, the court appeared to assume that the denial of First Amendment rights to aliens in the deportation setting serves *inadvertently* to render their rights meaningless outside that context. However, in his discussion of the threshold issue of standing, Judge Wilson concluded

that the government had purposefully "used the McCarran-Walter provisions to quell the [ ] First Amendment activities" of the aliens in this case. *Id.* at 1069.

205. *ADC*, 714 F. Supp. at 1084.

206. Following several rounds of appeals and remands, the Supreme Court concluded that intervening legislation had stripped the courts of jurisdiction to hear the case. *Reno v. Am.-Arab Anti-Discrimination Comm.*, 525 U.S. 471 (1999). The new provisions allow for deportation of aliens who have "engaged in terrorist activity," with "terrorist activity" very broadly defined. 8 U.S.C. § 1251 (a)(4)(B) (Supp. V. 1993). Although those new provisions are currently under challenge, they seem unlikely to be struck down on First Amendment grounds, particularly in the aftermath of 9/11. For general discussion, see David Cole, *Enemy Aliens* (New Press, 2003).

207. For a thorough theoretical exposition of the "circles of membership" position, see generally David Martin, "Due Process and Membershp in the National Community: Political Asylum and Beyond," 44 *Pittsburgh L. Rev.* 165, 210–15 (1983).

208. See generally, Charles Taylor, "Cross-Purposes: The Liberal-Communitarian Debate, in *Liberalism and the Moral Life* (Nancy L. Rosenblum, ed., Harvard U. Press, 1989).

209. Recall Justice Brennan's statement that the immigrant children's parents are persons "who elect to enter our territory by stealth and in violation of our law" and who consequently "should be prepared to bear the consequences, including, but not limited, to deportation." *Plyler v. Doe*, 457 U.S. at 220.

210. *See* Joseph H. Carens, "Immigration and the Welfare State," in *Democracy and the Welfare State* 207, 227 (Amy Gutmann, ed., Princeton Univ. Press, 1988) ("[A]ny restrictions on freedom of movement (even residency requirements) entail the subordination of an important liberal value to other concerns."); David C. Hendrickson, "Migration in Law and Ethics," in *Free Movement: Ethical Issues in the Transnational Migration of People and Money* 217 (Brian Barry and Robert E. Goodin, eds., Pennsyl. State U. Press, 1992) ("[T]he idea . . . that the free movement of individuals across borders often serves important human values" is "normally associated with liberalism."). The separation model might be said, therefore, to reflect a kind of nationalist liberalism. See discussion in chapter 6.

211. When I speak here of exclusion of persons on national grounds, I do not use the term national in the cultural but rather in the political sense. My point is that both the separation model and the convergence models endorse the right of the state to exclude legal outsiders to the national political community. See chapter 6 for further discussion.

212. Michael J. Perry, "Modern Equal Protection: A Conceptualization and Appraisal," 79 *Col. L. Rev.* 1023, 1061 (1979) (emphasis added).

213. *Id.* Among the justices, Chief Justice Rehnquist has most fully and consistently articulated the vision that alienage matters constitutionally. In his view, alienage matters because citizenship matters:

[T]he constitution itself recognizes a basic difference between citizens and aliens. That distinction is constitutionally important in no less than 11 instances in a political document noted for its brevity. . . . In constitutionally defining who is a citizen of the United States [in the Fourteenth Amendment], Congress obviously thought it was doing something, and something important. Citizenship meant something, a status in and relationship with a society which is continuing and more basic than mere presence or residence.

214. Perry, "Equal Protection, Judicial Activism, and the Intellectual Agenda of Constitutional Theory" at 335.

215. Of course, precisely what the contours of this "moment" are remains controversial. Strictly interpreted, Walzer's metic theory seems to suggest that the only relevant moment in the relationship between alien and government in the membership sphere is the moment of territorial admission (with the exception of the moment of admission to citizenship, which occurs sometime soon after territorial admission). Other proponents of the basic separation model concede that membership regulation may affect the life of the alien at various discrete moments in addition to territorial and political admission; they allow, for instance, that the government may deport aliens who commit certain crimes.

216. While I have characterized separation and convergence as the two principal models for thinking about the relationship between membership and personhood in current legal thought about alienage, I should emphasize that these are in fact models and are not meant to be understood as absolute and unvarying positions in practice. In fact, adherents of both models very often express their views in somewhat relative terms. Those who support a separation position rarely argue that government may not legitimately make *any* distinctions between citizens and aliens who reside in the society, something a pure separation position would require. On the other hand, many of those who endorse a convergence perspective tend to recognize that aliens are entitled to core constitutional rights as required by *Wong Wing* and *Yick Wo*.

217. Thinking in terms of spheres tends to sound archaic to the contemporary constitutional ear, and sphere-thinking might at some point pass from the scene in the immigration context as it has elsewhere (replaced, perhaps, by "balancing" approaches). For an account of the rise and fall of sphere-thinking in American legal thought, *see generally* Duncan Kennedy, "Toward an Historical Understanding of Legal Consciousness: The Case of Classical Legal Thought in America," *1850–1940, 3 Res. L. & Soc.* 3, 4–5 (1980) ("[T]he legal elite conceived [of legal relationships as] instances of a single general legal relation: each of them was an example of the delegation of legal powers absolute within their spheres. The role of the judiciary (its sphere of absolute power) was the application of a single, distinctively legal, analytic apparatus to the job of policing the boundaries of these spheres."); *see also* T. Alexander Aleinikoff, "Constitutional Law in the Age of Balancing," *96 Yale L.J.* 943, 949, 951 (1987) (arguing that in contrast to today's "balancing" methodology, under nineteenth and early twentieth century jurisprudence, disputes were resolved "in a categorical fashion. Supreme Court opinions generally recognized differences in kind, not degree. . . . [A]ttention to the strength of the state's interests was part of the process of categorization, not a balance of competing interests" (citations omitted)); Richard H. Fallon, Jr., "Individual Rights and the Powers of Government," *27 Ga. L. Rev.* 343, 348–49 (1993)

("Modern constitutional discourse tends to blur analysis of the *scope* of governmental power with assessment of practical necessity or the *weight* of governmental interests. . . . Today, historical limits on the scope of federal powers are generally viewed as anachronisms.") (emphasis added) (internal citations omitted).

On the other hand, one scholar has argued that despite their general abandonment of nineteenth century substantive commitments, contemporary courts have continued to employ a methodology of policing the boundaries of spheres in constitutional adjudication, and he has defended the merits of this approach in some contexts. *See* Richard H. Pildes, "Avoiding Balancing: The Role of Exclusionary Reasons in Constitutional Law," 45 *Hastings L.J.* 711 (1994). Pildes writes:

> The Constitution recognizes numerous distinct spheres of interaction, each governed by its own logic of norms that defines the kinds of reasons for which government can appropriately act. Constitutional adjudication (much more often than we recognize) is primarily about defining the normative structure of these different spheres. . . . Recapturing this method would entail understanding constitutional law as the effort to set the boundaries between separate spheres of authority. On this view, the Constitution makes certain values appropriate bases for state action in some arenas, and other values appropriate in other arenas. . . . If we focus . . . on the central role of "excluded reasons," constitutional law would become less a matter of rights versus state interests and more a matter of defining the boundaries on political authority in different arenas.

Id. at 712–15 (citing Joseph Raz, *Practical Reason and Norms* (2d ed., Princeton Univ. Press, 1990)).

We should also bear in mind that the regulatory spheres whose boundaries the field debates are social constructions; they reflect particular historical commitments which are bound to time and place and are therefore subject to change. Walzer himself acknowledges that both the content of the distributive spheres, and the location of the boundaries between them, are the product of "social meanings." *Spheres of Justice* at 9. Moreover, he recognizes that "[w]e never know exactly where to put the fences; they have no natural location." *Id.* at 319. As a substantive matter, Walzer finds our own "social meanings" as to the character and boundaries of spheres far more uniform and harmonious than I do, but his broader point remains: there is nothing intrinsically necessary about these spheres, their content, or the location of the boundaries between them. *See also* Pildes, "Avoiding Balancing" at 727 ("The boundaries between distinct spheres are, themselves, simply matters of cultural understandings. To enforce these boundaries is to enforce these understandings. . . .").

Some have argued that what Walzer calls the "membership sphere"—normatively embraced to a greater or lesser degree by both the convergence and separation perspectives—may eventually be replaced with some other, postnational way of thinking about social belonging. A growing body of literature is working in a variety of different ways to critique national understandings of membership and to establish the outlines of an alternative to nationally based models of belonging. For extensive discussion and citations, see Bosniak, "Citizenship Denationalized," 7 *Ind. J. Global Legal Stud.* 447 (2000) (symposium issue).

CHAPTER 4
CONSTITUTIONAL CITIZENSHIP THROUGH THE PRISM OF ALIENAGE

1. Alexander M. Bickel, "Citizenship in the American Constitution," 15 *Ariz. L. Rev.* 369 (1973).

2. The Supreme Court's 1999 decision in *Saenz v. Roe*, 526 U.S. 489 (1999), dramatically intensified the interest in the privileges or immunities clause and has fueled a debate over the question of whether the clause is likely to enjoy a full-scale renaissance. *See, e.g.*, Laurence H. Tribe, "*Saenz* Sans Prophecy: Does the Privileges or Immunities Revival Portend the Future—or Reveal the Structure of the Present?," 113 *Harv. L. Rev.* 110 (1999); F. H. Buckley, "Liberal Nationalism," 48 *UCLA L. Rev.* 221 (2000); Tim A. Lemper, Note, "The Promise and Perils of 'Privileges or Immunities': *Saenz v. Roe, 119 S. Ct. 1518 (1999),*" 23 *Harv. J.L. & Pub. Pol'y* 295 (1999).

3. This is the classic reading. *See, e.g., Slaughter-House Cases*, 83 U.S. (16 Wall.) 36, 94 (1872) (Field, J., dissenting) ("The first clause of this [the Fourteenth]Amendment determines who are citizens of the United States, and how their citizenship is created."); T. Alexander Aleinikoff, "Re-reading Justice Harlan's Dissent in *Plessy v. Ferguson*: Freedom, Antiracism, and Citizenship," 1992 *U. Ill. L. Rev.* 961, 964 (1992) ("[The Fourteenth Amendment] provided, for the first time, a constitutional definition of citizenship. . . .").

4. *See* Charles L. Black, Jr., *Structure and Relationship in Constitutional Law* 33–66 (Louisiana State Univ. Press, 1969). For additional citations to a fast-growing body of scholarship advancing such an "aggressive reading" of the clause, see Christopher Eisgruber, "Political Unity and the Powers of Government," 41 *UCLA L. Rev.* 1297, 1328, n.117 (1994).

5. Against the suggestion that the equal protection clause is not the appropriate textual home for the principle of equal citizenship, Kenneth Karst argued in 1977 that the clause "shows every sign of being able to bear the full meaning of the equal citizenship principle." Kenneth L. Karst, "Forward: Equal Citizenship under the Fourteenth Amendment," 91 *Harv. L. Rev.* 1, 43 (1977).

6. *The Slaughter-House Cases,* 83 U.S. (16 Wall.) at 36. As one commentator described the case, the Court held that the privileges or immunities clause of Section 1 of the Fourteenth Amendment "protected only what was already otherwise protected in the Constitution." Lino A. Graglia, "Do We Have An Unwritten Constitution?—The Privileges or Immunities Clause of the Fourteenth Amendment," 12 *Harv. J.L. & Pub. Pol'y* 83, 83 (1989).

7. *See* sources cited *infra* note 53.

8. Some progressives have suggested that a revival of the privileges or immunities clause could serve the interests of the marginalized and excluded. *See, e.g.*, Angela P. Harris, "Beyond Equality: Power and the Possibility of Freedom in the Republic of Choice," 85 *Cornell L. Rev.* 1181, 1183 (2000) ("[T]he Privileges or Immunities Clause was about freedom: specifically, the freedom of six million or so people of African descent. . . . [It was] an exercise in considering the relevance of [the already existing literature on natural rights] to the project of emancipation."). Harris describes this project in lamenting terms as the "road not taken." *Id.* at 1184.

Note, however, that proponents of a revitalization of the privileges or immunities clause have included supporters of limited government, judicial restraint, and laissez-faire constitutionalism. *See, e.g.*, Clarence Thomas, "The Higher Law Background of the Privileges or Immunities Clause of the Fourteenth Amendment," 12 *Harv. J.L. & Pub. Pol'y* 63 (1989); *see also* Phillip Kurland, "The Privileges or Immunities Clause: 'Its Hour Come Round at Last'?," 1972 *Wash. U. L.Q.* 405, 414 (1972) (describing support of "privileges or immunities as a means to establish a constitutional doctrine of laissez-faire with regard to industrial and commercial activities").

9. Linda Bosniak, "Citizenship Denationalized," 7 *Ind. J. Global Legal Stud.* 447, 450–453, 489–491 (2000); Nancy Fraser and Linda Gordon, "Civil Citizenship against Social Citizenship? On the Ideology of Contract-versus-Charity," in *The Condition of Citizenship* 90, 90 (Bart Van Steenbergen, ed., Sage, 1994) (describing citizenship as "a weighty, monumental, humanist word" that has "no pejorative uses").

10. One of these, as I have suggested earlier, is that the concept is so utterly flexible and protean in meaning that its usefulness in analytic discussion is sometimes compromised. See chapter 2.

11. Bickel, "Citizenship in the American Constitution."

12. Will Kymlicka and Wayne Norman, "Return of the Citizen: A Survey of Recent Work on Citizenship Theory," 104 *Ethics* 352, 354 (1994).

13. In chapter 3, I discuss the development and significance of the American jurisprudence of personhood and its impact on noncitizens. See also Linda S. Bosniak, "Exclusion and Membership: The Dual Identity of the Undocumented Worker Under United States Law," 1988 *Wis. L. Rev.* 955 [hereinafter Bosniak, "Exclusion and Membership"]; Aleinikoff, "Re-reading Justice Harlan's Dissent in *Plessy v. Ferguson*;" Hiroshi Motomura, "Immigration Law after a Century of Plenary Power: Phantom Constitutional Norms and Statutory Interpretation," 100 *Yale L.J.* 545 (1990). Recently, the Supreme Court reiterated its long-standing position that aliens enjoy fundamental rights as territorially present persons. "The Due Process Clause applies to all 'persons' within the United States, including aliens, whether their presence here is lawful, unlawful, temporary, or permanent." *Zadvydas v. Davis*, 533 U.S. 678, 693 (2001).

14. William N. Eskridge, "The Relationship between Obligations and Rights of Citizens," 69 *Fordham L. Rev.* 1721, 1742–49 (2001); *see also* Mark Strasser, "The Privileges of National Citizenship: On *Saenz*, Same-Sex Couples, and the Right to Travel," 52 *Rutgers L. Rev.* 553 (2000) (urging that the privileges or immunities clause be interpreted to protect the right of same-sex couples to wed).

15. *See* William E. Forbath, "Caste, Class, and Equal Citizenship," 98 *Mich. L. Rev.* 1, 7–9 (1999); Kenneth L. Karst, "The Coming Crisis of Work in Constitutional Perspective," 82 *Cornell L. Rev.* 523 (1997).

16. Linda S. Bosniak, "Universal Citizenship and the Problem of Alienage," 94 *Nw. U. L. Rev.* 963 (2000).

17. Laurence H. Tribe, *American Constitutional Law* § 7–6, at 1325 (3d ed., Foundation Press, 2000).

18. John Hart Ely, *Democracy and Distrust: A Theory of Judicial Review* 25 (Harvard Univ. Press, 1980).

19. *E.g.* Michael Kent, *Curtis*, "Historical Linguistics, Inkblots, and Life after Death: The Privileges or Immunities of Citizens of the United States," 78 *N.C.L. Rev.* 1071, 1149 (2000); William N. Eskridge, "The Relationship between Obligations and Rights of Citizenship"; Jeffrey Rosen, "Exclusion, Discrimination and the Making of Americans: America in Thick and Thin," *New Republic*, Jan. 5 & 12, 1998, 29, 36 (reviewing Rogers M. Smith, *Civic Ideals: Conflicting Views of Citizenship in U.S. History* (Yale U. Press, 1997).

20. Black, *Structure and Relationship in Constitutional Law* at 52–53. *See also* Kurland, "The Privileges or Immunities Clause" at 415:

> It is possible that for some the [Privileges or Immunities] clause was deemed inhospitable because by its language it confined its protection to citizens, while the equal protection clause and the due process clause afford sanctuary for all persons, including corporations, which the Supreme Court had specifically held to be outside the ambit of the privileges or immunities clause.

Id.

21. *See* Linda S. Bosniak, "The Citizenship of Aliens," *Social Text* at 29 (Fall 1998); Bosniak, "Universal Citizenship and the Problem of Alienage." Gerald L. Neuman expressed similar concerns in response to Judith Shklar's work on rights and American citizenship. *See* Gerald L. Neuman, "Rhetorical Slavery, Rhetorical Citizenship," 90 *Mich. L. Rev.* 1276, 1283–90 (1992) (reviewing Judith N. Shklar, *American Citizenship: The Quest for Inclusion* (1991)).

22. In his dissent in *Saenz*, Justice Thomas argues that before reinvoking the privileges or immunities clause as the basis for constitutional decision, the Court must, among other things, "consider whether the Clause should displace, rather than augment, portions of our equal protection and substantive due process jurisprudence." *Saenz*, 526 U.S. 489, 528 (Thomas, J., dissenting).

23. Kurland, "The Privileges or Immunities Clause" at 420.

24. *See, e.g.*, Kurland, "The Privileges or Immunities Clause" at 419 ("The equal protection clause has already required that classifications be rationalized so that differences in treatment between aliens and citizens would have to be particularly justified."). Tribe makes a similar argument: grounding new rights in the privileges or immunities or citizenship clauses would seem, he acknowledges, to leave aliens behind. Yet "by prohibiting discrimination in legal rights among all *persons*—citizens and aliens alike—[the equal protection clause could], in effect . . . secure the 'privileges or immunities of citizens of the United States' to all *persons* within the jurisdiction of a particular state." Tribe, *American Constitutional Law* at 1325. Under this approach, the equal protection clause would be used to piggyback onto the privileges or immunities clause to accomplish for aliens indirectly what cannot (by dint of text) be done directly. In the end, however, Tribe concludes that equal protection would not require perfectly identical treatment of citizens and aliens. "With respect to entitlement to at least some of the privileges or immunities of national citizenship, aliens and citizens may simply not be similarly situated," he writes. *Id.*

Of course, this supplementarity strategy raises various questions about exactly how rights would be divided up under a citizenship-centered rights regime: which rights would remain personhood rights and which would end up as rights of citizenship? If this approach left most of the rights enjoyed by aliens intact, it would seem to do little toward rationalizing our existing due process— and equal protection—based fundamental rights doctrine, the pursuit of which has been a prime motivator for citizenship revivalists in the first place.

25. The Fourteenth Amendment provides in part, "No state shall make or enforce any law which shall abridge the privileges or immunities of citizens of the United States." U.S. Const. amend. XIV, § 1.

26. Ely, *Democracy and Distrust* at 25.

27. Philip Bobbitt, *Constitutional Fate: Theory of the Constitution* 89 (Oxford Univ. Press, 1982); *see also* Note, "Membership Has Its Privileges and Immunities: Congressional Power to Define and Enforce the Rights of National Citizenship," 102 *Harv. L. Rev.* 1925, 1931 n.43 (1989):

> [Understanding citizenship] as a binding relationship between the individual and the political community, under which the polity is obligated to guard and respect certain fundamental rights of the individual . . . does not necessarily exclude aliens from the protection of these same fundamental rights. Aliens have generally been extended the same individual guarantees as those enjoyed by persons who have achieved the legal status of citizenship.

Id.

28. *See* Karst, "Forward" at 25 (describing alien rights cases of the 1970s as "promot[ing] the principle of equal citizenship").

29. For earlier articulations of the notion of the "citizenship of aliens," see Bosniak, "The Citizenship of Aliens" at 29–35; Bosniak, "Universal Citizenship and the Problem of Alienage"; *see also* Ruth Rubio-Marin, "National Limits to Democratic Citizenship," 11 *Ratio Juris* 51, 54–55 (1998) (urging recognition of the "democratic citizenship" of resident aliens); Virginie Guiraudon, "Citizenship Rights for Non-citizens: France, Germany and the Netherlands," in *Challenge to the Nation-State: Immigration in Western Europe and the United States* 272 (Christian Joppke, ed., Oxford Univ. Press, 1998) (describing civil, social and political rights enjoyed by aliens as "citizenship rights").

The concept of "alien citizenship" may resemble the sort of Zen Buddhist koan Charles Black refers to in describing the apparently paradoxical notion of "substantive due process." Black, *Structure and Relationship in Constitutional Law.* In a more postmodern vein, we might characterize "alien citizenship" as a "performative contradiction," one that serves "to expos[e] the contradictory characteri of previous conventional formulations of the universal" as expressed through the idea of citizenship. *See* Bosniak, "Universal Citizenship and the Problem of Alienage" at 981 (quoting Judith Butler, "Sovereign Performatives in the Contemporary Scene of Utterance," 23 *Critical Inquiry* 350, 366–67 (1997)).

30. In the nineteenth century, American political thought distinguished between natural rights, civil rights, political rights, and social rights, and citizenship was associated with only the first two of these. *See* Nancy F. Cott, "Marriage and Women's Citizenship in the United States, 1830–1934," 103 *Am. Historical Rev.* 1440, 1448–49 (1998); Earl Maltz, "Reconstruction Without Revolution: Republican Civil Rights Theory in the Era of the Fourteenth Amendment," 24 *Hous. L. Rev.* 221 (1987); Jeffrey Rosen, "Translating the Privileges or Immunities

Clause," 66 *Geo. Wash. L. Rev.* 1241 (1998). Political rights became integral to our conception of citizenship only over the course of the twentieth century. A number of scholars have recently urged expansion of the class of rights associated with citizenship still further by advocating recognition of what some have termed "economic citizenship." *See, e.g.*, Forbath, "Caste, Class, and Equal Citizenship"; Karst, "The Coming Crisis of Work in Constitutional Perspective"; Alice Kessler-Harris, *In Pursuit of Equity: Women, Men, and the Quest for Economic Citizenship in 20th Century America* (Oxford Univ. Press, 2001).

31. Cott, at 1448.

32. *Id.* at 1441–42.

33. Christopher Eisgruber, "The Fourteenth Amendment's Constitution," 69 *S. Cal. L. Rev.* 47, 71 (1995) ("[The clause's] declaration of citizenship decisively repudiates state sovereignty.").

34. *Dred Scott v. Sandford*, 60 U.S. (19 How.) 393 (1857).

35. Bickel, "Citizenship in the American Constitution" at 374.

36. *See The Slaughter-House Cases*, 83 U.S. (16 Wall.) 36, 72 (1872) (describing the first sentence of the first clause of the Fourteenth Amendment as providing "a definition of citizenship").

37. Mark Tushnet, *Taking the Constitution Away from the Courts* 191 (Princeton Univ. Press, 1999); *see also* Eisgruber, "The Fourteenth Amendment's Constitution" at 78 (arguing that the Fourteenth Amendment "articulat[es] citizen identity").

38. The citizenship clause declares as citizens all persons born or naturalized in the United States. Congress possesses naturalization power under Article I, Section 8, pursuant to which it may define the criteria for accession to citizenship after birth. It is, therefore, the citizenship clause, together with the naturalization decisions that Congress may make pursuant to the naturalization power, that defines the class of citizens.

Although there have been disputes over the years about the precise contours of the class of Fourteenth Amendment citizens—the most recent concerning the status of U.S.-born children of undocumented immigrants—on the whole, the amendment's definition of the citizenship class is relatively uncontroversial.

39. For the pro-incorporation position, see, e.g., Akhil Reed Amar, "The Bill of Rights and the Fourteenth Amendment," 101 *Yale L.J.* 1193 (1992); Michael Kent Curtis, *No State Shall Abridge: The Fourteenth Amendment and the Bill of Rights* (Duke Univ. Press, 1986); Kevin Christopher Newsom, "Setting Incorporationism Straight: A Reinterpretation of the *Slaughter-House Cases*," 109 *Yale L.J.* 643, 648 (2000) (arguing that "the Framers' purpose of incorporating Bill of Rights freedoms through the Privileges or Immunities Clause may be accomplished without disturbing the *Slaughter-House* precedent"). For arguments urging a narrower, nonincorporationist interpretation of the privileges or immunities clause, see Raoul Berger, *Government by Judiciary: The Transformation of the Fourteenth Amendment* 22, 31–32, 38 (Harvard Univ. Press, 1977); and Charles Fairman, "Does the Fourteenth Amendment Incorporate the Bill of Rights? The Original Understanding," 2 *Stan. L. Rev.* 5 (1949).

40. For arguments on behalf of an antidiscrimination reading of the privileges or immunities clause, see, e.g., John Harrison, "Reconstructing the Privileges or

Immunities Clause," 101 *Yale L.J.* 1385, 1388 (1992) (providing an "equality-based reading" of the privileges or immunities clause and concluding that "the main point of the clause is to require that every state give the same privileges and immunities of state citizenship . . . to all of its citizens"); Graglia, "Do We Have an Unwritten Constitution?" (arguing that the privileges or immunities clause, like the due process and equal protection clauses, was meant to ensure the protection of civil rights for blacks); Berger, *Government by Judiciary* at 20–36. For opposing views, see Ely, *Democracy and Distrust* at 24 ("[I]t is no small problem for the [antidiscrimination] interpretation of the privileges or immunities clause that it would render the equal protection clause superfluous. . . . [The Clause] seems to announce rather plainly that there is a set of entitlements that no state is to take away."); Michael Kent Curtis, "Resurrecting the Privileges or Immunities Clause and Revising the *Slaughter-House Cases* without Exhuming *Lochner*: Individual Rights and the Fourteenth Amendment," 38 *B.C. L. Rev.* 1 (1996) (reading the privileges or immunities clause to prohibit states from abridging a body of preexisting national rights); Note, "Membership Has Its Privileges and Immunities" at 1937 (suggesting a reading of "citizenship" as providing certain "nontextual guarantees" to members of the political community); Richard L. Aynes, "On Misreading John Bingham and the Fourteenth Amendment," 103 *Yale L.J.* 57, 104 (1993).

41. The debate is in part historical. Some scholars have argued the rights the framers sought to guarantee by way of the privileges or immunities clause were only civil, and not social or political rights. *See, e.g.*, Earl M. Maltz, "Citizenship and the Constitution: A History and Critique of the Supreme Court's Alienage Jurisprudence," 28 *Ariz. St. L.J.* 1135, 1190 (1996); Rosen, "Translating the Privileges or Immunities Clause" at 1245 (describing the Framers' "broader purpose . . . to extend civil rights (or privileges and immunities of citizenship), but not political or social rights, to all citizens, black and white, on equal terms"); *see also* Daniel J. Levin, "Reading the Privileges or Immunities Clause: Textual Irony, Analytical Revisionism, and an Interpretive Truce," 35 *Harv. C.R.-C.L. L. Rev.* 569, 571 (2000) (arguing that "the normative content of the 'privileges or immunities of citizens of the United States' is embedded in conceptions of structural participation of self-government rather than in more general notions of personal liberty") (citation omitted).

In contrast to these readings, a number of scholars have argued recently that the rights of citizenship should be understood, on historical and normative grounds, to entail economic rights. *See, e.g.*, William E. Forbath, "Why Is This Rights Talk Different from All Other Rights Talk? Demoting the Court and Reimagining the Constitution," 46 *Stan. L. Rev.* 1771 (1994); Karst, "The Coming Crisis of Work in Constitutional Perspective"; Bruce Ackerman and Anne Alstott, "Your Stake in America," 41 *Ariz. L. Rev.* 249 (1999).

42. Bickel, "Citizenship in the American Constitution."

43. *See, e.g.*, Maltz, "Citizenship and the Constitution" at 1190 ("The text, structure and history of the Constitution reflect a keen appreciation of the importance of the political relationships inherent in both state and national citizenship, as well as the potential relevance of those relationships to the allocation of a wide variety of rights and benefits.").

44. *See* Peter H. Schuck, "The Devaluation of American Citizenship," 3 *Geo. Immigr. L.J.* 1, 13 (1989).

> [T]he distinctive meaning of American citizenship . . . has been transformed in recent decades by a public philosophy that . . . [has] reduced almost to the vanishing point the marginal value of citizenship as compared to resident alien status. . . . Not only do aliens need or want [it] less; many of those who *do* want it for their children need expend remarkably little in order to get it.

Id. (emphasis added); *see also* Eskridge, "The Relationship between Obligations and Rights of Citizens."

Justice Rehnquist has penned what is probably the most pointed judicial articulation of this position:

> [T]he Constitution itself recognizes a basic difference between citizens and aliens. That distinction is constitutionally important in no less than 11 instances in a political document noted for its brevity. . . . In constitutionally defining who is a citizen of the United States, Congress obviously thought it was doing something and something important. Citizenship meant something, a status in and relationship with a society which is continuing and more basic than mere presence or residence.

Sugarman v. Dougall, 413 U.S. 634, 651–52 (1973) (Rehnquist, J., dissenting).

45. *See, e.g.*, Rogers M. Smith, *Civic Ideals: Conflicting Visions of Citizenship in U.S. History* 2 (Yale Univ. Press, 1997) (describing laws pertaining to acquisition and loss of citizenship status *and* laws pertaining to general rights of residents as "citizenship laws").

46. *Cf.* Bosniak, "Difference That Alienage Makes."

47. Bobbitt, *Constitutional Fate* at 88.

48. See discussion in text accompanying notes 24–27.

49. Alexander M. Bickel, *The Morality of Consent* 51 (Yale Univ. Press, 1975) (describing the "traditional minimal content of the concept of citizenship").

50. This characterization seems questionable: describing the clause as "defining citizenship" suggests that it provides a definition of what citizenship substantively entails. As Douglas Smith has written, the clause is better viewed as "defin[ing] the conditions sufficient for attaining the status of 'citizen.' " Douglas G. Smith, "Citizenship and the Fourteenth Amendment," 34 *San Diego L. Rev.* 681, 693 (1997).

51. *Minor v. Happersett*, 88 U.S. (21 Wall.) 162, 166 (1875).

52. The Supreme Court's recent decision in *Saenz v. Roe*, 526 U.S. 489 (1999) has been characterized by some scholars as representing a major step toward an unraveling of *The Slaughter-House Cases. See, e.g.*, Buckley, "Liberal Nationalism." Determining whether this reading of *Saenz* is overly optimistic will have to await further decisions from the Court.

53. For arguments that *Slaughter-House Cases* badly distorted constitutional rights doctrine by, in effect, forcing the equal protection and due process clauses to bear the weight for which they were, and are, ill-equipped, see, e.g., Tribe, *American Constitutional Law* at 1317 (noting that for many constitutional scholars, "the problems [associated with] the textual gymnastics arguably necessary

to find protection of *substantive* rights in a provision whose words seem most apparently concerned with *process*—have become insuperable"); Kurland, "The Privileges or Immunities Clause" at 406 ("[O]nly the privileges or immunities clause speaks to matters of substance; certainly the language of due process and equal protection does not."); and Ely, *Democracy and Distrust* at 18, 22–30 (arguing "that 'substantive due process' is a contradiction in terms—sort of like 'green pastel redness' " and urging new attention to the privileges or immunities clause as a source of substantive rights). For a contrary view on the effect of the *Slaughter-House Cases*, see Walter Dellinger, "Remarks on Jeffrey Rosen's Paper," 66 *Geo. Wash. L. Rev.* 1293, 1293 (1998):

> Although *Slaughter-House* was wrong, I have never agreed with the many scholars who believe that its fundamental error was that it eliminated the correct clause for the national protection of individual rights (the Privileges and Immunities Clause) thereby "forcing" later interpreters to rely upon the wrong clause (the Liberty/Due Process Clause). . . . Having the Due Process Clause do the work intended for the Privileges and Immunities Clause may be awkward, but it is not a constitutional tragedy.

Id.; *see also* Rosen, "Translating the Privileges or Immunities Clause" at 1242–43 (arguing that "the new conventional wisdom about the virtues of resurrecting the Privileges or Immunities Clause is wrong. . . . Overruling *Slaughter-House* would solve so few of the problems in modern Fourteenth Amendment jurisprudence that it's not clear that a textualist revival would be worth the trouble").

54. *Minor*, 88 U.S. (21 Wall.) at 165–66.

55. As the Court in *Slaughter-House* maintained, the reach of the privileges or immunities clause imparts only rights of national citizenship, which confers upon the individual the right

> " 'to come to the seat of government to assert any claim he may have upon that government, to transact any business he may have with it, to seek its protection, to share its offices, to engage in administering its functions' . . . [to] free access to its seaports . . . to the subtreasuries, land offices, and courts of justice in the several States.' . . . [and] to demand the care and protection of the Federal government over his life, liberty, and property when on the high seas or within the jurisdiction of a foreign government."

Slaughter-House Cases, 83 U.S. (16 Wall.) 36, 79 (1872) (quoting *Crandall v. Nevada*, 73 U.S. (6 Wall.) 35, 44 (1867)).

56. Bickel, "Citizenship in the American Constitution" at 378.

57. *See, e.g.*, Black, *Structure and Relationship in Constitutional Law* at 33–66; Rebecca E. Zietlow, "Belonging, Protection and Equality: The Neglected Citizenship Clause and the Limits of Federalism," 62 *U. Pitt. L. Rev.* 281 (2000); Jennifer S. Hendricks, "Women and the Promise of Equal Citizenship," 8 *Tex. J. Women & L.* 51 (1998); Arthur Kinoy, "The Constitutional Right of Negro Freedom," 21 *Rutgers L. Rev.* 387, 395 (1967):

> [T]he national citizenship bestowed upon the Negro by the first sentence of the Fourteenth Amendment contained as an essential attribute of this new

status the right to be free from the stigma of inferiority implicit in the institution of slavery, the right to be free from discrimination by reason of race in the exercise of rights or privileges generally available to white citizens.

See also D. Smith, "Citizenship and the Fourteenth Amendment" at 690 (arguing that "[t]he Citizenship Clause of Section 1 may be interpreted to represent a guarantee binding upon both the state and federal governments of certain fundamental rights inherent in the concept of citizenship as understood at the time of ratification of the Amendment"); Robert J. Kaczorowski, "Revolutionary Constitutionalism in the Era of the Civil War and Reconstruction," 61 *N.Y.U. L. Rev.* 863, 912–13 (1986) ("Understood within the context of the Declaration of Independence, natural rights theory, and nationalist constitutionalism, the Citizenship Clause of the fourteenth amendment delegated the constitutional authority to secure affirmatively the fundamental rights of American citizens."); Christopher L. Eisgruber, "Justice and the Text: Rethinking the Constitutional Relation between Principle and Prudence," 43 *Duke L.J.* 1, 45 (1993) (suggesting that Section 5 of the Fourteenth Amendment grants Congress the power to enforce the citizenship clause and ensure "the benefits government ought to provide to a free people—such as liberty, security and justice"); William Eskridge, Jr., "Destabilizing Due Process and Evolutive Equal Protection," 47 *UCLA L. Rev.* 1183 (2000) (urging that the due process and equal protection clauses "be read as guarantees fulfilling the promise of citizenship made in the first sentence of the Fourteenth Amendment"); Tribe, "*Saenz* Sans Prophecy" at 126–27 (describing the citizenship clause as "an underutilized constitutional provision if ever there was one").

58. As John Ely writes, "it was probably the clause from which the framers of the Fourteenth Amendment expected most." Ely, *Democracy and Distrust* at 22.

59. Karst, "Forward" at 4 (describing citizenship principle as giving "substantive content [to] the equal protection clause").

60. For arguments that the Fourteenth Amendment's protection of citizenship rights pertained only to civil rights, see Maltz, "Citizenship and the Constitution." But see Harris, "Beyond Equality," for a discussion of citizenship as political rights. For arguments that citizenship has to be understood to include economic and social rights, see Forbath, "Caste, Class, and Equal Citizenship"; Karst, "The Coming Crisis of Work in Constitutional Perspective" (discussing economic rights); and Balkin, "The Constitution of Status" (discussing social rights).

61. There is by now a substantial literature on the historical origins and political context of the Fourteenth Amendment, and many scholars have concluded that the Framers affirmatively intended to imbue the concept of citizenship with real constitutional effect. *See, e.g.,* Ely, *Democracy and Distrust*; Harrison, "Reconstructing the Privileges or Immunities Clause"; Maltz, "Reconstruction without Revolution"; Maltz, "Citizenship and the Constitution."

62. Some characterize the Constitution as embodying an anticaste ethic; in this view, the Fourteenth Amendment should be read as a response to the subordination of African Americans—and by implication, to other oppressed groups as well. The concept of equal citizenship—understood as full and meaningful membership for all—figures centrally in this narrative. See, e.g., Karst, "Forward" at 17:

[The Framers] chose to cast the amendment in general terms, declining to use the language of specific rights and particular groups that they had used in the 1866 Act. It was this choice that gave the principle of equal citizenship its capacity to grow into a protection of other groups and other rights.

See also, e.g., J. M. Balkin, "The Constitution of Status," 106 *Yale L.J.* 2313 (1997). Others regard constitutional citizenship as embodying commitments to democratic self-government and republican virtue. *See, e.g.*, Linda McClain and James E. Fleming, "Some Questions for Civil Society-Revivalists," 75 *Chi.-Kent L. Rev.* 301 (2000); Frank Michelman, "Law's Republic," 97 *Yale L.J.* 1493 (1988).

63. *See, e.g.*, Chantal Mouffe, "Democratic Citizenship and the Political Community," in *Dimensions of Radical Democracy: Pluralism, Citizenship, Community* 225, 227 (Chantal Mouffe, ed., Verso, 1992) (arguing that "liberalism . . . reduced citizenship to a mere legal status"); Sanford Levinson, "National Loyalty, Communalism, and the Professional Identity of Lawyers," 7 *Yale J.L. & Human.* 49, 53–54 (1995) (distinguishing between the concepts of "good citizens" and "mere citizens").

64. For a useful, and elaborate, characterization of "thin" and "thick" conceptions of citizenship, see Rainer Baubock, "Differentiating Citizenship," in *Inclusion/Exclusion* (Alison Woodward, ed., forthcoming). In contrast to the account here, however, Baubock characterizes as thin not merely conceptions of citizenship as status but also those conceptions of citizenship as rights that do not entail corresponding obligations or cultural commitments. *Id.* at 5–7. He propounds a conception of thick citizenship that is far more communitarian and nationalistic than the one I am describing here.

65. Karst describes the principle of equal citizenship not merely as a constitutional mandate but as "an ideal, a cluster of value premises." Karst, "Forward" at 5.

66. *Id.* at 5 (quoting Alexander M. Bickel, *The Morality of Consent* 54 (Yale Univ. Press, 1975)).

67. *Id.; see also* Kenneth L. Karst, *Belonging to America: Equal Citizenship and the Constitution* 10 (Yale Univ. Press, 1989) ("I agree that the bare legal status of citizenship is a constitutional trifle. . . .").

68. Karst, "Forward" at 5; *see also* Karst, *Belonging to America* at 10 ("[R]eal membership in the community is more than a legal status. . . .").

69. For other articulations of this see, e.g., Black, *Structure and Relationship in Constitutional Law* at 53 (arguing that the citizenship clause does not simply bestow an "honorific label" but also mandates, more substantively, "incorporation and participation in society"); Note, "Membership Has Its Privileges and Immunities" at 1946 ("Although the title of 'citizen' has been reduced to a mere legal status, the belief that 'citizenship means something' remains a powerful emotional and symbolic legacy in our political traditions.").

70. *See* Civil Rights Cases, 109 U.S. 3, 26–62 (Harlan, J., dissenting); Kinoy, "The Constitutional Right of Negro Freedom" at 403.

71. *See, e.g.*, Kenneth Karst, "Why Equality Matters," 17 *Ga. L. Rev.* 245, 288 (1983) (stating that formal citizenship never guaranteed full societal membership; " '[a]ctual membership was determined by additional tests of religion, perhaps, or race or language or behavior, tests that varied considerably among segments

and over time.' " (quoting Robert H. Wiebe, *The Segmented Society: An Introduction to the Meaning of America* 95 (Oxford Univ. Press, 1975))).

72. *Minor v. Happersett*, 88 U.S (21 Wall.) 162, 171 (1875). Proponents of "economic citizenship" today would argue that Congress and the courts have wrongfully excluded economic rights from the scope of substantive citizenship as well.

73. While most invocations of the idea of "second-class citizenship" counterpose the possession of formal citizenship status with the denial of substantive rights, the term has sometimes been used to describe the imposition of lesser forms of citizenship status itself. *See, e.g., Schneider v. Rusk*, 377 U.S. 163, 169 (1964) (holding that a statute that deprived naturalized citizens of their citizenship status if they resided abroad for three years in their place of original nationality or birth created "a second-class citizenship"); *see also Knauer v. United States*, 328 U.S. 654, 658 (1946) ("Citizenship obtained through naturalization is not a second-class citizenship."). Members of the Supreme Court have often used the concept of second-class citizenship in an offhand and unexamined way to refer to a condition of exclusion, stigma, or less favorable treatment experienced by a subject group (most often African Americans and other racial minorities; sometimes veterans, juveniles, or others). In one case, however, there is a brief exchange among the justices about the concept: Justice Black, dissenting in *Rogers v. Bellei*, argued that "[u]nder the view adopted by the majority today, all children born to Americans while abroad would be excluded from the protections of the Citizenship Clause and would instead be relegated to the permanent status of second-class citizenship, subject to revocation at the will of Congress." 401 U.S. at 839 (Black, J., dissenting). The majority, in response, described this characterization—that the holding imposes second-class citizenship—as a "cliché [that] is too handy and too easy, and, like most clichés, can be misleading." *Id.* at 835. Perhaps in part because second-class citizenship is an inherently critical term, it is far more often invoked in dissenting than in majority opinions.

74. *See* Ian F. Haney Lopez, *White by Law: The Legal Construction of Race* (NewYork Univ. Press, 1996); John Tehranian, "Performing Whiteness: Naturalization Litigation and the Construction of Racial Identity in America," 109 *Yale L.J.* 817 (2000); Cott, "Marriage and Women's Citizenship in the United States"; Leti Volpp, "Getting Married and Losing Citizenship," 52 *UCLA L. Rev.* (forthcoming, 2005).

75. *See generally Foreign in a Domestic Sense: Puerto Rico, American Expansion and the Constitution* (Christina Duffy Burnett and Burke Marshall, eds., Duke Univ. Press, 2001).

76. In a recent essay, Karst recognizes this point. *See* Kenneth L. Karst, "Citizenship, Law, and the American Nation," 7 *Ind. J. Global Legal Stud.* 595, 596 (2000) (arguing that while Alexander Bickel considered the status of citizenship "a trifling matter, . . . to an African-American living under Jim Crow, or to many a resident alien today, the status was and is a prize to strive for. . . . The formal status of citizenship can seem trifling only when you are able to take it for granted.").

77. *See generally* Bosniak, "Universal Citizenship and the Problem of Alienage."

78. Voting has not always been regarded as a necessary incident of citizenship. *See, e.g., Minor v. Happersett*, 88 U.S. (21 Wall.) 162, 178 (1875); *Pope v. Williams*, 193 U.S. 621, 628 (1904) ("Citizenship and suffrage are by no means inseparable; the latter is not one of the universal, fundamental, inalienable rights with which men are endowed by their Creator. . . ."). *See also* Cott, "Marriage and Women's Citizenship in the United States."

79. Gerald Neuman, *Strangers to the Constitution: Immigrants, Borders, and Fundamental Law* 63–71, 139–49 (Princeton Univ. Press, 1996); Jamin B. Raskin, "Legal Aliens, Local Citizens: The Historical, Constitutional and Theoretical Meanings of Alien Suffrage," 141 *U. Pa. L. Rev.* 1391 (1993); Gerald M. Rosberg, "Aliens and Equal Protection: Why Not the Right to Vote?," 75 *Mich. L. Rev.* 1092 (1977).

80. The concept of "relative autonomy" has often been used to describe the nature of a relationship between social domains or phenomena in empirical terms; it is meant to convey the idea that two domains (or phenomena) are neither entirely reducible to one other, nor entirely independent. The term has its origins in Marxist thought, and was a key concept of critical legal studies' accounts of law's relationship to other social fields. *See, e.g.,* Robert W. Gordon, "Critical Legal Histories," 36 *Stan. L. Rev.* 57, 101 (1984).

My use of the term here is meant to convey not an empirical but a logical or conceptual relationship. My argument is simply that in conventional constitutional thought, rights citizenship does not depend entirely on possession of status citizenship, nor does enjoyment of status citizenship entail, necessarily, enjoyment of citizenship rights. These dimensions of citizenship, in other words, are not collapsible one into the other; they are closely related and partly overlapping, but substantially independent as well.

81. Charles L. Black, Jr., "The Unfinished Business of the Warren Court," 46 *Wash. L. Rev.* 3, 10 (1970).

82. *Id.* at 10 n.38.

83. Ely, *Democracy and Distrust* at 25 (emphasis added). Ely recognizes that on its face, the clause's language appears to "limit its protection to United States citizens." *Id.* at 24–25. In response he writes:

> I certainly agree that we should defer to clear constitutional language: for one thing it is the best possible evidence of purpose. But when the usual reading is out of accord with what we are quite certain was the purpose, we owe it to the Framers and ourselves at least to take a second look at the language. . . . Since everyone seems to agree that [the non-exclusionary] construction would better reflect what we know of the purpose, and since it is one the language will bear comfortably, it is hard to imagine why it shouldn't be followed.

Id.

84. *Id.*

85. Bobbitt, *Constitutional Fate* at 89.

86. 8 U.S.C. § 1101(a)(3) ("The term 'alien' means any person not a citizen or national of the United States.").

87. Bobbitt writes that the relationship between citizen and alien is not necessarily an "antinomy." Bobbitt, *Constitutional Fate* at 88. It is, rather, "a chiaroscuric relationship," one "which may be found in Aristotle but is not a relationship established anywhere in the Constitution." *Id.*

88. Karst, "Forward" at 42–46.

89. *Id.* at 42–44.

90. *Id.* at 43–44.

91. *Id.* at 43.

92. *Id.* at 44.

93. *Id.* at 44–45.

94. *Id.*. *at 44.*

95. *Id.* at 45. Karst suggests that noncitizens may rightly be denied political (though not other) rights: "[since] we are a political community, and aliens are members of other political communities, it may be permissible for a state to restrict political participation. . . ." *Id.* Of course, many citizens—increasing numbers of them—are members of other political communities as well, yet we do not disenfranchise them on this basis. For a useful recent overview of the subject of dual nationality in fact and in law, see generally Peter J. Spiro, "Dual Nationality and the Meaning of Citizenship," 46 *Emory L.J.* 1411 (1997).

96. *See* Ely, *Democracy and Distrust.*

97. One way of expressing this divide in textual terms might be to say that while aliens are clearly not "Fourteenth-Amendment-first-sentence citizen[s]," *Rogers v. Bellei*, 401 U.S. 815, 827 (1971), they are in many respects Fourteenth-Amendment-second-sentence citizens.

98. Michael Kent Curtis, "Historical Linguistics, Inkblots, and Life after Death: The Privileges or Immunities of Citizens of the United States," 78 *N.C. L. Rev.* 1071, 1149 (2000). On interpreting the closely analogous privileges and immunities clause of Article IV, Justice O'Connor observed, "[t]he word 'Citizens' suggests that the Clause also excludes aliens. Any prohibition of discrimination aimed at aliens . . . must derive from other constitutional provisions." *Zobel v. Williams*, 457 U.S. 55, 74 n.3 (1982) (O'Connor, J., concurring) (citations omitted).

99. Michael Kent Curtis, "Two Textual Adventures: Thoughts on Reading Jeffrey Rosen's Paper," 66 *Geo. Wash. L. Rev.* 1269, 1272 (1998).

100. Akhil Reed Amar, *The Bill of Rights: Creation and Reconstruction* 364 n.42 (Yale Univ. Press, 1998) (emphasis in original). For a similarly skeptical discussion of Ely's reading, see Michael J. Perry, "Brown, Bolling and Originalism: Why Ackerman and Posner (among Others) Are Wrong," 20 S. *Ill. U. L.J.* 53, 61 n.44 (1995). *See also* T. Alexander Aleinikoff, "Citizenship Talk: A Revisionist Narrative," 69 *Fordham L. Rev.* 1689, 1694 n.32 (2001) (assuming that noncitizens cannot claim the protection of the privileges and immunities clause); Levin, "Reading the Privileges or Immunities Clause" at 586 ("The 1866 [Civil Rights] Act envisioned a different set of beneficiaries than the Amendment did. The Amendment returned to the language of citizenship . . . [whereas] the civil rights enumerated in the 1866 Act inured to the 'inhabitants of every race.' "); Karst, "Forward" at 42 ("[T]he privileges and immunities clause [*sic*] is addressed explicitly to the rights of citizens.").

101. Bosniak, "Universal Citizenship and the Problem of Alienage"; Bosniak, "The Citizenship of Aliens" at 29–36.

102. For example, *The American Heritage Dictionary of the English Language* 245 (Houghton-Mifflin, 1969), defines *citizenship* as "the status of a citizen, with its attendant duties, rights and privileges."

103. As one theorist has written, "Within civil republicanism, citizenship is an activity or a practice, and not simply a status, so that not to engage in the practice is, in important senses, not to be a citizen." Adrian Oldfield, "Citizenship and Community: Civic Republicanism and the Modern World," in *The Citizenship Debates: A Reader* 75, 79 (Gershon Shafir, ed., Univ. Minnesota Press, 1998).

104. T. Alexander Aleinikoff, *Between Principles and Politics: The Direction of U.S. Citizenship Policy* 46 (Carnegie Endowment for Int'l Peace, 1998); *see also* Schuck, "The Devaluation of American Citizenship."

105. *See, e.g.,* Georgie Ann Geyer, *Americans No More* (Atlantic Monthly Press, 1996).

106. Rosen, "Exclusion, Discrimination and the Making of Americans: America in Thick and Thin"; *see also* Frederick Schauer, "Community, Citizenship, and the Search for National Identity," 84 *Mich. L. Rev.* 1504, 1515 (1986) (arguing that citizenship status serves as the principal mechanism for social cohesion and common identity in the United States, and arguing that citizenship status must therefore count for something in order to serve this "community-bonding function"); Schuck, "The Devaluation of American Citizenship."

107. William N. Eskridge, Jr., "The Relationship Between Obligations and Rights of Citizens" at 1726. Eskridge goes on to write that "the Court's jurisprudence ought to read the Equal Protection Clause differently, in some respects, for citizens than for noncitizens." *Id.* at 1727.

108. *See Slaughter-House Cases*, 83 U.S. at 114 (Bradley, J., dissenting) ("In this free country . . . citizenship means something.").

109. William Rogers Brubaker, "Introduction," in *Immigration and the Politics of Citizenship in Europe and North America* 1, 4 (William Rogers Brubaker ed., Univ. Press of America, 1989) (citizenship in its ideal form will be "consequential," among other things, meaning that it "should entail important privileges").

110. *But see* text accompanying notes 78–79 (discussing alien voting as an historical matter).

111. See chapter 3. *See also* Peter H. Schuck, "Citizenship (Update 1)," in *Encyclopedia of the American Constitution* 366, 366 (Leonard W. Levy and Kenneth L. Karst, eds., 2d ed., Macmillan Reference USA, 2000) ("As a result of a steady expansion of the Equal Protection and Due Process principles, legal resident aliens today enjoy almost all the significant rights and obligations that citizens enjoy.").

112. It is this assumption that has rendered the post-9/11 establishment of military tribunals for accused noncitizen terrorists highly controversial. By design, these tribunals provide an adjudicative process stripped of important due process guarantees for the accused. These procedures would, in ordinary circumstances, be deemed to violate basic precepts of constitutional law, at least as to those aliens within the United States. *See Wong Wing v. United States*, 163 U.S. 228, 238 (1896) (all persons within the territory of the United States are entitled to the protections guaranteed by the Fifth and Sixth Amendments). Times of declared

national emergency are not ordinary times, however, and few commentators expect that the courts will soon invalidate the order establishing the tribunals.

113. *See, e.g.*, Bosniak, "Exclusion and Membership"; Bosniak, "Difference That Alienage Makes"; Linda S. Bosniak, "Immigrants, Preemption, and Equality," 35 *Va. J. Int'l L.* 179 (1994); Linda Bosniak, "Opposing Proposition 187: Undocumented Immigrants and the National Imagination," 28 *Conn. L. Rev. 555* (1986); Bosniak, "Universal Citizenship and the Problem of Alienage."

114. The concern is that noncitizens not be locked permanently into alienage status. See discussion in chapter 3.

115. Others have formulated arguments structured in this way. *See, e.g.*, Aleinikoff, "Re-reading Justice Harlan's Dissent in *Plessy v. Ferguson*" at 977 ("In his dissent in *Plessy v. Ferguson*, Harlan eloquently envisions a national polity of free persons equally enjoying the fundamental rights of citizenship.").

116. Christopher L. Eisgruber, "The Fourteenth Amendment's Constitution" at 71.

117. Karst, "Forward" at 15 (explaining that the Fourteenth Amendment's framers "[made] no serious effort to differentiate the functions of the various clauses" of Section I).

118. *See, e.g.*, Levin, "Reading the Privileges or Immunities Clause" at 609–11, 614 (arguing that the privileges or immunities clause is concerned with "the majoritarian, structural, and participatory rights of citizens," and embodies commitments to "civil republicanism and participatory virtues," unlike the due process and equal protection clauses, which address "the substantive rights of personhood," namely, rights to private autonomy).

119. *See, e.g.*, Berger, *Government by Judiciary* at 240 ("All in all, it will not do to read the rights of 'persons' more broadly than those that were conferred on 'citizens.' "). *But see* Earl M. Maltz, "The Constitution and Nonracial Discrimination: Alienage, Sex, and the Framers' Ideal of Equality," 7 *Const. Comment* 251, 264, 271 (1990); Rosen, "Translating the Privileges or Immunities Clause" at 1245 ("There seems to have been a general consensus that, whatever the Equal Protection Clause guaranteed, it was something narrower than the Privileges or Immunities Clause.").

120. Karst, "Forward" at 5.

121. Karst, "Why Equality Matters" at 248.

122. Karst, *Belonging to America* at 1.

123. Bosniak, "Universal Citizenship and the Problem of Alienage."

124. T. Alexander Aleinikoff, "Citizenship (Update 2)," *Encyclopedia of the American Constitution* 368 (Leonard W. Levy and Kenneth L. Karst, eds., Macmillian Reference USA, 2000).

125. Brubaker, "Introduction" at 22; *see also* Charles R. Beitz, *Political Theory and International Relations* (Princeton Univ. Press, 1979).

126. Michael Walzer, "Citizenship," in *Political Innovation and Conceptual Change* 211, 217 (Terence Ball et al., eds., Cambridge Univ. Press, 1989, 1995) .

127. This is true of most political and social theory concerned with citizenship as well. *See generally* Bosniak, "Universal Citizenship and the Problem of Alienage."

128. I should note that it is not only constitutional scholars who tend to ignore citizenship's threshold aspects. Immigration scholars, for the most part, reciprocally fail to engage with the kind of equal citizenship discourse generated in mainstream constitutional theory. See dicussion in chapter 6.

129. In the Supreme Court's recent decision in *Saenz*—a case regarded by many commentators as breathing new life into the privileges or immunities clause—the majority opinion concludes with what F. H. Buckley calls "a paean to national unity." Buckley, "Liberal Nationalism" at 233. As Justice Stevens writes, "The Fourteenth Amendment, like the Constitution itself, was, as Justice Cardozo put it, 'framed upon the theory that the peoples of the several states must sink or swim together, and that in the long run prosperity and salvation are in union and not division.' " *Saenz v. Roe*, 526 U.S. 489, 511 (1999) (quoting *Baldwin v. G.A.F. Seelig, Inc.*, 294 U.S. 511, 523 (1935)).

130. Karst, "The Coming Crisis of Work in Constitutional Perspective" at 549.

131. *Id.*

132. Karst, Why Equality Matters" at 280.

133. Karst, "The Coming Crisis of Work in Constitutional Perspective" at 571; *see also* Karst, *Belonging to America* at 2 ("Equality and belonging are inseparably linked: to define the scope of the ideal of equality in America is to define the boundaries of the national community.").

134. *See, e.g.*, Buckley, "Liberal Nationalism" at 223–24, 232 (proposing a "nationalist account of the Privileges or Immunities Clause" according to which "basic constitutional liberties are constitutive of the American identity and deserve support as a symbol of American nationalism"); Mark Tushnet, "Thinking About the Constitution at the Cusp," 34 *Akron L. Rev.* 21, 34 (2000) ("In important ways the Constitution, with its opening words 'We the People of the United States,' is a document *about* national unity; a document that tries to create—at least through rhetoric—a single people of the United States, notwithstanding our wide differences.") (emphasis in original); Eisgruber, "Political Unity and the Powers of Government" at 1336 (describing "political unity" as a central constitutional principle); Black, *Structure and Relationship in Constitutional Law*; Eskridge, "The Relationship between Obligations and Rights of Citizens."

135. This is made especially clear in Karst, *Belonging to America* at 177–81.

136. While the term can no doubt be used in both senses, its double meaning or double connotation is inescapable, notwithstanding that its users in this context do not intend to deploy the term this way. The claim I make here is that certain political phrases do certain kinds of rhetorical work quite independently of the speaker's intention.

137. Mark Tushnet articulates an explicit version of this argument. In a recent book, he endorses a vision of constitutional law in which people are committed to a national community rather than a universal one. He urges that

[T]he people *of the United States* continue to constitute ourselves by a commitment to universal human rights. We are citizens of the United States—not citizens of the world at large, or cosmopolitans indifferent to the place we happen to find ourselves in—because of that commitment. . . . Whatever the ultimate scope of the Declaration's principles, the people of the United States do not yet have general responsibility for the well-being of people all over the world. At least for the time being, we can limit the benefits of *our* welfare state to those who are in some meaningful sense part of us.

Mark Tushnet, *Taking the Constitution Away from the Courts* 191, 193 (Princeton Univ. Press, 1999) (emphasis in original).

138. This is implicit in communitarian theory, and sometimes made explicit. *See* Oldfield, "Citizenship and Community" at 81:

Citizenship is exclusive: it is not a person's humanity that one is responding to, it is the fact that he or she is a fellow citizen, or a stranger. In choosing an identity for ourselves, we recognize both who our fellow citizens are, and those who are not members of our community, thus who are potential enemies.

Id.

139. On these views, there is a substantial literature. For a sampling, see *Global Justice: Nomos XLI* (Ian Shapiro and Lea Brilmayer eds., New York Univ. Press, 1999).

140. See chapter 3.

141. *See, e.g.,* Rogers Brubaker, *Citizenship and Nationhood in France and Germany* 21 (Harvard Univ. Press, 1992) ("Although citizenship is internally inclusive, it is externally exclusive.").

142. See chapter 3.

143. Karst, *Belonging to America* at 45.

144. *Id.* Karst's argument does not hold up given that we today consider dual citizens—who likewise maintain allegiance to other states—as entitled to vote in this country.

145. *Mathews v. Diaz*, 426 U.S. 67, 77 (1976).

146. I refer to the contrast drawn in Justice Brennan's opinion in *Plyler v. Doe* between "innocent children," who deserve special protection, and their culpable parents, who "elect to enter our territory by stealth and in violation of our law" and who "should be prepared to bear the consequences, including, but not limited to, deportation." *Plyler v. Doe*, 457 U.S. 202, 220 (1982). For discussion, see chapter 3. *See, e.g.,* Schuck, "The Devaluation of American Citizenship"; Rogers M. Smith, *Civic Ideals: Conflicting Visions of Citizenship in U.S. History* (Yale Univ. Press, 1997); Christopher L. Eisgruber, "Birthright Citizenship and the Constitution," 72 *N.Y.U. L. Rev.* 54, 96 & n.110 (1997) (stating that while the people subject to the U.S. government's sovereign power "deserve a fair share of the benefits that result from the collective enterprise in which they participate, . . . [i]llegal aliens, who have violated the laws of the collective enterprise, may forfeit any claim to share in the common good").

147. Efforts to enact a new amnesty or legalization program, which in the early part of 2001 looked promising, were shelved after the terrorist attacks of September 11, 2001. As of 2005, the debate on legalization is tied up with the debate over enactment of a possible temporary worker program. Critics have characterized proposed programs that would permit acquisition of lawful status after some period of progam participation as covert "amnesties" and therefore illegitimate. See

Linda Bosniak, "Comment, Working Borders: Linking Debates about Insourcing and Outsourcing of Capital and Labor," 40 *Tex. Int'l. L.J.* 691, 729 (2005).

148. See discussion in chapter 3.

149. Bosniak, "Exclusion and Membership" at 986–87.

150. Smith, *Civic Ideals* at 13. Smith goes on to write that "American citizenship . . . has always been an intellectually puzzling, legally confused, and politically charged and contested status." *Id.* at 14.

151. By citizenship laws, Smith means "the statutes and judicial rulings that have defined what American citizenship [is] and who is eligible to possess it." *Id.* at 2.

CHAPTER 5
BORDERS, DOMESTIC WORK, AND THE AMBIGUITIES OF CITIZENSHIP

1.These scholars employ the language of citizenship in largely liberal terms to describe rights and entitlements that individuals hold against the state. The rights-based approach to citizenship was most influentially elaborated in the contemporary period by sociologist T. H. Marshall and has subsequently been extended by many commentators across the disciplines. Arguments for "economic citizenship" sometimes also have republican overtones: the claim in some work is that basic economic rights are a necessary condition for the achievement of engaged, republican citizenship in the national polity. These uses should be distinguished from claims on behalf of "workplace citizenship," which have also recently proliferated in the legal and sociological literature: here, the idea of citizenship is deployed explicitly in republican terms to refer to active democratic engagement in the life of the political community. The community at issue, however, is not the polity, as in classical articulations of republican citizenship, but the firm.

2. There are other strands of the economic citizenship literature. One group urges public provision of a financial stake in society to all Americans at the age of majority. Bruce Ackerman and Ann Alsott, for example, have proposed a provision to all Americans of an economic stake in society in the form of a public lump-sum transfer of $80 thousand at the age of majority. In Ackerman and Alsott's vision, economic citizenship requires creation of a stakeholder society in order to ensure equality of opportunity—the opportunity for "every American to better themselves." Bruce Ackerman and Ann Alsott, *The Stakeholder Society* (Yale Univ. Press, 1999). A second strand emphasizes more familiar welfare strategies that ensure a right to decent livelihood. *See, e.g.*, Joel F. Handler, "Questions about Social Europe by an American Observer," 18 *Wis. Int'l L.J.* 437 (2000); Charles Black, *A New Birth of Freedom: Human Rights, Named and Unnamed* (Grosset/ Putnam, 1994); Nancy Fraser and Linda Gordon, "Contract vs. Charity: Why Is There No Social Citizenship in the United States?" in *The Citizenship Debates* (Gershon Shafir, ed., Univ. of Minnesota Press, 1998).

3. William E. Forbath, "Why Is This Rights Talk Different from All Other Rights Talk? Demoting the Court and Reimagining the Constitution", 46 *Stan. L. Rev.* 1771, 1790 (1994). Kenneth Karst describes the goal as "the fair distribution of work." Kenneth L. Karst, "The Coming Crisis of Work in Constitutional

Perspective," 82 *Cornell L. Rev.* 523, 559 (1997). John Denvir similarly argues that the constitutional rights of citizenship must entail "the opportunity to earn a living." John Denvir, *Democracy's Constitution: Claiming the Privileges of American Citizenship* 50 (Univ. of Illinois Press, 2001).

4. *See* Forbath, "Why Is This Rights Talk Different from All Other Rights Talk?"

5. *See* Judith Shklar, *American Citizenship: The Quest for Inclusion* (Yale Univ. Press, 1991).

6. *See* Vicki Schultz, "Life's Work," 100 *Colum. L. Rev.* 1881 (2000).

7. J.G.A. Pocock, "The Ideal of Citizenship since Classical Times," in *The Citizenship Debates* 31–42 (Gershon Shafir, ed., Univ. of Minnesota Press, 1998).

8. Michael Walzer, "Citizenship," in *Political Innovation and Conceptual Change* (Terrence Ball, James Farr, and Russell Hanson, eds., Cambridge Univ. Press, 1989).

9. Marx, "On the Jewish Question," in *Karl Marx: Early Writings* (Vintage, 1975).

10. *See, e.g.,* Bryan Turner, *Citizenship and Capitalism* (Allen & Unwin, 1986); Nancy Fraser and Linda Gordon, "Civil Citizenship against Social Citizenship? On the Ideology of Contract vs. Charity," in *The Condition of Citizenship* (Bart van Steenbergen, ed., Sage, 1994); Alice Kessler-Harris, *In Pursuit of Equity: Women, Men, and the Quest for Economic Citizenship in 20th Century America* (Oxford Univ. Press, 2001). These efforts represent part of a broader resurgence of interest among scholars in the subject of citizenship in recent years. For an overview, see generally chapter 2; *see also* Linda Bosniak, "Citizenship," in *Oxford Handbook of Legal Studies* (Peter Cane and Mark Tushnet, eds., Oxford Univ. Press, 2003).

11. The idea of "cultural citizenship" was once similarly regarded as an impossible conjoining of concepts, but the concept is in wide use today.

12. Kessler-Harris, *In Pursuit of Equity* at 283.

13. *See* Schultz, "Life's Work."

14. Carole Pateman, *The Disorder of Women: Democracy, Feminism and Political Theory* 10 (Polity Press, 1989).

15. Kessler-Harris, *In Pursuit of Equity* at 12–13.

16. Terms are contested. See Joan Williams for a critique of the idea of "care work" as "still ha[ving] the little pink bow and the sacralizing heritage, of domesticity." She prefers the term "family work," in part because it serves to "use the legitimate claims of family life as a pivot to redefine the ideal worker." Joan Williams, "From Difference to Dominance to Domesticity: Care as Work; Gender as Tradition," 76 *Chi.-Kent L. Rev.* 1441, 1446 (2000–2001).

17. *Care Work: Gender, Labor, and the Welfare State* 3 (Madonna Harrington Meyer, ed., Routledge, 2000).

18. Linda McClain, "Contract and Care," 76 *Chi.-Kent L. Rev.* 1403, 1437 (2001); Linda McClain, "Care as a Public Value: Linking Responsibility, Resources and Republicanism," 76 *Chi.-Kent L. Rev.* 1673, 1681 (2001); Deborah Stone, "Why We Need a Care Movement," *The Nation*, Mar. 13, 2000, at 13, 15.

19. Achieved either through thoroughgoing state-sponsored programs of child care provision or through more gradualist (though in today's political environment, still utopian) proposals to "eliminate the ideal-worker norm in the benefits

related to market work," thus ensuring that receipt of benefits to unemployment insurance, Social Security, and the like are not "contingent on ideal worker schedules that mothers do not work." Joan Williams, "From Difference to Dominance to Domesticity," 76 *Chi.-Kent L. Rev.* 1441, 1456 (2001).

20. Professor McClain has some doubts about the strategy. "It is a fair question whether a tradition with a history that so vividly links citizenship to independence, to political participation, to manhood, and to certain forms of 'productive' work (e.g., the yeoman farmer, the independent producer) is useful in an attempt to ground public responsibility for care." McClain, "Care as a Public Value, and Contract and Care." The approach raises questions about the politics of sexual difference, and in particular whether it is women's biological capacity to give birth that underlies the significance of the politics of care invoked here. On this subject, *see* Carole Pateman: "Only women can give physical life to new citizens, who, in their turn, give life to a democratic political order." Pateman, "Equality, Difference, Subordination: The Politics of Motherhood and Women's Citizenship," in *Beyond Equality and Difference: Citizenship, Feminist Politics and Female Subjectivity* 29 (Gisela Bock and Susan James, eds., Routledge, 1992).

21. A growing literature on the family as a "school for citizenship" has emerged in recent years. *See, e.g., Seedbeds of Virtue: Sources of Competence, Character, and Citizenship in American Society* (Mary Ann Glendon and David Blankenhorn, eds., Madison Books, 1995). For a useful discussion of the history of the construction of republican motherhood as a form of women's citizenship, see Pateman, "Equality, Difference, Subordination."

22. *E.g.*, Katharine Silbaugh, "Turning Labor into Love: Housework and the Law," 91 *Nw. U. L. Rev.* 1 (1996); Martha M. Ertman, "Commercializing Marriage: A Proposal for Valuing Women's Work Through Premarital Security Agreements," 77 *Tex. L. Rev.* 17 (1998). For earlier statements of this position, see essays in *The Politics of Housework* (Ellen Malos, ed., Schocken, 1980).

23. Some feminists have argued that women's citizenship cannot be achieved without a revaluing and recognition of women's work in the domestic sphere. Here, women's citizenship is defined at least in part as a function of the performance of care work. Others respond that achievement of citizenship requires work outside the home. *See* Schultz, "Life's Work." Schultz argues that domestic work as currently organized leads to isolation and lack of opportunities for cooperation and adult connection necessary to citizenship.

24. *See, e.g.*, Kessler-Harris, *In Pursuit of Equity.*

25. Feminists have advanced various reasons for this, including internalized gender roles and "gatekeeping." *See, e.g.*, Arlie Russell Hochschild, *The Second Shift: Working Parents and the Revolution at Home* (Viking, 1989); Naomi R. Cahn, "Gendered Identities: Women and the Household," 44 *Vill. L. Rev.* 525 (1999).

26. *E.g.*, Joan Williams, *Unbending Gender: Why Family and Work Conflict and What to Do about It* (Oxford Univ. Press, 2000), especially chapter 3. *See also* Gillian Hadfield, "Households at Work: Beyond Labor Market Policies to Remedy the Gender Gap," 82 *Geo. L.J.* 89 (1994).

27. See http://censtats.census.gov/cgi-bin/eeo/eeojobs.pl.

28. Ruth Milkman, Ellen Reese, and Benita Roth, "The Macrosociology of Paid Domestic Labor," 25 *Work and Occupations* 483–510 (Nov. 1998).

29. *Id.* Milkman et al. describe what they call "a partial reversal of the decline," and emphasize that "paid domestic labor is far more widespread in some metropolitan areas than others," including Los Angeles, Miami, Houston, and New York. According to these authors:

> female labor force participation generally has contributed to the rapid growth of the personal services sector, of which paid domestic labor is one important component. We expect demand for such services to be especially extensive in households with young children where the mother is in the labor force, and indeed, the labor force participation rates of mothers of preschool children have risen dramatically in recent years. Although the availability of group child care has increased, high quality child care remains scarce and is often available for limited hours. . . . More generally, the persistence of the traditional gender division of household labor, as well as the increased number of households headed by females, suggests that men have not increased their contributions to domestic labor significantly. For these reasons, we expect that metropolitan areas, with higher maternal labor force participation rates, will have greater demand for domestic servants than other metropolitan areas.

Id. at 495.

Other commentators describe the degree of occupational growth in the domestic labor sphere in less qualified terms. *See generally* Pierrette Hondagneu-Sotelo, *Domestica: Immigrant Workers Cleaning and Caring in the Shadows of Affluence* (Univ. of California Press, 2001). Note, however, that, as Peggie R. Smith has written, "[t]he paid household workforce does not lend itself easily to statistical quantification because underreporting is widespread and facilitated by the informal nature of domestic service work. . . . Underreporting in paid household work reflects both the entry of undocumented workers into the occupation as well as legal workers who are disinclined to report their earnings because of tax related concerns and fear about the impact of earnings on eligibility for government benefits." Peggie R. Smith, "Organizing the Unorganizable: Private Paid Household Workers and Approaches to Employee Representation," 79 *N.C. L. Rev.* 45, 110, n.25 (2000).

30. Judith Rollins, *Between Women: Domestics and Their Employers* 104 (Temple Univ. Press, 1985), *reprinted in Working in the Service Society* (Cameron Lynn Macdonald and Carmen Sirianni, eds., Temple Univ. Press, 1996) ("The middle-class women I interviewed were not demanding that their husbands play a greater role in housekeeping; they accepted the fact that responsibility for domestic maintenance was theirs, and they solved the problem by hiring other women to assist.").

On the other hand, defenders respond that the commodification of care work ultimately operates to the advantage of women as a group because it is a "society-wide mechanism for allocating [household labor]'s costs rather than continuing to impose them on individual family members (too often women.) (Schultz, "Life's Work" at 1901) and because it challenges "the idea that women are inclined to serve and to gift their work." Kathryn Silbaugh, "Commodification and Women's Household Labor," 9 *Yale J.L. & Feminism* 81, 108 (1997) (While it may often be that "commodification invites exploitation, [i]t seems just as plausible to argue that pricelessness invites exploitation.") On this view the trouble is not commercialization per se but the poor conditions under which many domestic employees labor—something that can and should be addressed through social policy and collective organizing.

31. Mary Romero, "Unraveling Privilege: Worker's Children and the Hidden Costs of Paid Childcare," 76 *Chi.-Kent L. Rev.* 1651, 1654 (2001). *See also* Milkman et al., "The Macrosociology of Paid Domestic Labor" at 485 ("Paid domestic labor is in many respects a microcosm of the growing class inequality among women. The elite corps of professional and managerial women, whose ranks have expanded so dramatically in recent years, can now purchase on the market much of the labor of social reproduction traditionally relegated to them as wives and mothers. And the workers who perform this labor are typically women on the lower rungs of the economic ladder, often women of color and/or immigrants.").

Often, these domestic workers perform what Dorothy Roberts has described as the most "menial" functions of housework. Dorothy Roberts, "Spiritual and Menial Housework," 9 *Yale J.L. & Feminism* 51 (1997). But many in addition perform other, more traditionally honored domestic work, including the emotional, physical, and managerial aspects of caring for the employer's children. *See* Williams, "From Difference to Dominance to Domesticity" at 1462–65 for a useful disaggregation of care work into seven component parts, which she calls "growth-work, housework and yardwork, household management, social capital development, emotion-work, care for the sick, and daycare." For discussions of the effects on employers of the delegation to third parties of the more "spiritual" aspects of domestic work (including those related to the emotional and managerial tasks related to the raising of children) (Roberts, "Spiritual and Menial Housework"), see Sharon Hays, *The Cultural Contradictions of Motherhood* (Yale Univ. Press, 1996); Hondagneu-Sotelo, *Domestica*.

32. As Mary Romero poses the question: "who takes care of the maid's children?" She notes that "[t]he higher quality, paid reproductive labor the employers' families receive produces, as a direct consequence, lower amounts of unpaid reproductive labor in their own families." Romero, "Unraveling Privilege" at 1652–53.

33. Grace Chang, *Disposable Domestics: Immigrant Women Workers in the Global Economy* 57 (South End Press, 2000) ("Members of *Mujeres Unidas y Activas* (MUA), a support group for Latina immigrant domestic workers, report that they commonly endure conditions approaching slavery or indentured servitude."). Some analysts have challenged this kind of characterization as overstated. As Milkman et al. remark, "in comparison to working in a garment sweatshop, in agriculture, or even as a minimum-wage fast food server, this occupation may be relatively attractive to workers." They raise cautions about "the frequent claims in the microsociological literature on domestic service that this occupation is uniquely exploitative." Milkman et al., "The Macrosociology of Paid Domestic Labor," at 489.

34. Evelyn Nakono Glenn, "Cleaning Up/Kept Down: A Historical Perspective on Racial Inequality in 'Women's Work'," 43 *Stan. L. Rev.* 1333, 1341 (1991).

35. Milkman et al., "The Macrosociology of Paid Domestic Labor," Table 4 ("African Americans, Latinas and the foreign born . . . are all overrepresented in this occupation."). These authors insist, however, that income inequality is an

important variable predicting rate of employment of private household workers which functions "independent of factors like race."

Historically, women of color have often performed what Dorothy Roberts terms the menial dimensions of care work, with "spiritual aspects retained by white women." Today, however, these domestic workers perform more of the "spiritual" work related to childrearing as well (Roberts, "Spiritual and Menial Housework"). The psychic ramifications of this delegation for both the employer and employee are complex and sometimes painful. *See especially* Hondagneu-Sotelo, *Domestica*.

36. Milkman et al., "The Macrosociology of Paid Domestic Labor."

37. Hondagneu-Sotelo, *Domestica*; *Global Woman: Nannies, Maids and Sex Workers in the New Economy* (Barbara Ehrenreich and Arlie Russel Hochschild, eds., Metropolitan Books, 2003).

38. Many of the immigrants who perform this care work also have families in their countries of origin. The transfer of care work from the family of origin to the family of employment in the developed country has been described by some commentators as a global care chain. Arlie Hochschild, "The Nanny Chain," 11 *American Prospect* (2001). *See* Pierrette Hondagneu-Sotelo, "International Division of Caring and Cleaning Work," in *Care Work: Gender, Labor and the Welfare State* 149–162, 160 (Madonna Harrington Meyer, ed., Routledge, 2000) (In a new system of "transnational mothering," domestic workers experience "separations of space and time from their communities of origin, homes, children, and sometimes husbands. In doing so, they must cope with stigma, guilt and criticism from others. As they do care work and cleaning work for others, they lose the right to do care work and cleaning for their own families.").

39. Iris Marion Young, "Polity and Group Difference: A Critique of the Ideal of Universal Citizenship," 99 *Ethics* 250 (1989).

40. *E.g.*, Young, "Polity and Group Difference."

41. Young, "Polity and Group Difference" at 250.

42. *E.g.*, Schultz, "Life's Work" at 1885 ("In order to make paid work the basis for equal citizenship, we will have to take steps to ensure that what the market produces is both substantively adequate and universally available for everyone.").

43. Ayelet Shachar, *Children of a Lesser State: Sustaining Global Inequality Through Citizenship Laws* (2003) (N.Y. Univ., Jean Monnet Working Paper 2/03) (criticizing the institution of birth-right citizenship, which assigns citizenship status by reason of birthplace and/or genetic inheritance, as entirely inconsistent with liberal values). For a similar critique (though one framed and animated by different political commitments), see Peter Schuck and Rogers Smith, *Citizenship Without Consent: Illegal Aliens in the American Polity* (Yale Univ. Press, 1985).

44. Analysts estimate that close to half of all private household workers in the United States are immigrants, of whom more than two-thirds are noncitizens. Randolf Capps et al., "A Profile of the Low-Wage Immigrant Workforce," in *Policy Briefs/Immigrant Families & Workers* (Oct. 27, 2003). In major urban areas, the concentration of immigrant low-wage workers, including domestic workers, is far higher than in the country as a whole. *Id.*

45. Zoe Baird, President Clinton's first nominee for attorney general in 1993, was compelled to withdraw from consideration for the post when it came to light

that she had employed undocumented domestic workers in her home and had failed to pay taxes associated with their employment. "The Zoe Baird problem," as it has come to be known, has derailed several other high-level nominees since then, including nominee for chief of the Department of Homeland Security, 9/11 hero Bernard Kerick. *See* Mike Allen and Jim VandeHei, "Homeland Security Nominee Kerik Pulls Out: Ex-Police Official Says He Failed to Pay Taxes for Nanny Who May Have Been Illegal Immigrant," *Washington Post*, Dec. 11, 2004, at A1.

46. *See* Mary Romero, *Maid in the U.S.A.* 9–17 (2d ed., Routledge, 2002).

47. *E.g., id.* at 1 ("[U]ndocumented women are more likely to face the lowest wages in the occupation and are more vulnerable to abuses including employers refusing to pay, increasing their workload, not paying on time, and threatening to call the INS.").

48. *See, e.g.,* "Hidden in the Home: Abuse of Domestic Workers with Special Visas in the United States," Human Rights Watch, June 2001, *available at* http://hrw.org.reports/2001/usadom/.

49. *E.g.,* Hondagneu-Sotelo, *Domestica* at 13 ("Immigration status has clearly become an important axis of inequality, one interwoven with relations of race, class, and gender, and it facilitates the exploitation of immigrant domestic workers."); Mary Romero, "Immigration, The Servant Problem, and the Legacy of the Domestic Labor Debate: Where Can You Find Good Help These Days?" 53 *U. Miami L. Rev.* 1045, 1062–63 (1999) (Due to the intersection of their "race, class, gender, immigration and citizenship status," Latina immigrant women are not only "less expensive than employees hired by agencies, but . . . more easily exploited for additional work, and need not be provided any benefits.").

50. Like most other theorists of economic citizenship, Schultz treats the United States as a largely self-contained community.

51. For a particularly stark and in some respects overly simplified, statement of the position, see Chang, *Disposable Domestics* at 35 ("The efforts of primarily white, middle-class professional women to 'have it all,' including careers . . . [and] leisure . . . are secured by exploiting immigrant women and women of color as cheap laborers. . . . The employment of undocumented women in dead-end, low-wage, temporary service jobs makes it possible for middle-and upper-class women to pursue salaried jobs and not have to contend with the 'second-shift' when they come home."). For a critique of this kind of framing of the issue, see Romero, "Immigration, the Servant Problem, and the Legacy of the Domestic Labor Debate" at 1062 (characterizing the domestic labor question "as an elite-class issue . . . completely ignore[s] the realities of the working poor, working class and lower-middle class. Although child care options for these classes are limited by finances, they too face overtime and long commutes to and from work making day care center options less than adequate.").

52. Bridget Anderson, *Doing the Dirty Work? The Global Politics of Domestic Labor* 195 (Zed Books, 2000).

53. *See, e.g.,* Hondagneu-Sotelo, *Domestica*; Romero, "Immigration, the Servant Problem, and the Legacy of the Domestic Labor Debate"; Hochschield, "The Nanny Chain"; Rhacel Salazar Parrenas, "The Care Crisis in the Philippines: Children and Transnational Families in the New Global Economy," in *Global Woman.*

54. Arlie Hochschild, "Love and Gold," in *Global Woman: Nannies, Maids, and Sex Workers in the New Economy* 15–38 (Metropolitan Books, 2003).

55. Hannah Arendt, *The Origins of Totalitarianism* (Harcourt, Brace Jovanovich, 1968) (1951); *Perez v. Brownell*, 356 U.S. 44, 64 (1958) (Warren, J., dissenting).

For an extended discussion of the idea of the "right to have rights," see Seyla Benhabib, *Transformations of Citizenship: Dilemmas of the Nation State in the Era of Globalization* (Spinoza Lectures), (Koninklijke Van Gorcum, 2001). In Benhabib's reading, the second use of the word "right" in the phrase is premised upon the first: as Benhabib writes: "The second use of the term . . . is built upon th[e] prior claim of membership" as expressed in the first. *Id.* at 16.

56. *See, e.g.*, Paul Johnston, "The Emergence of Transnational Citizenship among Mexican Immigrants in California," in *Citizenship Today: Global Perspectives and Practices* (Carnegie Endowment for International Peace, 2001); Jennifer Gordon, "Let Them Vote: A Response to Owen Fiss's 'The Immigrant as Pariah,' " *Boston Review* (1999); Linda Bosniak, "Citizenship Denationalized," 7 *Ind. J. Global Legal Stud.* 447 (2002).

57. *See generally* Michele Wucker, "Civics Lessons from Immigrants: What Happens to the Working-Class Political Voice When Many of Its Speakers Aren't Citizens?," 14 *American Prospect* (7) (July 3, 2003). For further discussion of democratic political organizing by and on behalf of noncitizens, see chapter 6.

58. See discussion in chapter 4.

59. See discussion of Walzer and membership boundaries in chapter 3.

60. This separate-spheres model of citizenship basically rearticulates Michael Walzer's understanding of membership. See generally chapter 3.

61. As argued in chapter 4, the ideals and institutions and practices of equal/democratic citizenship are not always confined to the national inside but operate as well at the territorial borders. This transposition of regime values from inside to border can be seen in democratic states' sometimes liberal asylum and refugee policies and in the norms of due process required in deportation proceedings, among other things. Furthermore, the universalist norms associated with citizenship in the inward-looking sense arguably extend beyond national borders. The international human rights regime, transnational political advocacy networks, and commitments to cosmopolitan ethics, to give three examples, have all been described and are plausibly described as forms of citizenship that take place across or beyond national borders. See further discussion in Bosniak, "Citizenship Denationalized."

62. This is conflict not merely across but within spheres. *Cf.* Michael Walzer, *Spheres of Justice* (Basic Books, 1983).

63. *Cf.* Stephen H. Legomsky, "Why Citizenship?," 35 *Va. J. Int'l L.* 279 (1994) (suggesting that "international law provides some compelling rationales for use of the concept of 'nationality' " as distinct from "citizenship").

64. *E.g.*, Linda Bosniak, "The Citizenship of Aliens," *Social Text* 56, 29–35 (1998).

65. For general discussion, see *Political Innovation and Conceptual Change* (Terrence Ball, James Farr, and Russell L. Hanson, eds., Cambridge, 1989).

66. See chapter 2.

CHAPTER 6
SEPARATE SPHERES CITIZENSHIP AND ITS CONUNDRUMS

1. *See generally* Hiroshi Motomura, *Americans in Waiting: The Lost Story of Immigration and Citizenship in the United States* (Oxford Univ. Press, forthcoming) (continuum); David A. Martin, "Reforming Asylum Adjudication: On Navigating the Coast of Bohemia," 138 *U. Pa. L. Rev.* 1247 (1990) (concentric circles).

2. *See generally* Motomura, *Americans in Waiting*; Martin, "Reforming Asylum Adjudication"; Noah Pickus, *True Faith and Allegiance: Immigration and American Civic Nationalism* (Princeton Univ. Press, 2005); Peter H. Schuck, *Citizens, Strangers and In-Betweens: Essays on Immigration and Citizenship* (Westview Press, 1998). *See also* Joseph Carens, "On Belonging: What We Owe to People Who Stay," *Boston Rev.* 16, 18 (Summer 2005) ("As people stay longer, their moral claims grow stronger, and after a while they pass a threshold that entitles them to virtually the same legal status as citizens." Carens's statement is notable when read in light of his well-known liberal critique of national immigration controls. *See* Joseph Carens, "Aliens and Citizens: The Case for Open Borders," 49 *Rev. Pol.* 251 (1987). In the more recent essay, he treats immigration control as legitimate in principle and asks what follows for those who are territorially present.).

3. T. Alexander Aleinikoff, *Semblances of Sovereignty: The Constitution, The State and American Citizenship* 177 (Harvard Univ. Press, 2002). Aleinikoff criticizes arguments on behalf of "necessary differences" between citizens and aliens as based "on a conceptualization of membership as a set of concentric circles."

4. Like Walzer, most separation scholars allow for membership consequences to be visited upon resident aliens in the domain of voting, and recognize the right of the government to deport resident aliens in at least some circumstances. See discussion in chapter 3.

5. In other words, a frontal challenge to border control itself is not on the agenda. Indeed, avowed open-borders advocates on the left and right are hard to come by. Progressives are often critical of immigration restrictions, both substantively and procedurally, but for both strategic and principled reasons rarely affirmatively advocate a full open-borders regime. *See* Linda Bosniak, "Opposing Proposition 187: Undocumented Immigrants and the National Imagination," 28 *Conn. L. Rev.* 555 (1996). There is a group that supports increased immigration on the right (e.g., Wall Street Journal free-marketers), but they tend to seek enhancement of business interests through expansion of temporary employment programs rather than through open borders. Those few who articulate support of the latter tend to be dismissed as utopian eccentrics.

6. As I have made clear in earlier chapters, I am not arguing that the practice of citizenship "inside" the political community is fully universalist and inclusive as a matter of fact. To the contrary, I am fully aware of, and sympathetic to, the critiques that universalist commitments in liberal democratic societies remain radically unfulfilled in some ways and often function coercively. However, for the moment, I am taking the claims of inside "softness" in the discourse over alienage and immigration at face value, and deconstructing them on their own terms.

7. They differ, for example, about whether, to be liberal, national citizenship must take a "civic" form, or whether forms of cultural nationalism qualify.

8. E.g., Rogers Smith, *Civic Ideals: Conflicting Visions of Citizenship in U.S. History* (Yale Univ. Press, 1997); Kenneth L. Karst, *Belonging to America: Equal Citizenship and the Constitution* (Yale Univ. Press, 1989); David Miller, *On Nationality* (Oxford Univ. Press, 1995); David Miller, *Citizenship and National Identity* (Polity Press, 2000); Michael Lind, *The Next American Nation: The New Nationalism and the Fourth American Revolution* (Free Press, 1995); David A. Hollinger, *Postethnic America: Beyond Multiculturalism* (Basic Books, 1995); Chantal Mouffe, *The Democratic Paradox* (Verso, 2000).

9. Samuel Scheffler, *Boundaries and Allegiances: Problems of Justice and Responsibility in Liberal Thought* 36, 79 (Oxford Univ. Press, 2001).

10. Henry Shue, *Basic Rights: Substance, Affluence and American Foreign Policy* 132 (Princeton Univ. Press, 1980).

11. Bounded solidarity need not be motivated by hatred or xenophobia or hostility toward the other. Alternative motivations might include selfishness, self-interestedness, or indifference.

12. Louis Michael Seidman also uses the term "bounded caring" to characterize normative nationalism in an essay on immigration. Louis Michael Seidman, "Fear and Loathing at the Border," in *Justice in Immigration* 136–46 (Warren F. Schwartz, ed., Cambridge Univ. Press, 1995).

13. For examples of the cosmopolitan justice position, see Martha Nussbaum, "Patriotism and Cosmopolitanism," in *For Love of Country* (Joshua Cohen, ed., Beacon Press, 1996); Thomas Pogge, "Introduction: Global Justice," in *Global Justice* (Thomas W. Pogge, ed., Blackwell, 2001); Charles Beitz, "Does Global Inequality Matter?," in *Global Justice* (Thomas W. Pogue, ed., Blackwell, 2001); Brian Barry, "Statism and Nationalism: A Cosmopolitan Critique," in *Global Justice* (Nomos XLI) (Ian Shapiro and Lea Brilmayer, eds., New York Univ. Press, 1999); Debra Satz, "Equality of What among Whom? Thoughts on Cosmopolitanism, Statism and Nationalism," in *Global Justice* (Ian Shapiro and Lea Brilmayer, eds., New York Univ. Press, 1999).

14. Even if we put to one side the many kinds of struggles that arise over the location of the territorial and political boundaries which define the inside and outside of political communities, and even if we assume the existence of relatively fixed and agreed-upon frontiers, we will have to come to terms with fact of the movement of people *across* these borders—in particular, the efforts of those on the outside to join the national inside. And in doing so, we must, in turn, face the question of how political communities, including liberal democratic political communities, are going to respond to those movements. This may make the state sound too passive. State policies often cause transnational population movement, directly and indirectly, as well as respond to those movements.

15. Subject to certain, relatively minimal constraints of justice: see discussion of Walzer on admissions in chapter 3.

Notably, when outsiders are prevented from entering or joining the community, political communities effect a double exclusion that perpetuates itself: exclusion from opportunities and benefits that presence and inclusion bring, but also exclusion from the normative community of people and exclusion from the community of people to whom we feel special responsibility. *See* Scheffler, *Boundaries and Allegiances* at 74 ("if participation in rewarding groups and relationships does indeed give rise to associative duties, then . . . non-participants lose out twice; in addition to missing out on the other rewards of participation, their claims on the participants for assistance become weaker"). *See also* Aleinikoff, *Semblances of Sovereignty* at 168 ("The concept of national membership is thus doubly exclusive. It designates nonmembers by defining members. It also recognizes an association that is expected to exercise power in the interests of members with less concern for the interests of nonmembers.").

16. Self-interested admissions policies may be more or less restrictive. There may be times when national self-interest is understood to dictate a relatively open immigration policy. In other words, normative nationalism and immigration restriction are not necessarily mutually entailing.

17. *But see* Mae Ngai on the exaggerated antiracist reading of the national origins reforms of the 1960s. Mae M. Ngai, *Impossible Subjects: Illegal Aliens and the Making of Modern America* (Princeton Univ. Press, 2004). According to Ngai, the Immigration Act of 1965 "was not inclusionary toward all. By extending the system of formal equality in admissions to all countries, the new law affected the immigration from the Third World differently—creating greater opportunities for migration from Asia and Africa but severely restricting it from Mexico, the Caribbean and Latin America." *Id.* at 263. Ngai points out, furthermore, that on balance, "the Immigration Act of 1965 did not 'open' immigration, for it continued and, indeed, extended the reach of numerical restriction, a policy that would reproduce the problem of illegal immigration, especially from Mexico to the present day." *Id.* at 228.

18. See generally, Motomura, *Americans in Waiting*.

19. "I am not surreptitiously questioning the validity of laws regulating the admission of immigrants to this country. For present purposes, I am prepared to assert that these laws are just." Owen Fiss, "A Community of Equals: The Constitutional Protection of New Americans," in *Boston Rev., published as A Community of Equals: The Constitutional Protection of New Americans* 16 (Beacon Press, 1999). See response by Mark Tushnet, "Open Borders," in *A Community of Equals* 69 ("Owen Fiss's proposal doesn't go far enough. He assumes that an immigration policy founded on creating legal barriers to people's entry into this country is just.").

20. Fiss, "A Community of Equals" at 16.

21. *Id* at 17.

22. *Id.* at 4. "Yet as long as naturalization remains a viable and fairly economical option, as it indeed is in the United States . . . it seems sensible for the law to require completion of the formal process of affirmation before granting immigrants the right to vote." For a different view, see Jamin Raskin, "Legal Aliens, Local Citizens: The Historical, Constitutional and Theoretical Meanings of Alien Suffrage," 141 *U. Pa. L. Rev.* 1448 (1992); Gerald Neuman, "We Are the People: Alien Suffrage in German and American Perspective," 13 *Mich. J. Int'l L.* 259 (1992) ; Gerald M. Rosberg, "The Protection of Aliens from Discriminatory Treatment by the National Government," *Sup. Ct. Rev.* 329 (1977).

23. Fiss, "A Community of Equals" at 16.

24. Aleinikoff, *Semblances of Sovereignty* at 161.

25. *Id.* at 172. This is both a descriptive and a normative claim.

26. The full benefit of Aleinikoff's soft interior, however, would extend only to "lawful, settled members of a polity." *Id*. at 174. This raises questions about what is to happen to those territorially present persons who are neither lawful nor, perhaps, settled. It is precisely here, at the point of discussion of undocumented immigrants, where the model of citizenship as hard shelled container tends to break down. See discussion in chapter 3 and later in this chapter.

27. As is the case with Walzer and Fiss, Aleinikoff's separation commitment is not absolute; he is willing to accept that noncitizens may appropriately suffer certain disabilities, including political disenfranchisement (*id*. at 172), although elsewhere he indicates some support for extending voting rights to lawful permanent residents in local communities on the grounds that "local voting by immigrants does not drain citizenship of its meaning." *Id*. at 179.

Peter Spiro also reads Aleinikoff as seeking to "save citizenship as an institution" rather than abandon it. *See* Peter Spiro, "The Impossibility of Citizenship," 101 *Mich. L. Rev*. 1492, 1500 (2003) (reviewing Aleinikoff, *Semblances of Sovereignty*).

28. *See* Smith, *Civic Ideals*; Karst, *Belonging to America*.

29. See discussion in chapter 3.

30. Michael Walzer, *Spheres of Justice: A Defense of Pluralism and Equality* 21, 318–19 (Basic Books, 1983). *See also* Michael Walzer, "The Art of Separation," 12 *Pol. Theory* 328 (Aug. 1984) ("We have to argue, then, about the location of the line and fight (democratically) to draw it differently. Probably we will never get it exactly right. . . ."); *id*. at 327 ("What goes on in one institutional setting influences all the others; the same people, after all, inhabit the different settings.").

31. The problem of indefinite alienage is not limited to the class of irregular or undocumented immigrants; sometimes legal residents are affected as well. In some countries, naturalization requirements are stringent, and many aliens are ineligible. Even in the United States—a country known for its relatively lenient naturalization requirements—the path to citizenship is obstructed for many lawful permanent residents. For example, recent immigration reforms have barred from naturalization, on grounds of their past criminal convictions, many resident aliens who previously would have been eligible. This occurs even when such convictions are decades old, relatively minor, and there is evidence of rehabilitation. Furthermore, some long-term resident aliens are ineligible to naturalize because they are illiterate or because they are deemed mentally incapable of completing the oath of allegiance. Some will also choose to remain aliens, rather than naturalize, if the laws of their home state treat naturalization elsewhere as an act of expatriation. *See* Linda Bosniak, "Universal Citizenship and the Problem of Alienage," 94 *Nw. U. L. Rev*. 963, 976 (2000).

32. An alternative proposal advanced by the Democrats would establish a guest worker program that ensures a path to eventual citizenship. *See* Safe, Orderly, Legal Visas and Enforcement Act ("SOLVE"), S. 2381, 108th Cong. (2004) (As of June 2005, this bill is awaiting review in the Senate Judiciary Committee.).

33. Ruth Rubio-Marin, *Immigration as a Democratic Challenge: Citizenship and Inclusion in Germany and the United States* 6 (Cambridge Univ. Press, 2000):

[T]o the extent that the enjoyment of a full and equal set of rights and duties within the political community of the state remains attached to the recognition of the formal status of national citizenship, after a certain residency period permanent resident aliens, both legal and illegal, ought to be automatically, and thus unconditionally, recognized as citizens of the state, regardless of whether or not they already enjoy the status of national citizens in some other community, and hence, whether that second citizenship makes of them dual or multiple nationals.

34. This is a proposition that Rubio-Marin seeks to refute in earlier chapters of her book.

35. Rubio-Marin includes undocumented long-term residents in this class, although she also maintains that it is legitimate to impose longer waiting periods and greater restrictions on them. See her chapter 5.

36. Rubio-Marin considers various theoretical and practical objections to the argument, which I will not address here.

37. These two strategies are not mutually exclusive but can be seen as complementary. Each works to ameliorate the limits of the other: We may strive to make citizenship more widely and easily accessible to residents, but also to limit the difference that lack of citizenship makes in the life of a person without such access. Both are modes of reducing the disjuncture: the one by making everyone a citizen as soon as possible, the other by making very little depend on the possession of citizenship.

On the other hand, each of these strategies can lead to different rhetorical politics in any given situation. When enjoyment of a right is made contingent upon citizenship, where exactly does the harm lie? Is the problem that citizenship status is being made to count for too much? Or is the problem that citizenship status is too hard to come by in a society in which citizenship rightfully counts for a good deal?

38. Instead of redressing exclusion from the game, this approach attacks disadvantage within the game.

39. This contrasts with analysts like Peter Schuck, David Jacobson, and David Abraham, who criticize the "devaluation" of citizenship and want to make citizenship status count for more, not less. See Schuck, Citizens, Strangers and In-Betweens; David Jacobson, Rights across Borders: Immigration and the Decline of Citizenship (Johns Hopkins Univ. Press, 1996); David Abraham, "The Good of Banality? The Emergence of Cost-Benefit Analysis and Proportionality in the Treatment of Aliens in the US and Germany," 4 Citizenship Studies 237 (2000).

40. For a comprehensive discussion of separate spheres ideology in relation to the status of women historically, see Linda K. Kerber, "Separate Spheres, Female Worlds, Woman's Place: The Rhetoric of Women's History," in Toward an Intellectual History of Women (Univ. of North Carolina Press, 1997).

41. See the debate over the idea of "ascriptive nationalism" generated by Rogers Smith's book, Civic Ideals. E.g., Bonnie Honig, Democracy and the Foreigner (Princeton Univ. Press, 2001), at 12 ("Ascriptive ideologies distinct from liberalism are responsible for the nativist, sexist and racist citizenship laws and arguments catalogued by Smith. Thus liberalism is insulated from implication in the

unsavory elements of American political history. The real culprits, those other 'traditions,' are set up as Girardian scapegoats. Made into the bearers of all that liberalism seeks to disavow, they can now be cast out of the polity, which is then (re-)unified around this purging of its pollutants.").

42. Iris Marion Young, "Polity and Group Difference: A Critique of the Ideal of Universal Citzienship," in *Theorizing Citizenship* (Ronald Beiner, ed., SUNY Press, 1995).

43. This literature is concerned, in one way or another, with the persistent non-alignments between the population and the people, or between the society and the democratic community, which characterize modern liberal states. See Calhoun, *Critical Social Theory* (Blackwell Press, 1995) (population and the people); Jack Balkin, "The Constitution of Status," 106 *Yale L.J.* 2313 (1997) (society and democratic community).

44. Aleinikoff, *Semblances of Sovereignty* at 173–74 ("The statutes in Graham should be invalidated not because aliens are a defenseless group needing judicial protection, but rather because—at least from the state's perspective—they are indistinguishable from other residents of the state." *See also* Aleinikoff's response to Fiss's claim about the "immigrant as pariah." T. Alexander Aleinikoff, "First Class," in Owen Fiss, *A Community of Equals: The Constitutional Protection of New Americans* (Beacon Press, 1999).

45. *E.g.*, Kevin Johnson, "Fear of an 'Alien Nation': Race, Immigration, and Immigrants," 7 *Stan. L. & Pol'y Rev.* 111 (1995–1996).

46. *E.g.*, David Cole, *Enemy Aliens* (The New Press, 2003).

47. *See, e.g.*, Leti Volpp, "The Citizen and the Terrorist," 49 *UCLA L. Rev.* 1575 (2002); Susan M. Akram and Maritza Karmely, "Immigration and Constitutional Consequences of Post-9/11 Policies Involving Arabs and Muslims in the United States: Is Alienage a Distinction without a Difference?" 38 *U.C. Davis L. Rev.* 609 (2005).

Alienage interacts with gender in distinct ways as well, as chapter 5 makes clear. For a useful general overview, see Joan Fitzpatrick, "The Gender Dimension of U.S. Immigration Policy," 9 *Yale J.L. & Feminism* 23–49 (1997).

48. The classic example of the ameliorative case in the U.S. context is that of the lawfully present northern European alien, whose privileged race and national origin often figure more significantly than noncitizenship in his or her social experience.

49. Some immigration scholars do so increasingly, especially by incorporating concepts from critical race theory. *But see* George Martinez, "Race and Immigration Law: A Paradigm Shift?" 2000 *U. Ill. L. Rev.* 517; Kevin Johnson, "Race Matters: Immigration Law and Policy Scholarship, Law in the Ivory Tower, and the Legal Indifference of the Race Critique," 2000 *U. Ill. L. Rev.* 525 (arguing that immigration scholars have been inadequately race-conscious).

50. One prominent example of a political theorist who has focused recently on issues of alienage is Seyla Benhabib. *See* Seyla Benhabib, *The Rights of Others: Aliens, Residents and Citizens* (The Seeley Lectures) (Cambridge Univ. Press, 2004).

51. Honig, *Democracy and the Foreigner*, at 4 (asking "What problems does foreignness solve for us?").

52. In moral philosophy, this ethically particularist view is often described as patriotism. According to Charles Jones, "patriots express their love of their country by showing greater care and concern for their country and compatriots than they do for other countries and noncompatriots, though the latter also count for something. 'Greater care and concern' here means that some concern should be shown to noncompatriots, but the level of concern will be less than that accorded to compatriots." Charles Jones, "Patriotism, Morality and Global Justice," in *Global Justice* (Nomos XLI) (Ian Shapiro and Lea Brilmayer, eds., New York Univ. Press, 1999).

53. John Dunn, *Western Political Theory in the Face of the Future* 67 (Cambridge Univ. Press, 1979).

54. *Id.* at 68.

55. In addition to ethical cosmopolitanism, there are traditions on the left that focus on transnational solidarity among classes, including versions of internationalist labor solidarity in socialist thought, and other visions focusing on cross-national solidarity of the oppressed.

56. *Id.* at 58.

57. As I have argued, some inward-looking citizenship theorists make their normative nationalism explicit. Others enact a tacit normative nationalism through background presumptions of the nation as complete and closed system. If there is no national outside, then of course there are no questions of responsibility to outsiders to contend with.

58. In the United States, the constitutionalization of birthright citizenship marked the end of the system of chattel slavery and a legal regime in which blacks could not be deemed citizens by law. See discussion in chapter 4. In countries such as Germany, citizenship was hereditary until quite recently, and aliens likewise passed their status down by descent, so that alienage commonly remained a perpetual condition, not merely within an individual's lifetime but across the generations. It was the democratic and institutional problems associated with perpetual alienage that Germany sought to redress with the 2000 reform of its Nationality Law.

59. Scholars have shown, however, that the introduction of *jus sanguinis* (citizenship via descent) was adopted by many countries that sought to break away from the feudal tradition of *jus soli*, which linked subject to a particular land and lord. Patrick Weil, "Access to Citizenship: A Comparison of Twenty-Five Nationality Laws," in *Citizenship Today: Global Perspectives and Practices* 17–35 (T. Alexander Aleinikoff and Douglas Klusmeyer, eds., Brookings Institution Press, 2001). *See also* Ayelet Shachar, "Children of a Lesser State: Sustaining Global Inequality Through Citizenship Laws," in *Nomos XLIV: Child, Family and the State* 13 (Stephen Macedo and Iris Marion Young eds., New York Univ. Press, 2002) (describing perception of jus sanguinis upon its advent as "fresh and radically egalitarian"). As part of their brief for abandonment of the birthright citizenship rule in the United States, Peter Schuck and Rogers Smith made this antifeudal argument central. *See* Peter Schuck and Rogers Smith, *Citizenship without Consent: Illegal Aliens in the American Polity* (Yale Univ. Press, 1985).

60. Birthright citizenship rules are based both on territory and on blood; both *jus soli* and *jus sanguinis* are hereditary citizenships.

61. Shachar, "Children of a Lesser State." Shachar makes clear that her argument should not be read as a brief against birthright citizenship within states. "[T]he desire to ensure equality among all children who reside *within* the same polity still does not relieve us of the moral responsibility to address the basic question of why *these* children deserve such entitlements, whereas others are deprived of them." *Id.* at 6. *See also* Rainer Baubock, "Political Boundaries in a Multilevel Democracy" (contribution to the conference, Identities, Affiliations and Allegiances, New Haven, Oct. 3–5, 2003) (manuscript on file with author) ("From a liberal perspective, it is hard to justify that the arbitrary fact of being born in a particular state determines to a large extent individual well-being and autonomy."); Carens, "Aliens and Citizens."

62. Shachar's claim is part of a larger argument that we should begin to view citizenship as a form of property. It is property in the sense that it entails rights to make claims and receive entitlements, and rights to exclude others.

63. And once again, most also urge that opportunities for naturalization be made more accessible to more lawful resident noncitizens.

64. Most observers, including most liberals, take the operation of national borders entirely for granted. There are exceptions, however; *see, e.g.,* Carens, "Aliens and Citizens"; *see also* essays in *Free Movement: Ethical Issues in the Transnational Migration of People and Money* (Brian Barry and Robert E. Goodin, eds., Univ. of Pennsylvania Press, 1992). For a comprehensive review of the literature in political theory, *see* Kevin Johnson, "Open Borders?" 51 *UCLA L. Rev.* 193, 205–14 (2003). Johnson, in addition, offers a powerful (largely consequentialist) brief on behalf of the open borders position. *Id.*

65. Scheffler, *Boundaries and Allegiances* at 74 ("If participation in rewarding groups and relationships does indeed give rise to associative duties, then . . . nonparticipants lose out twice: in addition to missing out on the other rewards of participation, their claims on the participants for assistance become weaker.").

66. Kunal Parker makes a similar point about the moral significance of presence in liberal thought. Kunal Parker, "Thinking Space, Thinking Community: Lessons from Early American 'Immigration History,' " in *Repositioning North American Migration History: New Directions in Modern Continental Migration, Citizenship and Community* (Marc S. Rodrigues, ed., U. Rochester Press, 2004), at 287 (In liberal migration theory, "there is an ineluctable moral weight to be accorded existing and shared spatial presence ('being already there'), a moral weight that must 'trump' all the historically specific exclusionary communal narratives of the 'Promised Land' variety.").

67. Many have also endorsed legalization policies that would allow some undocumented immigrants to convert their "hereness" into lawful residence.

68. E.g., desert deaths, drowning deaths, cargo-hold deaths; smuggling abuses. For discussion, see Johnson, "Open Borders?" (outlining the growing trend of "death at the border").

69. Heightened border enforcement efforts since the mid-1990s, however, have served to deter many undocumented immigrants from returning home. These immigrants choose to remain because they fear the prospect of apprehension and deportation upon attempted reentry into the United States. This decline in the rate of return migration has in turn produced in an increase in the total population of

undocumented immigrants in the country. See generally Douglas Massey, "Backfire at the Border: Why Enforcement Without Legalization Cannot Stop Illegal Immigration," 29 *Trade Policy Analysis* (June 13, 2005).

70. Parts of this paragraph were first published in Linda Bosniak, "Opposing Proposition 187," at 594–95. For a similar argument, see also Peter Spiro, "The Impossibility of Citizenship" at 1507 ("It is not clear why territorial location should be determinative of rights."). A recent article examining the general authoritative force of what the author calls "legal spatiality" in American law raises this question at a broader level of generality: "What is the legal magic of American soil?" *See* Kal Raustiala, "The Geography of Justice," 73 *Fordham L. Rev.* 101, 142 (2005).

71. This is the crux of the argument made in Linda Bosniak, "Exclusion and Membership: The Dual Identity of the Undocumented Worker under U.S. Law," 1988 *Wis. L. Rev.* 955.

72. For a discussion of nonterritorially based national ties, see Peter Spiro, "The Citizenship Dilemma," 51 *Stan. L. Rev.* 597, 621–25 (1999). *See also* Linda Bosniak, "Multiple Nationality and the Postnational Transformation of Citizenship," 42 *Va. J. Int'l L.* 979, 983–991 (2002) (reviewing literature on modes of deterritorialized nation-building).

73. Ngai, *Impossible Subjects.*

74. For a perceptive discussion of the process of criticism from within, see Michael Walzer, *Interpretation and Social Criticism* (Harvard Univ. Press, 1987), at 64–65 ("We become [social] critics naturally, as it were, by elaborating on existing moralities and telling stories about a society more just than, though never entirely different from, our own.").

75. *Cf.* Bonnie Honig, "Difference, Dilemmas and the Politics of Home," 61 *Soc. Res.* 563 (Fall 1994), who writes about the realities of "dilemmatic spaces" and the persistent desire of liberal theory to "keep dilemmas at bay." *See also* William Connolly, *Politics and Ambiguity* (Wisconsin Univ. Press, 1987).

Index

Made in the USA
San Bernardino, CA
20 December 2018